Alethea Hayter was born in Cairo. On leaving Oxford, she joined the editorial staff of *Country Life*, had a wartime job in Gibraltar, Bermuda and Trinidad and worked for the British Council in Athens, Paris and Brussels. A member of the Board of Governors of the Old Vic and Sadler's Wells Theatres, and of the Society of Authors' Committee of Management, she was elected Fellow of the Royal Society of Literature in 1962. In 1970 she was awarded the OBE. She lives in London.

Biographer and critic, Alethea Hayter is the author of *Mrs Browning: A Poet's Work and Its Setting*, *Elizabeth Barrett Browning*, *Opium and the Romantic Imagination*, *Horatio's Version*, *A Voyage in Vain: Coleridge's Journey to Malta in 1804* and *Portrait of a Friendship: Drawn from New Letters of James Russell Lowell to Sybella Lady Lyttelton 1881–1891*.

D0721873

BENJAMIN ROBERT HAYDON. Self Portrait, 1846

A SULTRY MONTH

Scenes of London Literary Life in 1846

ALETHEA HAYTER

Robin Clark
LONDON

First published in 1965 by Faber & Faber Limited, London

First published in paperback by Robin Clark Limited 1992
A member of the Namara Group
27/29 Goodge Street
London W1P 1FD

Reissued in 1994

A catalogue record for this book is available from the British Library

ISBN 86072 146 9

Printed and bound in Great Britain by
Cox & Wyman Ltd
Reading, Berks

CONTENTS

Foreword and Acknowledgements *page* 11

Chapter I Thursday 18th June 15

II Thursday 18th June 25

III Thursday 18th June 32

IV Thursday 18th June 39

V Friday 19th June 47

VI Saturday 20th June 58

VII Sunday 21st June 68

VIII Monday 22nd June 77

IX Monday 22nd June 82

X Monday 22nd June 93

XI Tuesday 23rd June 102

XII Wednesday 24th June 108

XIII Wednesday 24th June 114

XIV Wednesday 24th June 121

XV Thursday 25th June to Monday 29th June 130

XVI Tuesday 30th June 137

XVII Wednesday 1st July and Thursday 2nd July 146

XVIII Saturday 4th July 153

XIX Sunday 5th July 160

XX Monday 6th July 167

XXI Tuesday 7th July 175

XXII Wednesday 8th July 183

XXIII July to September 188

XXIV Monday 13th July 196

Appendix 203

List of sources 207

Index 219

LIST OF ILLUSTRATIONS

Frontispiece: BENJAMIN ROBERT HAYDON. Self Portrait, 1846
National Portrait Gallery

THOMAS CARLYLE by John Linnell, 1844
Scottish National Portrait Gallery

JANE WELSH CARLYLE by Karl Hartmann, 1850
National Trust

SAMUEL ROGERS, MRS NORTON AND MRS PHIPPS
by Frank Stone, *c.* 1845
National Portrait Gallery

RICHARD MONCKTON MILNES by Caroline Smith, 1848
By courtesy of Mr James Pope-Hennessy.
Photograph by Cecilia Gray

NAPOLEON MUSING AT ST HELENA by B.R. Haydon
Devonshire Collection. By courtesy of the Trustees of the Chatsworth Settlement

WELLINGTON MUSING ON THE FIELD OF WATERLOO
by B.R. Haydon
Devonshire Collection. By courtesy of the Trustees of the Chatsworth Settlement

'A VILE CARICATURE OF B.R. HAYDON BY MR KEATS':
a page of drawings by Keats and Haydon
National Portrait Gallery

MACREADY AS KING LEAR with Helen Faucit as Cordelia
Raymond Mander and Joe Mitchenson
Theatre Collection

PARLOUR OF THE CARLYLES' HOUSE IN CHEYNE ROW
Photograph by E.A. Fleming Hewett.
National Trust and Gordon Fraser Gallery

ANNA JAMESON by John Gibson
National Portrait Gallery

WILLIAM WORDSWORTH ON HELVELLYN
by B.R. Haydon, 1843
National Portrait Gallery

THOMAS NOON TALFOURD by H.W. Pickersgill
National Portrait Gallery

CURTIUS LEAPING INTO THE GULF by B.R. Haydon
Royal Albert Memorial Museum, Exeter

FOREWORD

Nothing in this book is invented. Every incident, every sentence of dialogue, every gesture, the food, the flowers, the furniture, all are taken from the contemporary letters, diaries and reminiscences of the men and women concerned, nearly all of them professional writers with formidable memories and highly trained descriptive skills. Many of the anecdotes and personal descriptions are all too familiar to any student of the period. My object—like that of the Pop Artist who combines scraps of Christmas cards, of cinema posters and of the Union Jack to make a picture—has been to create a pattern from a group of familiar objects. It seemed possible to show a set of authors—all of whom have had their separate portraits painted many times at full length—as a conversation piece of equals, existing in relationship to each other at a particular moment, encapsulated with one dramatic event in an overheated political and physical climate.

While writing this book I have always had before my eyes the warning of Max Beerbohm's "Savonarola" Brown and his tragedy, whose stage directions read: "Enter Lucrezia Borgia, St Francis of Assisi and Leonardo da Vinci . . . Enter Dante . . . Andrea del Sarto appears for a moment at a window. Pippa passes . . . Enter Bocaccio, Benvenuto Cellini and many others". My characters, unlike Mr Brown's, all belong to the same century; but the mere fact that two events happen simultaneously in time does not give them a significant relationship. At the moment in June 1846 when this book starts, the second volume of *Modern Painters* had been out for two months, *Poems by Currer Ellis and Acton Bell* for one month, Mary Ann Evans' translation of *Leben Jesu* for just a week; *Vanity Fair* and *Mary Barton* were being worked on, *Wuthering Heights*, *Agnes Grey* and *The Professor* were going the round of the

11

publishers. But neither Ruskin nor George Eliot, neither the Brontës nor Mrs Gaskell, were in touch with the principal figures in this sketch at this period, and Thackeray not very closely at this particular moment, so these great names in Victorian literature will hardly be mentioned in this book. Others, who now seem to us minor writers, have been given the importance accorded to them by their contemporaries.

The last three volumes of the complete diaries of Benjamin Robert Haydon, in Professor Willard Pope's monumental edition, were published when this book was already partly written, but I have drawn largely on them and on Professor Pope's notes. The other primary sources for this book are the *Life of B. R. Haydon, Historical Painter, from his Autobiography and Journals*, edited by Tom Taylor; *B. R. Haydon, Correspondence and Table Talk*, with a Memoir by F. W. Haydon; and the many sets of letters by Thomas and Jane Welsh Carlyle and by Robert Browning and Elizabeth Barrett, above all their letters to each other. Among recent biographical studies, there are three to which I owe much—Mr Eric George's *The Life and Death of B. R. Haydon*, Mr and Mrs Hanson's *Necessary Evil: the Life of Jane Welsh Carlyle*, and Mr James Pope-Hennessy's *Monckton Milnes, the Years of Promise, 1809–1851*. A list of these and other sources will be found at the end of the book. I have also included in an appendix a few notes on some dates and identifications.

I am most grateful to the following publishers for permission to quote copyright material: the Harvard University Press for *The Diary of Benjamin Robert Haydon*, edited by Professor Willard Pope; the Clarendon Press, Oxford, for *Letters of William and Dorothy Wordsworth: the Later Years*, edited by Professor E. de Selincourt; the Oxford University Press for *Anna Jameson: Letters to Ottilie von Goethe*, edited by G. H. Needler; the Oxford University Press, New York, for *Elizabeth Barrett: Letters to B. R. Haydon*, edited by Professor M. H. Shackford; Messrs John Murray for *Jane Welsh Carlyle: Letters to Her Family, 1839–1863*, edited by Leonard Huxley, for *E. B. Browning: Letters to Her Sister, 1846–1859*, edited by Leonard Huxley, and for *Elizabeth Barrett to Miss Mitford*,

Foreword

edited by Betty Miller; the University of Illinois Press for *Letters of the Brownings to George Barrett*, edited by Paul Landis; the Nonesuch Press for *Letters of Charles Dickens*, edited by Walter Dexter. I am also very grateful to the Master, Fellows and Scholars of Trinity College, Cambridge, for allowing me to consult the Houghton Papers in the Library, and for permission to quote some unpublished material from them.

I have chosen as illustrations to this book the portraits of its leading characters which are nearest in date to 1846, rather than the best-known likenesses or the best as paintings. I have not succeeded in tracing any unquestionable portrait of Robert Browning or Elizabeth Barrett which dates from the mid-1840's, so there are no portraits of them in this book. The portraits of Haydon, Samuel Rogers and Mrs Norton, Wordsworth, Talfourd, the bust of Mrs Jameson, and Keats' drawing of Haydon are reproduced by permission of the National Portrait Gallery; the portrait of Carlyle by permission of the Scottish National Portrait Gallery; the portrait of Mrs Carlyle by permission of the National Trust; the photograph of the parlour of the Carlyles' house by permission of the National Trust and the Gordon Fraser Gallery; Haydon's picture of *Curtius Leaping into the Gulf* by permission of the Royal Albert Memorial Museum, Exeter; the print of Macready as King Lear by permission of the Raymond Mander and Joe Mitchenson Theatre Collection. The two panels by Haydon of Wellington and Napoleon are from the Devonshire Collection, Chatsworth, and are reproduced by permission of the Trustees of the Chatsworth Settlement. I am most grateful to Mr T. S. Wragg, the Librarian of Chatsworth, for help and advice. I have also had much help and information from the staff of the National Portrait Gallery, specially Mrs Isherwood Kay; the Scottish National Portrait Gallery; the Royal Albert Memorial Museum, Exeter; the Reading Museum and Art Gallery; and the Henry E. Huntington Library and Art Gallery, California. Professor Kathleen Tillotson gave me most valuable advice about a possible drawing of Elizabeth Barrett by Thackeray. Mr James Pope-Hennessy has kindly given me permission to reproduce the drawing of Monckton Milnes by Caroline Smith which he owns. Mr Carlos van Hasselt drew my attention to the un-published letter by Haydon in the Collection Frits Lugt, Institut Néerlandais, Paris, and gave me permission to publish it as an illustration to this book.

Many other friends have helped me in the writing of this book. Mr and Mrs Basil Gray allowed me to stay in their hospitable house in the British Museum for weeks together, while I was working in the Reading Room. Lady Mynors found and despatched to Paris many heavy tomes for which I appealed at the shortest notice. Mrs Warriner drove me round London in her car, to identify the sites of the houses where the characters in this book lived. Mrs Lewis advised me about Serjeant Talfourd's legal career. My sister Mrs Napier verified what flowers known to Victorian England would be actually in bloom in a heat-wave in June.

Paris, 1964

On Thursday 18th June 1846 the painter Benjamin Robert Haydon deposited at the door of 50 Wimpole Street five pictures and three trunks, which the poet Elizabeth Barrett, his friend by correspondence, had agreed to take in for a time. The pictures were portraits of the Duke of Wellington, of Wordsworth, of Mary Russell Mitford, and of Haydon's wife and son. The trunks contained papers and the twenty-five vellum-bound folio volumes and odd note-books which contained Haydon's journals—all but the current volume.

Haydon wanted to get these treasures out of his own house in Burwood Place, just off the Edgware Road, because he expected that at any moment he would be arrested for debt, and all his possessions seized. On the previous Saturday a loan of £1,000 which he had been expecting had fallen through, desperate letters to his patrons asking for commissions had produced little result, and by the end of the month he had to pay a quarter's rent—£30—to his landlord William Newton, to whom he already owed a great deal of money, perhaps as much as £1,200. And there were other sums owing all round, due to be repaid within the month—to the bank, to the baker, to the bookseller. That morning his landlord had called for the rent, but Haydon had explained that he could not pay it, and had wheedled the landlord into promising not to put an execution for debt into the house.

The situation was not at all an unusual one for Haydon. He had been arrested for debt seven times in the last twenty-five years, and had been sent to a debtors' prison four times. His dress suit, his wife's and daughter's clothes, his books, his few silver spoons, had often disappeared to the pawnbroker. He had written hundreds of begging letters, and had been lent hundreds of pounds. Yet he was a temperate domesticated man with no very luxurious tastes; he was energetic and hard-working, he was acquainted with nearly all the leading states-men, writers and painters of the day, and his own name was at any rate widely known. As a young man he had painted three huge pictures, *The Judgement of Solomon, Christ's Entry into Jerusalem* and *The Raising of Lazarus* which had brought him much acclaim. Wordsworth had praised his genius and nobility of soul; John Hamilton Reynolds had told him in a crashing sonnet that he was born to immortality and that whole nations would bend over his sublime works; Keats had classed him with Wordsworth and Leigh Hunt as a "Great Spirit" and had contrasted his Magian wisdom with the brainless idiotism of those who failed to recognize the beauty of the Elgin Marbles. Haydon's vehement advocacy, or so he himself and many of his contemporaries believed, forced the public to acknowledge the authenticity and splendour of the Elgin Marbles, and en-sured that they remained in Britain and are now in the British Museum. He was a pioneer in art education, both for practi-tioners and appreciators. He was sure the English people had the taste and feeling to appreciate great art if they were given the chance to see it and hear about it. He was a popularizer in the good sense; he would today be a very successful broad-caster. In his own day he was notorious rather than successful. He wrote letters to successive Prime Ministers and to the Press; he got questions and petitions put to the House of Commons; he gave lectures and formed committees and led pressure groups. He agitated for the reform of the Royal Academy, the foundation of art schools in the provinces, the improvement of industrial design; for State patronage of the arts by the purchase of famous works of art for national mu-seums and galleries, by the commissioning of pictures for public buildings and of monuments for national heroes. He argued, he exhorted, he reproached, he repeated himself. He was irritating, embarrassing, boring; he was also often a true prophet; many of his ideas are now accepted as obvious and inevitable.

One of the projects which he had advocated most ardently—the commissioning of paintings to decorate public buildings—

came to fruition four years earlier than this summer of 1846. In April 1842 the Royal Commission which had been set up in the previous year to encourage art in England, with special reference to the new Houses of Parliament then rebuilding after the fire, announced a competition for cartoons, a qualifying test whose winning designs were to be executed in fresco in the House of Lords. This was what Haydon had been hoping and working for all his life; he entered two cartoons, *The Curse on Adam and Eve* and *Edward the Black Prince Entering London with John of France*—and when the result of the competition was announced in June 1843, Haydon heard that his cartoons were not among the prize-winners. "It is a thunderbolt to him" wrote Elizabeth Barrett to a friend. He had partly foreseen a reverse, but when it happened he was dazed and wounded by the ingratitude of his pupils and friends whom he believed to have sided against him, and indignantly shocked at the injustice of passing over the very man whose efforts had made such a competition for State-commissioned painting possible. "Degraded, insulted and harassed" he wrote in his journal. He tried to put a good face on it, and generously praised some of the other cartoons in the exhibition; but an unfriendly critic who met him there saw him suddenly changed into an old man, and added with grudging compassion "Every competition has its dark side: dark with a red light as of the nether pit shining through it".

This red light flickers intermittently round Haydon in the 1840's. The idea of Satanic beauty, of a being magnificent but doomed, haunted him as he painted his cartoon of *The Curse on Adam and Eve* and then a picture of *Uriel Revealing Himself to Satan*. One Sunday afternoon, on a rather surprising expedition to the Zoo with Wordsworth and the handsome sardonic Lockhart, he noticed Lockhart looking at the old poet and "smiling at the Purity of his Nature with something the look the Devil looked at Adam and Eve. That's a fine Idea—an Idea I will use in my cartoon. Caroline Norton's Eyes, Lockhart's Melancholy, Byron's Voluptuousness, Napoleon's mouth, Haydon's forehead, and Hazlitt's brows, will make a very fine Devil". He began the cartoon and the idea of the devilish head

17

haunted him. "I have now got Satan's head to do—in the middle of the night, I saw his large, fiery, cruel rimmed eye and kept staring in the dark where nothing was for an hour". In 1844 when he was working on the "Uriel" picture, "the real expression of Satan flashed on my inward Eye", but six months later he was worrying as to whether he might not lead the public astray by "encasing Evil in beauty . . . my object in painting him is not *admiration* but *terror*, and I have a sublime delight in dwelling on and developing such sensations".

The notion of fallen, ruined beauty was not uncongenial to Haydon. His own forehead was to contribute to the Satanic portrait, and he would have approved the description which his son Frederic gave of his father's flaming glance—"a keen, restless, azure-grey eye, the pupil of which contracted and expanded, rose and fell as he talked, just as if some inner light and fire was playing on his brain".

Most of Haydon's contemporaries, however, did not think he looked fatal or devilish. There are descriptions of him during a visit which he paid to Edinburgh in February and March 1846 which present him in a more cheerful light. It was a successful visit. He gave lectures on Fuseli, on Wilkie, on fresco, on decoration and cartoons, on the Elgin Marbles. He reported that the lectures were "heroically received" by entranced, breathlessly silent audiences. He showed the engraving of his portrait of Wordsworth to admiring friends. He examined Walter Scott's manuscripts. He collected some gratifying fan letters and anecdotes of admirers of his paintings. He was asked twice to Lord Jeffrey's famous suppers.

These were on Tuesdays and Fridays during the winter; they lasted from about nine to midnight and consisted of ten or twenty guests who were placed at small round tables and provided with a light supper and conversation of formidable acuteness. Haydon's first evening there, on 3rd March, began rather seriously with his having to take a very talented, travelled and bluestocking lady in to supper, but on his other side at table he found a beauty, wife of the American actor Edwin Forrest—who, the previous evening, had launched one of the fiercest theatrical feuds of the nineteenth century by hissing the great Macready, who was then playing Hamlet in Edinburgh. Haydon's evening passed pleasantly in talking to his sweet and beautiful neighbour, whose formidable black-moustached husband was at another table. When Haydon left, Jeffrey said to him—"Haydon, you look fat and well, the sure signs of prosperity". Haydon thought of his unpaid bills, and of how much even one's affectionate old friends go by appearances.

The second evening at Jeffrey's was a week later. "Macready and Haydon the lions" reported Miss Elizabeth Rigby, who was later to marry Charles Eastlake, Haydon's pupil who had had to break to him the news that his competition cartoons had not won a prize. Macready's was the fatal and devilish appearance that evening. Haydon describes him "looking as if he had just escaped from the tortures of the damned, and that his features had not yet recovered the calmness of humanity". It was not surprising that Macready looked so tormented; Edwin Forrest had been back again at other performances by Macready in the last week, talking through his big scenes, laughing when he waved his handkerchief at a pathetic moment. Macready, gaunt, grizzled, with heavy lines running down from his nose to his square jaw, might well look scorched by flames of agony when he appeared at Jeffrey's supper party. Haydon, on the other hand, looked unromantic to Miss Rigby's eye. As a child she had been fascinated by a drawing of Haydon's handsome youthful face, but now she thought that beautiful outline was obscured by fat and no longer interesting.

At sixty, Haydon was a fresh-coloured beaky-nosed man with a fine curved mouth and a great bald forehead. He was extremely short-sighted, and sometimes wore three pairs of spectacles, one on top of the other, but his blue-grey eyes were clear and searching. He was upright and energetic in his movements, and seemed to fatten on anxiety and care. In May 1846, on seeing a sketch of himself in 1805, he came to the conclusion, in which his wife supported him, that he was better-looking at sixty than at nineteen, and on 9th June he dashed off a black and white chalk sketch of himself, under which he wrote Μεγα Φρονεων, and then gave it to his old friend the painter Samuel Prout.

Thursday 18th June

Μεγα Φρονεων, "meditating great things"—that was how he liked to see himself. Wordsworth once asked Haydon's wife what his chief pleasure was. "Feeding on his own thoughts!" replied Mary Haydon, with an irony quite lost on her husband, who commented "What a beautiful compliment! and how sincere from a beautiful Woman, who ought to imagine her divine face should be the chief pleasure".

The great things that Haydon was meditating at this time were the six cartoons which, in defiance of his failure in the competition, he had decided to paint as an example of what the Parliament frescoes ought to be. His dejection of 1843 had not lasted many months. Waking one morning in depression, he suddenly said to himself "Is this B. R. Haydon? I'll see if I will be conquered by Cartoon", and by the end of the year he rose from his prayers "my heart beating in anticipation of a greater work and a more terrific struggle. This is B. R. Haydon—the *real* Man—may he live a thousand years!" He convinced himself that his failure in the competition had been due to the malice and persecution of his enemies—the Queen and Prince Albert wanted German painters to have supremacy, the Prime Minister Sir Robert Peel had a grudge against him over past financial transactions, the Royal Academy intrigued against him because he had attacked their privileges, their inefficiency and indolence. But he would show them that the true lovers of art, the faithful British public, recognized his genius. Unfairness, ill-treatment, opposition, invigorated him; he said of himself that he almost relished ruin as a stimulus to activity. All through 1844 and 1845 he toiled on at two huge pictures, *The Banishment of Aristides* and *Nero at the Burning of Rome*, destined in his mind to adorn the walls of the House of Lords and to illustrate the Injustice of Democracy and the Heartlessness of Despotism. In between, he painted portraits, and small replicas of his previous pictures, to stave off his increasing liabilities; but these were only pot-boilers—his great pictures were what mattered, and would exalt the noble tradition of historical painting in Britain.

In April 1846, soon after his return from his visit to Edinburgh, he decided to exhibit *Aristides* and *Nero*, with some portraits and drawings, at a one-man show at the Egyptian Hall. The startling façade of this vanished exhibition hall, squeezed between the sober Georgian houses of Piccadilly, was a fitting drop-curtain for the ludicrous tragedy that was now played behind it. A menacing cornice and three monumental first-floor windows, crowded with giant statues and sphinxes, scarabs and hawks' wings and lotus capitals, weighted down a low ground floor, with an entrance fit for the entombment scene in *Aida*.

Haydon's pictures were installed on the first floor of the Egyptian Hall, to the right. He sent out four hundred invitations to the Private View, which was on 4th April. It poured with rain all that day, and only four people came. *The Times* and the *Herald* gave good notices to Haydon's pictures; he himself wrote and published a flamboyant advertisement of it; but day after day the attendance was wretched, the receipts almost nothing.

Meanwhile in the same building a very different exhibition was in progress. The American circus proprietor Barnum was showing "General Tom Thumb, the midget", actually an eight-year-old boy called Stratton, only thirty-one inches tall. Tom Thumb was no novelty to London—he had appeared at the Egyptian Hall two years earlier, and had put on an act of "Napoleon Musing at St Helena" for the benefit of the Duke of Wellington, who went to see him. Haydon, who had painted a well-known series of pictures with the title of *Napoleon Musing at St Helena*, had prophetically noted in his diary at the time "I do not like this". Novelty or not, Tom Thumb was an immense attraction when he reappeared at the Egyptian Hall in 1846, to everyone up to Queen Victoria, who sent for him three times to the Palace, thus enabling Barnum to put a notice on the door of the Egyptian Hall each time saying "Closed this evening, General Tom Thumb being at Buckingham Palace by the command of Her Majesty". The Tom Thumb show at the Egyptian Hall ran from 20th March to 20th July 1846, and such were the crowds that came to see him that Barnum made up to 500 dollars a day out of it. "They rush by thousands to see Thumb. They push, they fight, they scream, they faint, they cry help and murder, and oh and ah. They see my bills, my boards, my caravans, and don't read them. Their eyes are open but their sense is shut. It is an insanity, a Rabies, a madness, a Furor, a dream. I would not have believed it of the English people!" wrote Haydon in his journal. It was not only the mob who went to see Tom Thumb. On 2nd May a group of men, most of them acquaintances of Haydon's—Charles Dickens, Samuel Rogers, the painters Landseer and Stanfield, the actor Macready, the barrister and dramatist Talfourd—met at the opening day of the Royal Academy. Dickens persuaded them to go and see General Tom Thumb, but Macready, who records this in his diary, makes no mention of their going to see Haydon's pictures in the same building. The American writer Bayard Taylor, on his way to see Tom Thumb, saw Haydon standing outside the door of his exhibition room. "He was stout, broad-shouldered . . . rather shabbily dressed, with a general aid of dilapidated power. There was something fierce and bitter in the expression of his face, as he glanced across to the groups hurrying to see Tom Thumb". In one week 12,000 people went to see Tom Thumb; in the same week 133 adults and a little girl went to see Haydon's pictures. On 18th May he closed his exhibition; it had been a disastrous failure and he had lost £111 by it. It was a month later, on 18th June, when no more money had come in and his creditors were besieging him, that he sent his journals and pictures to Elizabeth Barrett for safe keeping.

Mary Russell Mitford had introduced Haydon to the Barrett family. Elizabeth Barrett's sisters Henrietta and Arabel had visited his studio in 1842, to see the *Adam and Eve* cartoon on which he was working for the competition, and had seen at the same time an unfinished portrait of Wordsworth.

"Oh how my sister would like to see this!" said Arabel Barrett.

"Then she *shall* see it," said Haydon, and sent it round to Wimpole Street for Elizabeth Barrett. She wrote a sonnet about it, which she sent to Haydon who showed it to Wordsworth, much to Miss Barrett's gratification. From then on, for about a year, Haydon and Miss Barrett kept up a brisk correspondence. They wrote about genius and fame, about the problem of evil, about idea and subject in painting, about Plato and Wordsworth, about the date of Chaucer's birth, the odiousness of Lady Byron, Haydon's walk with Keats in Kilburn Meadows, Miss Mitford's care of her dying father. Haydon called Miss Barrett "my dear Aeschylus Barrett" because she had translated *Prometheus Bound*; he gave her the manuscript of part of Keats' poem *I stood tip-toe upon a little hill*; he sent drawings for his big pictures to give her an idea of them, since at this time she was a sofa-bound invalid who could never leave the house to visit an exhibition or a studio.

Their greatest bond was the conviction which they shared, that the creative artist's calling was sacred. Haydon knew that he had been called by God to raise his country's tastes, to vindicate the principles of High Art. High Art was historical painting; portraits, landscapes, were just for pot-boiling; the only real art was huge pictures of the heroic actions of history— Curtius leaping into the gulf, the Judgement of Solomon, Alexander taming Bucephalus. To bring back this great tradition into English art he had defied the Royal Academy, petitioned one Prime Minister after another, given up security and easy rewards, begged and borrowed and gone to prison. When his cartoons failed in 1843, financial disaster seemed more imminent than ever—"We shall be ruined" his wife said when she heard the news—and then for the first time he sent some boxes and papers to Miss Barrett for safe-keeping, with two jars of twenty-seven-year-old oil. At the time she kept this trust a secret even from Miss Mitford, and a month or two later, Haydon's immediate money embarrassments being postponed, he sent for his boxes again, and after this their correspondence died down, though it never stopped altogether.

Now, in June 1846, an execution for debt again seemed near. Haydon sent Miss Barrett a gaily-worded request for her permission to send his belongings to her for protection, with an offer to let her have his portrait of Miss Mitford to keep, as a remembrance of their common friendship with her. A second note followed this, desiring Miss Barrett not to think him guilty of want of feeling because of the lightness of his first letter. In a third letter, sent with the trunks and pictures, he said that after all he could not make up his mind to part permanently with the picture of Miss Mitford, but would leave it with Miss Barrett for a time. He referred to his money troubles, and said that Sir Robert Peel had just sent him a cheque for £50, but he wanted employment, not charity. He spoke of the new background which he was putting into the picture on which he was then engaged, another one in his cartoon series, representing *Alfred and the First British Jury*. He told her how, as he was painting it, he felt as if his soul had wings. It was glorious to be a painter, if only for the neglect which was the reward of the true artist. And then he spoke of Napoleon, and of how youth had all the luck, and how precarious fame was, and how uncertain the public's interest, and how the dwarf had triumphed. But he would write more lectures, six more sets of them, six whole volumes. He hoped his brain would not turn. And he repeated, as he had so often said before to Elizabeth Barrett, that he couldn't and wouldn't die.

Elizabeth Barrett sent a note to Haydon to acknowledge the
arrival of his boxes and pictures; but that Thursday she had
received a letter which was much more interesting to her than
anything that Haydon could write. It was from Robert Browning, to whom she was secretly engaged to be married. His
letter, written that morning in answer to one received from her
by the first post, reached her in time for her to be able to write
to him again that same evening. Posts in London were quicker
then. Browning and Elizabeth Barrett were going to see each
other on Saturday, but still they needed to write to each other
daily—often twice daily.

Robert Browning's letter of 18th June was full of love, full
of plans about where they were to live in Italy when they were
married. It had a few sentences about friends—Samuel Rogers
and Anna Jameson; and it enclosed a note he had had from
Mrs Carlyle, inviting him to dinner next week.

In her note Jane Welsh Carlyle must have repeated with
approval some pronouncement by her husband Thomas Carlyle,
a pronouncement that Browning didn't agree with—perhaps one
condemning women writers as a class; Browning would be
bound to resent that for Elizabeth Barrett's sake. "To my
mortification I find that the wise man is not so peremptory on
the virtue of one of Ba's qualities as I, the ignorant man, must
continue to be. Never mind, perhaps 'in the long run' I may
love you as if you were exactly to Mrs Carlyle's mind" he told
Miss Barrett. She took no offence when she read Mrs Carlyle's
letter. "How I like Mrs Carlyle's note!" she wrote in reply
that evening, and urged him to accept the invitation to dinner.
Miss Barrett and Mrs Carlyle had not yet met, but Miss Barrett
admired Mrs Carlyle's mordant letters which Browning had

25

sometimes shown her, though she thought them more remarkable for intelligence than for sensibility.

The admiration was not returned. A visitor to the Carlyles reported a conversation during which Mrs Carlyle made it clear that "Of Miss Barrett she has a low—in my mind, altogether too low—opinion. She says *she* could not read her". The tone of Browning's reference to "Mrs Carlyle's mind" indicates his relationship to her. He and she did not appreciate each other much. He thought her too prone to pick holes in everyone, and was never sorry if he found that she was away in the country when he called on Thomas Carlyle, and that he was free to listen to Carlyle's bracing and tremendous talk, sitting in the little garden of the Carlyles' Cheyne Row house while Carlyle smoked his pipe; Carlyle would then walk part of the way home to New Cross with Browning at night, along the river as far as Vauxhall Bridge.

Mrs Carlyle was equally unenthusiastic about Browning. She thought him a sham, and she had a very low opinion of his poetry. It was she who made the famous comment on his poem *Sordello* that she had read it through without discovering whether Sordello was a man, a city or a book, and when Browning sent Carlyle a copy of *Pippa Passes*, the first of his *Bells and Pomegranates* series, Mrs Carlyle, who had opened the parcel in Carlyle's absence, wrote to her husband "God only knows what such names can mean".

Browning had got off on the wrong foot with the house-proud Mrs Carlyle by spoiling a new carpet of hers during an early visit to Cheyne Row. He had jumped up to get the kettle off the fire for her when she was making tea—a gesture which Carlyle, who was present, had not thought of making. As Browning went on talking with the kettle in his hand, Mrs Carlyle told him to put it down—which he did on the carpet. Mrs Carlyle cried out at him at once, but by the time he picked it up again it had burnt a round mark on the carpet.

Such disasters were apt to happen in the Carlyle household. Dexterous and notable as Mrs Carlyle was, the couple were somehow accident-prone. Simmering marmalade boiled over and set the chimney on fire, a maid poured boiling water over Mrs

Carlyle's foot, floods of soot came down the chimney when the kitchen floor had just been scrubbed, workmen fell through the floors when the house was being redecorated. And there were worse disasters than that; the manuscript of the first part of Carlyle's *French Revolution* was burnt by a friend's careless housemaid, Mrs Carlyle was run away with in a carriage in Liverpool and later seriously hurt in a street accident. Even her dogs got run over and fell out of windows.

Browning's accident with the tea kettle when he was trying to help Mrs Carlyle may be compared with Geraldine Jewsbury's possibly apocryphal story about the Carlyles when they were marooned in the lonely farmhouse at Craigenputtock during a snowstorm. Mrs Carlyle had to do all the housework because their maid had gone off for a holiday and could not get back because of the snow. Mrs Carlyle decided to wash the kitchen floor; having gone down on her knees and scoured half of it, she summoned Carlyle and installed him in an armchair by the fireplace to watch her progress. "He regarded her beneficently, and gave her from time to time words of encouragement".

In Mrs Carlyle's eyes this comparison would not have been in Browning's favour. She liked to be praised but left alone to do things efficiently herself, not to be chivalrously but inefficiently helped. "He *will* help the kettle and never fails to pour it all over the milk pot and sugar basin" she complained of another friend. When in 1844, to the scandal of some of their friends, Carlyle went off to stay with Lady Harriet Baring and left Jane Welsh Carlyle alone in the house to cope with one of her protégés, barely out of a lunatic asylum, she wrote to her cousin "Everybody else was *terrified* for my being left alone in the house with him. But C. has no idle apprehensions; he paid me the compliment of supposing that I had presence of mind and clearness enough to manage perfectly well without any protection—and I am quite of his opinion". She could not see why, when men were supposed to be able to exist by their own resources, women should be thought incapable of it, and to need "always to be borne about on somebody's shoulders, and dandled and chirped to". She did not feel lonely or neglected

27

when Carlyle went away in the summer and left her to cope with the redecoration of the house. She was glad not to have him under her feet, hating the whole business of household "earthquakes" as he did; and she thought that this was the rational attitude for any woman to take.

So Browning did himself no good by his attempted chivalry, and got a bad mark for the ruined carpet which was the result. But they had to keep up some pretence of getting on with each other, since she knew that Carlyle was fond of him, and he was devoted to Carlyle. To keep on terms with her he wrote polite acceptances of invitations, and bread-and-butter letters for previous ones—"How good you were to me that day. Ever yours and his faithfully, R. Bg"; and one October evening, calling at Cheyne Row and finding Carlyle away, but Mrs Carlyle at home, he stayed to tea and they sustained the conversation by anecdotes. He told her a good story about an eighty-four-year-old Unitarian, a ninety-two-year-old "Carlyleist", and the Pursuit of Truth, which she passed on in a letter to Carlyle, who was in Scotland; while she regaled him, as he told Elizabeth Barrett, with "characteristic quaintnesses" about her parents-in-law.

Mrs Carlyle's anecdotal style was her highly personal art, with which she subjugated her admirers. It did not work with quite everyone; at the Barings' she seems to have been occasionally thought a bore, with her Haddingtonshire accent (much less pronounced than her husband's broad Annandale one, but still noticeable—specially when she spoke of "Cárlyle", with the accent on the first syllable, as she always called her husband) and her stories that took so long to come to the point. You needed to know her well, to be in her circle, to appreciate the delicate effects of suspense, the telling details, by which she built up to her dazzling little climaxes. It was all constructed out of nothing, or nearly nothing, like the whole novel-plot which she piled up for Dickens and Forster from the outside look of a house in Cheyne Row. As Carlyle said, it was *coterie-sprache* of the closest kind, full of nicknames, turns of speech caught up from Mazzini's erratic English—"thanks God", "*here* down", "a mad"—or some old Scottish acquaintance's malapropisms; a vivid secret language which must have given intense pleasure to the initiates. They had to pick up rapidly that "Hell and Tommy" (by an obscure reference to a picture by John Martin and to Tom o' Bedlam) stood for some chaotic moment, that "Shuping Sing" (a Chinese character in a novel, who could see through millstones) was shorthand for the faculty of perception, and that "to make wits" was to make clever conversation with an effort, the opposite of their own spontaneous style. "Hardly, I think in any house, was there *more* of *Coterie-sprache*, shining innocently, with a perpetual expressiveness and twinkle generally of quiz and real humour about it, than in ours" wrote Carlyle after his wife's death. "She mainly was the creatress of all this . . . shedding such a lambency of 'own fireside' over everything, if you are in the secret".

The Carlyles' private language was pre-eminent, but it was an age of *coterie-sprache*. Some families, like the Glynnes, had a complete tribal language of their own. The use of abbreviations for Christian names was common at all levels, up to the highest; the Empress Frederick's letters are sprinkled with the ludicrously familiar nicknames—Mossy and Fishy, Missy and Tutsiman—of her royal relations all over Europe. Everybody had nicknames. Forster was "Fuz" or "The Hippopotamus" or "The Beadle of the Universe"; Cruikshank was "Genial George"; Dickens was "The Inimitable" and his children had innumerable and ever-changing nicknames such as "Chicken-stalker" or "Plornishmaroontigonter"; Mrs Procter was "Our Lady of Bitterness"; Macready was "Mac" or "The Eminent Tragedian" to his friends, "Sergeant Macready" or "The Bashaw" to his enemies. The use of nicknames for a socially successful figure like Richard Monckton Milnes was almost a status symbol; you might give yourself away by not recognizing him under references to "The Cool of the Evening" or "London Assurance" or "The Bird of Paradox"—or equally by continuing to use those particular nicknames when they had got too widespread and had begun to bore their originators.

Mrs Carlyle's nicknames for her friends were her own invention; her secret society was a small, devoted but fairly frequently changing band of callers in Cheyne Row, and all the passwords came from her. Browning neither belonged nor wanted to belong to the secret society. But he was affectionately devoted to Carlyle—"dear Carlyle", "dear generous noble Carlyle" he warmly calls his friend in his letters to Elizabeth Barrett. "I dined with dear Carlyle (catch me calling people 'dear' in a hurry, except in letter-beginnings!) yesterday. I don't know any people like them" he told a friend. Carlyle's opinion of Browning—allowing for the difference between a bilious pessimistic temperament and a sanguine optimistic one —was equally cordial. He told a friend that Robert Browning "had a powerful intellect, and among the men engaged in literature in England just now was one of the few from whom it was possible to expect something. . . . He had strong ambition and great confidence in himself".

Carlyle's extraordinary talk was a feast to Browning, whether it was a diatribe against the actor's profession or a rhapsody over an old folk song. Browning helped Carlyle to get hold of an MS letter needed for his book on Cromwell; Carlyle wrote and talked kindly to Browning about his *Bells and Pomegranates* poems—though his kindness took the rather odd form of suggesting that Browning would do better to write his next book in prose. But Carlyle gave the same advice to most of his poet friends and acquaintances—to Elizabeth Barrett, for instance, who received the advice with humility but, said Carlyle, "wrote me so touching a rejoinder that I had to draw in my horns". She felt ruffled, so she told Browning, that Carlyle should think so ill of poetry, and persisted in regarding Carlyle himself as a "poet unaware of himself", a "great prose poet", one who "fills the office of a poet—by analysing humanity back to its elements, to the destruction of the conventions of the hour". She had never met Carlyle, but she had long admired and been influenced by his works. She had a print of him hung up on the wall of her bedroom, she had contributed (though anonymously) to a study of him in R. H. Horne's *A New Spirit of the Age*, and had ventured to send him a copy of her 1844 Poems, which he had praised for "insight and veracity".

In this month of June 1846, Carlyle was fifty, Mrs Carlyle forty-four, Miss Barrett forty, Browning thirty-four. The

Carlyles had been married for nearly twenty years. Browning and Elizabeth Barrett had been secretly engaged for nine months and hoped to get married towards the end of the summer. The younger couple's relationship was moving to a climax. The older couple were nearing a crisis of another kind.

Elizabeth Barrett had spent this stifling hot Thursday of 18th June alone in her room, thinking of Browning all day; Haydon and his boxes had not stayed long in her mind. When all her family were having dinner, and her maid Wilson was away for her afternoon off, Miss Barrett suddenly decided she must go out for a little. This was more of a decision than it sounds; Miss Barrett never went out walking alone—hardly went out of the house at all, even in summer. So it was a stroke of great independence, even for a forty-year-old woman, to put on her bonnet and go out into the street alone with her dog Flush, and walk up and down at eight o'clock in the evening. Flush distracted her by refusing to come when she called him, and insisting on walking on the opposite side of the street, making her nervous lest the valuable little golden cocker spaniel should once again be snatched away by the dog-stealers. But they both got back safely to the house, and then came the late evening post with Browning's letter enclosing Mrs Carlyle's invitation. Miss Barrett sat down to write her late night reply to him. She talked of the Carlyles' invitation, she told him what she had been doing and thinking all day, she talked of their next meeting in two days' time. "If I am happy on any day it is through you wholly, whether you are absent or present, dearest, and ever dearest".

The dinner party to which the Carlyles invited Browning was to be in honour of the German novelist Gräfin Ida Hahn-Hahn, who was on a visit to London during this month. She had various lines to the Carlyles: through her compatriot Amely Bölte, for whom Mrs Carlyle had found jobs as a governess; through the German historian and diplomat Karl August Varnhagen von Ense, with whom Carlyle had been corresponding for some years; through Richard Monckton Milnes and Anna Jameson. Everyone was giving parties for Gräfin Hahn-Hahn in London that month, and the Carlyles felt obliged to do so too.

Ida von Hahn, daughter of Count Karl Friedrich von Hahn, of a very old Mecklenburg family, was born in 1805 and in 1826 married her cousin Graf Adolf von Hahn-Hahn. The marriage was unhappy, and in 1829 she was divorced on her own application. She lived in various parts of Germany and wrote a series of novels and travel books. Her most ambitious journey, calling for a good deal of enterprise and courage, was a voyage down the Danube to the Black Sea, thence to Turkey, the Aegean Islands, Cyprus, Syria, Palestine, Egypt and Nubia. In the book she wrote about this journey she showed herself a sensible hard-working observer, with little imagination, rather opinionated and not without some humour. She had what her mother, as she herself relates, called a "repulsive sincerity".

In 1840 Gräfin Hahn-Hahn had an operation on one eye to remove a squint, but lost the eye as well as the squint. She cannot have been a very glamorous beauty when she visited England at the age of forty-one. She apparently had false teeth as well as only one eye, since Lady Harriet Baring was heard to say that "Madame Hahn-Hahn's teeth quivered like the diamonds our grandmothers used to wear on their heads". The only picture of Ida Hahn-Hahn which I have been able to see dates from many years later than 1846; it is a photograph of her in a nun's habit—a motherly little bundle, with a face like a squashed muffin.

It is very unfair that women novelists who create radiant ethereal heroines are expected to be radiant and ethereal themselves; but such must have been the expectation about Gräfin Hahn-Hahn felt by the English readers who had been keenly devouring her novel *Gräfin Faustina* since it appeared in 1841—specially since Gräfin Faustina's life-story was an etherealized version of Gräfin Ida's. Faustina, too, had escaped from a distasteful early marriage to live with an intellectual lover. Young and dazzlingly beautiful, she is such an enchantress that before the story ends she has acquired a second husband, and also a passionate young adorer so despairingly devoted to her that he blows his brains out while holding her hand in farewell. The story ends with Faustina entering a convent; and here art anticipated life, for the novelist as well as her heroine ended as a nun.

Die Gräfin Faustina is ludicrous but not negligible. It has force and some originality, in the imagery, the dialogue, the minor characterization. No one but a student of the history of taste is likely to read it now, at any rate in translation, but it is possible to see why it had a great success in England, as it certainly did. "The English readers are fallen in love with Countess Hahn-Hahn's books, everybody reading them" wrote Mrs Jameson to Ottilie von Goethe in 1845. The high-minded Charlotte Williams-Wynn acknowledged to Varnhagen von Ense that Gräfin Hahn-Hahn's novels interested her exceedingly, and were valuable contributions towards the emancipation of women. That not-easily-pleased reader Mrs Carlyle wrote to her cousin that she had been doing nothing "except occasionally mend my stockings and read in the dreamy novels by the Gräfin Hahn-Hahn (Countess Cock cock! What a name!). She is a sort of German George Sand *without the genius*—and *en revanche* a good deal more of what we call in Scotland *gumtion*—a clever woman, really—separated from her husband of course, and on the whole very good to read when one is in a state of moral and physical collapse". Mrs Carlyle was sophisticated enough to recognize *Gräfin Faustina* as pure escape reading, a narcotic for a moment of mental strain. Mrs Jameson, too, read it at a moment of anxiety, during her father's last illness, "and it has fixed my attention and amused me from time to time as I am sure no other book could have done. . . . I have not for a long time read a book which has so chained and captivated my attention". Both Mrs Carlyle and Mrs Jameson were then in their middle forties; both were perhaps sexually unsatisfied by their marriages; one can understand why Faustina, that remote but ardent sylph, made pleasurable reading for them. Browning's comments, when he finally got round to reading the book (which he only did because he kept meeting the authoress at parties) were different. "What a horrible book . . . such characters as Faustina produce the very worst possible effect on me—I don't know how they strike other people—but I am at once incited *debellare superbos*—to try at least and pull down the arrogant—*contempt* would be the most Christian of all the feelings possible to be called forth by such a woman". Elizabeth Barrett did not agree: "but there is much beauty in Faustina—oh, surely!" she wrote back.

Gräfin Hahn-Hahn had already made some English friends in Germany before she decided to come to England. "Our poet Monckton Milnes—one of the *young England* set—has been to Berlin . . . he is very much enchanted with the Gräfin Ida" wrote Anna Jameson in February 1845 to her friend the volatile Ottilie von Goethe, whom Mrs Jameson considered very like Faustina. Milnes was in Berlin from December 1844 to February 1845, meeting many German writers in the circle of Varnhagen von Ense and Bettina von Arnim. Six months later Mrs Jameson herself met Gräfin Hahn-Hahn in Dresden and found her "very agreeable and lady-like". When Gräfin Hahn-Hahn came to London in the summer of 1846, it was mainly these two English writers, Milnes the poet M.P. and Anna Jameson the art historian, who sponsored the German novelist and introduced her to their friends.

Unluckily, the Gräfin did not come to England alone. She

brought a travelling companion with her, Oberst Baron Adolph von Bystram. She had met him in 1829, and they had been travelling about Europe together for years. The dedication of *Gräfin Faustina* reads—

"TO BYSTRAM

'For five months have I languished in the two-fold captivity of blindness and ill-health; for five months hast thou watched over me unweariedly, tending and soothing me, whispering of hope and peace, wiping the tears from mine eyes, and the damps of anguish from my brow,—lending me both sight and action; that I did not sink into despair, imbecility and apathy, I thank thee!"

This was very exciting for the readers of *Gräfin Faustina*, who easily identified Baron Andlau, Faustina's intellectual lover in the novel, with Baron Bystram. The editor of Milnes' letters to Varnhagen says firmly "This peculiar relationship, of whose innocence there is no doubt, was not understood by the prudish English". Gräfin Hahn-Hahn had said of her heroine Faustina that "she had, by the mere force of her individuality, brought things to that pass, that the world tacitly acknowledged her connexion with Baron Andlau as a legal one". No doubt she thought that she herself had forced the world to accept her own connexion with Bystram in the same way. But the prudish English couldn't help doubting whether it was as innocent as all that. "I fear Countess Hahn-Hahn cannot have liked her visit to England as far as society went" wrote Milnes later to Varnhagen. "She evidently saw she had made a mistake in coming there with Bystram to whom it was impossible to attach a character agreeable to our conventional morality; at first he was called her cousin, then her secret husband, then her guardian, then I don't know what, but as 'travelling companion' it was not considered decorous that he should be known. If she had been handsomer, we might have permitted it; but as it was, the public mind was offended! If she had come alone she would have done much better, and her social qualities would have been more appreciated".

Amely Bölte told the same story in a letter to Varnhagen.

Thursday 18th June

"The Gräfin Hahn-Hahn has greatly surprised and embarrassed the English public by her unexpected appearance. She brought with her letters of introduction from very important people, but she also brought—Colonel Bystram. She herself seemed not to have the slightest idea of the existing prejudice against her".

Gräfin Hahn-Hahn was indeed perfectly unconscious of having shocked anyone. She considered her visit as the greatest success. "Everything is going well" she wrote to a friend in Germany "and up till now I am well satisfied with my journey. Particularly with London! London surpasses all one's ideas and expectations. I imagined I should find a huge city, and I found a world—where every step, every pace, reminds one of its immensity. I passed five of the most tumultuous weeks of my life there, like a particle whirled about in this world of diamonds and mud". She attributed her not having been received by Queen Victoria simply to the fact that the Queen had just had a baby and was in the Isle of Wight, and therefore there were no drawing-rooms. However, everyone else had been extremely welcoming. "You can have no idea at all what English hospitality is like; one becomes more intimate with people here in two weeks than we do in two years". She had met Disraeli, Mrs Norton, Bulwer, Lady Morgan—the two last she described as "quite deformed and made idiotic by vanity".

She certainly was invited out a great deal, though possibly not quite for the reasons she supposed. "Very much fêtée, very fashionable" Mrs Jameson wrote about her. Annabel Crewe (who was afterwards to marry Milnes) described in her diary an evening at Lord Palmerston's where she saw for the first time "the lion Madame Hahn-Hahn". The German visitor certainly provided a good deal of entertainment to her more satirical English acquaintances such as the Barings and Milnes. Milnes' gratitude for the hospitality which he had received in Germany two years earlier made him accept responsibility for introducing anyone recommended to him by his German friends—and besides, he liked arranging things, manipulating people, doing good turns which allowed him to exercise his social skill, to show how many strings he was able to pull. He had just promised Browning to find him a post as Ambassador

if Browning wanted one. The previous year, at Carlyle's insti-
gation, he had helped to induce Sir Robert Peel to give Tennyson a Civil List pension. The much-quoted account of the conversation between Milnes and Carlyle about this is a perfect
illustration of the easy relationship between these unlikely
friends. When Tennyson lost what money he had, and his
friends began looking round for ways to help him, Carlyle said
to Milnes—

"When are you going to get that pension for Alfred Tennyson?"

"My dear Carlyle, the thing is not so easy as you seem to
suppose. What will my constituents say if I do get the pension
for Tennyson? They know nothing about him or his poetry,
and they will probably think he is some poor relation of my
own, and that the whole affair is a job".

"Richard Milnes, on the Day of Judgment, when the Lord
asks you why you didn't get that pension for Alfred Tennyson,
it will not do to lay the blame on your constituents; it is *you*
that will be damned".

Carlyle—lantern-jawed, grizzled, all but six foot tall, with
brilliant blue eyes and a "bilious-ruddy" complexion, with his
foot-long clay pipe and his old plaid dressing-gown—felt a
certain virile contempt for Milnes, that "pretty little robin-
redbreast" as he called him. Milnes was short and plump and
dapperly dressed, "a most bland-smiling, semi-quizzical, affectionate, high-bred, Italianized little man, who had long olive-
blonde hair, a dimple, next to no chin, and flings his arm round
your neck when he addresses you in public society" said Carlyle,
in one of his hard faithful flashlight-photograph likenesses.

But the two men got on very well, largely thanks to Milnes
who had a great talent for friendships with difficult men, but
partly also because of Carlyle's underlying generosity. It was a
friendship without obligation or patronage, which benefited
both their very unlike temperaments. They rode about London
together at night, Carlyle went to Milnes' breakfast parties
and stayed with him at his parents' house in Yorkshire, Milnes
dined in Cheyne Row. He was fond of Carlyle, laughed at him,
was not afraid of him; it was pleasantly relaxing for the moody

philosopher. Milnes was a tease; he would trail his coat, putting forward opinions which he knew would provoke Carlyle into furious contradictions, "reminding me" said a spectator "of a naughty boy rubbing a fierce cat's tail backwards and, getting in between furious growls and fiery sparks, he managed to avoid the threatened scratches".

Carlyle teased back. He mocked Milnes' occasional despondency—"Don't you think that a little gentlemanly melancholy is going to be sorrow enough for you in life?"; his social activity—"If Christ were again on earth Milnes would ask Him to breakfast, and the clubs would all be talking of the good things Christ had said"; his political standing—he ends a letter to Milnes "and so once more I address myself to the Honourable Member for Pomfret, and say 'Oh, Hon. Mem., speak to me!'"

Milnes even succeeded—at least at intervals—in the fundamentally much more difficult task of securing Mrs Carlyle's liking. Her suspicion that he must be snobbish, insincere and insolent was deeply lodged, but she was disarmed by his delightful little notes, his invulnerable good humour, his verbal acrobatics. She records an evening when he dined at Cheyne Row and made himself so pleasant—no showing-off, no disdain of the Carlyles' modest style of living—that the whole evening "went off like a sort of firework—crackers of wit exploding in every direction—Darwin spoke only in epigrams—Carlyle in flights of genius—Milnes in poetical paradoxes". Everyone had shone, including Mrs Carlyle herself; it had been an evening to remember.

Would the Carlyles' party for Gräfin Hahn-Hahn on 24th June be equally successful? It did not seem very likely. Among Milnes' experiments in introducing the German novelist to his English friends, this was perhaps the most daring. How delightful, in any case, for a tease like Milnes, to let loose an opinionated improper one-eyed woman writer on this captious and explosive couple.

Gräfin Hahn-Hahn's political opinions, like her appearance and
her marital status, must have caused some embarrassment to
her English hosts. She was entirely on the side of Disraeli and
the right-wing Tories about the Repeal of the Corn Laws.
England, she thought, powerful and active as it was, was being
corrupted by "strange ideas of philanthropy and forbearance".
The passing of the bill repealing the Corn Laws was "the work
of the canker-worm", because it would weaken the power of the
landowners and the old aristocracy on which, she considered,
England's strength at home and greatness abroad were based,
and would open avenues for the advance of democracy. Since
her return from the Near East in 1844 she had been worrying
about the advance of Communism. "I shudder when I think of
the next fifty years. Nothing can remain where it now stands—
neither Church, nor State, nor society. The work of dissolution
has commenced". She read books by Communists to try and
understand their ideas, and attempted to arouse her friends who
"denied the real existence of Communism and its propaganda"
from their complacent calm.

These McCarthy-ite opinions in the year 1846 must have
been coolly received by many of the writers with whom Gräfin
Hahn-Hahn was in touch in London. Browning was a Radical
and a Republican. Elizabeth Barrett had published a poem in
support of Corn Law Repeal, and had been praised for it by
Cobden. Macready had allowed anti-Corn Law meetings to be
held in Covent Garden Theatre when he was its manager.
Mrs Carlyle was a friend of Mazzini and other political exiles
who were preparing revolution in Italy. Carlyle's opinions
differed violently both from Gräfin Hahn-Hahn's and from those
of her opponents. He wanted the Corn Laws repealed; he was
not likely to join with Gräfin Hahn-Hahn in lamenting the

dissolution at work to undermine the Church, or in deploring the
weakened power of the old aristocracy. But when she peered
apprehensively down those great avenues along which democracy was sweeping forward, Carlyle was misgivingly at her
side; in his eyes, too, "Democracy . . . advances irresistible
with ominous ever-increasing speed", flinging aside the True
Guidance with the False, unable to discern the veritable Hero
who should have been leading the van of that onrush.

Gräfin Hahn-Hahn's chief sponsor, Monckton Milnes, was
also—though with some hesitation—against her on the question
of the Repeal of the Corn Laws. In the summer of 1846 Milnes
was politically a disappointed man. He had long been hoping
for the post of Under-Secretary of State for Foreign Affairs,
and in January of that year he had seemed to have a good hope
of getting it. But the Prime Minister, Sir Robert Peel, gave the
post to another man, and one whom Milnes particularly disliked. Milnes, who had ceased for some time to feel much
admiration or reverence for Peel, was exasperated by the
Prime Minister's action in passing him over for the coveted
Ministerial post. "Peel has not belief enough in him to be a
humbug—he is not even a hypocrite of sincerity" he wrote in
his Commonplace Book. "You abuse Peel like a woman; you
become *Miss* Milnes" said Lady Harriet Baring with her
habitual cruelty. Throughout the spring and early summer of
1846, Milnes was on the verge of leaving the Tory party and
joining the Whigs, and meanwhile was vacillating about
whether to support Peel over the Repeal of the Corn Laws.

These middle days of June 1846 were critical for Peel. His
Bill abolishing the Corn Laws had been passed by the House of
Commons on 15th May, and was now about to be passed by the
Lords, with the reluctant but loyal support of the Duke of
Wellington. Meanwhile in the Commons Peel was being in-
cessantly harassed and insulted by the Protectionist section of
his own party, led by Disraeli and Lord George Bentinck, who
vilified him as the betrayer of the landed interest which the
Conservative Party had undertaken to defend. The unanswerable arguments of Cobden and Bright, and the still more
unanswerable argument of the Irish potato blight and the

famine that followed, had changed Peel's convictions. The Whigs, given their chance in December 1845 to take office and abolish the Corn Laws, had lost their nerve and failed to form a government, so their leader Lord John Russell had "handed back with courtesy the poisoned chalice to Sir Robert".

How poisonous it was, Peel was now finding, as he carried grimly on with the Corn Bill and the Irish Coercion Bill, while Disraeli's venomous eloquence nightly splashed scorching round his head in the House of Commons. Disraeli compared Peel to the Turkish admiral who steered his fleet into the enemy's port and surrendered, to the nurse who murdered the baby in her charge. Peel was taunted with having invented, or at least exaggerated, the Irish famine. He was abused, hooted at, interrupted and shouted down by the Protectionists till sometimes his voice failed him to go on speaking, or he was too exhausted at the end of a debate to rise from his place.

Even when the Corn Bill was through the House of Commons, the violent and ruthless Bentinck suddenly accused Peel in the House of having "hunted an illustrious relative of his to death", a distorted reference to Canning and Peel's part in Catholic Emancipation. So unexpected and vicious was this attack that Peel at first could say little in reply. The papers which he needed to prove the injustice of the charge were at his country house, Drayton. On this evening of 18th June, he told the House of Commons that he would make a statement next evening on the accusation of base and dishonest conduct towards his old chief Canning which Bentinck had brought against him.

The House and the public were agog with expectation of the next night's debate. The political situation, like the weather, was in full heat wave. Sides were taken over the Corn Law question with a violence exceeding any normal political reaction. Fathers and sons quarrelled about it and did not speak to each other for years afterwards. Milnes' father was a Protectionist, and took an active part against his son in Yorkshire political activities. It was not only the old landowners like Robert Milnes who were dismayed; all the old men felt that their world was crumbling. "As to public affairs I cannot bear to think of them. Sir Robert Peel is infatuated; he is playing the part of that weak man, Necker, in the beginning of the French Revolution" wrote Wordsworth from Westmorland.

But the middle-aged and the young felt differently. Even those who normally stood aloof from party politics felt moved to take sides at this crucial moment. On this Thursday 18th June, Carlyle took a copy of his book *Cromwell*, the second edition of which had just appeared, and sat down to write a letter to send with it to Sir Robert Peel.

"Let this poor labour of mine be a small testimony . . . to a late great and valiant labour of yours, and claim reception as such. . . . By-and-by, as I believe, all England will say what already many a one begins to feel, that whatever were the spoken unveracities of Parliament, and they are many on all hands, lamentable to gods and men, here has a great veracity been *done* in Parliament, considerably our greatest for many years past—a strenuous, courageous, and needful thing, to which all of us that so see it are bound to give our loyal recognition and furtherance as we can.

> I have the honour to be, Sir,
> Your obliged fellow-citizen
> and obedient servant
> T. Carlyle".

A good letter to get, if you were a Prime Minister at the crisis of your career, from the foremost historian and political philosopher of the day, who not so long ago had been denouncing you as Sir Jabesh Windbag.

Even Haydon, whose former keen interest in politics had faded away into the self-absorption of his troubles, was pierced by some recognition of what Peel was enduring in these critical days. He had written a begging letter to Peel, latest of many, and others to the Duke of Beaufort and Lord Brougham. "Who answered first? Tormented by D'Israeli, harassed by public business, up came the following letter" and Haydon goes on to quote in his diary a letter from Peel expressing, with his customary chilly formality, sympathy for Haydon's financial distress, and enclosing a cheque for fifty pounds.

Haydon's diary entry for 18th June began "O God bless me through the evils of this day. Amen. Great anxiety" and went on to speak of his debts to the landlord and the failure of his other appeals for money. "No reply from Brougham, Beaufort, Barry or Hope!—and this Peel is the man who has *no heart*". He recorded writing a letter to his friend Commissioner Evans, offering to paint a picture of *Byron Musing at Harrow* for fifty guineas, and he attached to his diary Evans' reply asking him to dinner on Sunday to discuss it. He noted his delivery of his journals and pictures to Miss Barrett, and her letter acknowledging their safe receipt. And he added, thinking of his portrait of Wellington now lodged in Wimpole Street, "I have the Duke's boots and hat".

A long and often embarrassing story lies behind this reference. Wellington was one of Haydon's tutelary deities, one of the avatars between whom his faith oscillated. "The Wellington system—principle and prudence, the groundworks of risk. Mine the Napoleon—audacity, with a defiance of principle, if principle was in the way. I got into prison. Napoleon died at St Helena. Wellington is living and honoured" he wrote once in his diary, trying to trace out the pattern of his life. In his correspondence with Keats in 1817 the contrast between the characters of Wellington and Napoleon was thrashed out, and twenty-five years later he was still poring over the same contrast in his letters to Elizabeth Barrett. He was always writing to the Duke—asking for money, for commissions, for permission to dedicate pamphlets to him, for his support in getting funds voted for the encouragement of art. Wellington always replied, promptly and in his own hand, and invariably said No. Haydon was always painting pictures of Wellington—nearly as many as of Napoleon: *Wellington Musing on the Field of Waterloo* (five of these), *George IV and Wellington Visiting Waterloo* (two of these), and in order to get the details right he tried to borrow Wellington's clothes, boots, hat, saddle; he even got at the Duke's valet. He also visited Waterloo and made a sketch of the battlefield, and saw the monument to Lord Anglesey's leg.

In the end his persistence secured for him an invitation to

Walmer to do a sketch of the Duke for a large picture of *Wellington on the Field of Waterloo* commissioned by the City of Liverpool. Haydon's portrait sketch, now at Stratfield Saye—showing the Duke in profile "like an Eagle of the gods . . . silvery with age and service . . . Riding had made him rosy and dozy"—is one of Haydon's more successful likenesses. After this, Wellington's image was one of Haydon's sources of income; like Napoleon, Lord Grey and Byron, he did a great deal of "musing" in pictures and engravings. And Haydon still had his hat and boots.

Haydon could have chosen no more appropriate day than this 18th June for thinking of Wellington and his clothes and his horse Copenhagen, for this was Waterloo Day, the anniversary of the battle, and the Duke, as he had done every year for the last thirty years, was giving his Waterloo Banquet to com-memorate the great day. Wellington was still Commander-in-Chief and was in the Cabinet, supporting Peel over the Repeal of the Corn Laws in order to hold the Conservative Party to-gether, though unconvinced that the measure was really neces-sary, or anything more than just a panic of Peel's. But on this night of 18th June his attention was not on the imminent fate of the Government of which he was a member, but on the events of thirty-one years ago.

Carriages were queueing up in Piccadilly to get to Apsley House, and traffic was held up for half an hour by the arriving guests and the crowds assembled to watch them. The biggest cheer from the crowd went to "One-Leg", Lord Anglesey, the splendid beaky-nosed white-whiskered old hero who had lost a leg at Waterloo and was a close friend of the Duke's, and very like him to look at; the two deaf old men used to carry on shouted conversations with each other in the House of Lords during other peers' speeches. Anglesey was Master-General of the Ordnance, and had recently been up to no good; he had been involved in an unsuccessful intrigue between the Protec-tionists and the Whigs to get Peel out. But if Wellington knew of this, it made no difference tonight; at the Waterloo Banquet Anglesey was inevitably a guest of honour, and was placed on the right of Prince Albert.

Wellington, in Field-Marshal's uniform, was on the steps of Apsley House at half-past seven to meet Prince Albert as he got out of his carriage. The Prince was incongruous among the Waterloo veterans. Though he wore the uniform of Colonel of the Scots Fusiliers and looked a very fine figure in it, he was too young, even if he had not been a Royalty, ever to have known war. The seventy-seven-year-old Duke and the twenty-seven-year-old Prince went up together to the big banqueting gallery on the first floor and sat down to dinner at a quarter to eight, the Duke with Prince Albert on his right and the Neapolitan Minister Prince Castelcicola on his left.

The low sunset light of that fiercely hot day came in through the six westward-facing windows of the Waterloo Gallery, competing with the light of the serried candles in the candelabra of the huge silver-gilt Portuguese Service, crowded with dancing nymphs, allegorical figures of the Continents, camels, horses, scorpions, which stretched the whole length of the table. The colours were all fierce and bright—scarlet uniforms, shining white tablecloth, harsh yellow damask on the walls staring out between the crowded frames of the pictures captured in Joseph Bonaparte's carriage at the Battle of Vittoria.

There was gold and sheen everywhere—gilding on the doors and ceiling, shutters lined with looking-glass, epaulettes, decanters, medals, picture frames, chandeliers, everything glared and glittered; but the chairs on which the guests sat were of light cheap-looking wood. It was the room of a man and a soldier, with whom no female advice, not even Mrs Arbuthnot's, could prevail against his imperious unregarding taste, which called for crowded magnificence but did not notice inelegance of detail.

The band played martial tunes and the Overture and Aria from Verdi's *Nino*. The new statuettes of Wellington and Napoleon by Count d'Orsay which adorned the table were admired. There were toasts—a great many toasts—and speeches of thanks, twenty-two of them altogether. But it was all over by half-past ten, and the tireless old Duke—who could still go without both luncheon and dinner for days together if he were busy—went on to a reception at Lady Londonderry's, just round the corner at Holdernesse House.

At Vauxhall Gardens, crowded with strolling people on this sultry night, there was a Waterloo Fête with an illumination of Wellington's name with a ducal coronet and laurels. The orchestra played military tunes, there were fireworks, there was a salute of twenty-one guns, and finally another illumination of coloured fires and Wellington's head in a star surrounded by martial trophies.

Carlyle, if he was out that evening on one of his habitual night walks along the river to Vauxhall Bridge, would have an unappreciated grandstand view of the illuminations and fireworks. Browning was at home at New Cross that evening; he had bought a copy of Gräfin Hahn-Hahn's *Faustina* on his way home, but had not yet forced himself to start reading it. Miss Barrett, refreshed by her airing in the street with Flush, was writing her late night letter to Browning. Haydon, who slept very badly in this stifling weather, was completing his full share of "the Evils of this day".

This June was the hottest summer month that anyone could remember. For the first twenty-two days of the month the average day temperature was 84° in the shade, 105° in the sun. Kent had had six weeks without rain and midday temperatures of 104° to 116°. On the morning of Friday 19th June the temperature in some parts of the country reached 96° in the shade. The heat had begun in the very first days of the month. Already by 2nd June Browning was complaining that it was very warm, and warning Elizabeth Barrett to be careful of her health. By the 5th the temperature in her room was 80°, and though she loved the heat she could do nothing but lie on the sofa and drink lemonade and read *Monte Cristo*. "Oh—it is so hot" she wrote to Browning. "There is a thick mist lacquered over with light—it is cauldron-heat, rather than fire-heat". He meanwhile was at Church, and seeing people faint with the heat. A week later it was still "too hot to laugh"; even the mornings burned and dazzled in white heat; it was so overcoming that even Flush was cross, and Miss Barrett had to take him out in the carriage at half-past seven in the evening to get a breath of coolness by the silvery water of the Serpentine in the dusk of Hyde Park.

It was murderous weather. Wherrymen, out in boats on the Thames all day, died of sunstroke; farm-labourers died of heat-stroke after a day's mowing; many people all over the country were drowned while bathing. There were rumours of Asiatic cholera at Hull and Leeds, there were typhus outbreaks in London. There were proclamations that dogs must go muzzled, for fear of rabies. Anyone not in robust health suffered and sickened in the stifling weather. "The great heat of London . . . made me quite ill again" complained Mrs Carlyle, and from Manchester she heard from Geraldine Jewsbury "The Heat is

terrible, for our air is so thick and heavy that, when heated, it
is like a casing of hot lead''.

For the hay harvest the weather was a boon, and by the third
week in June the hay in the south of England was all cut, and
much of it stacked. The wheat crop was doing well, but the
prolonged drought was destroying the barley and oats, there
were heath fires all over the country, and the gardeners were
in despair. Grass everywhere was burnt brown, the peas and
beans were wilting, the mignonette in the London window-
boxes was withered and dry. It was a wonderful year for roses,
though; Browning brought Elizabeth Barrett bunches of them
from his parents' garden in New Cross, and she herself actually
drove out to Hampstead Heath and picked a dog rose there,
quite early in the month. Everything was early—Miss Mitford's famous strawberry parties at Three Mile Cross were
already collecting all her neighbours. But hot and fine as it was,
one could not reckon safely on the weather for outdoor parties;
there were sudden and violent storms all over the country,
many people were killed by lightning, in some places the very
air smelt of fire, and the raindrops that fell were the largest
ever seen. Dickens, who left England with his family on 31st
May and travelled up the Rhine in a heat "more intense than
any I have ever felt", described the huge thunderstorms that
boomed and rumbled among the Swiss mountains. The wooden
walls and floor of the pretty lake-side house which he had taken
at Lausanne were hot to the touch all the night through, and
his children were so tanned that they looked "as if they were
in one perpetual sunset".

The stored-up heat of the houses caused many fires in London,
and there were other disagreeable effects of town life in the
heat. On this 19th June "a correspondent requests us to call the
attention of the authorities to the offensive condition of the
sewers, the effluvia from which, in this hot weather, is most
offensive" announced the *Daily News*, the paper which Dickens
had founded a few months earlier. The rapid development of
London in recent years had overstrained the sewers, as everyone could now perceive. "The Heat has been so savage that not
only we Italians, but the East Indians, have suffered much from

it. I never knew hot nights so oppressive and hot days so little agreeable" wrote Milnes to a friend, while his future wife Annabel Crewe, whose spelling was not always perfectly reliable, recorded in her diary on 19th June "Heat of weather quite unparralled in England".

The only pleasant thing to contemplate was ice. A ship called the *Ilizaide* came into St Katharine's Docks with 664 tons of ice in large blocks; little boys hung all day round the depots of the Wenham Lake ice, as though the mere sight of the great white blocks would cool them; sherry coblers with ice (and no doubt quantities of typhoid germs) in them were a favourite drink. But it was impossible to keep cool, or look as if you were cool. "This hot weather puts us all into Falstaff's state" wrote Wordsworth to Crabb Robinson, conjuring up an unlikely vision of the stately old poet "larding the lean earth" with his sweat as he pottered about Rydal Mount. The papers were full of advertisements for clothes to keep cool in. "The Delightful Coolness of the Golden Flax Cravat Collar, together with its perfect fit, however loosely tied on, recommend it especially during this weather". For the women "dresses of the most aerial textures, tulles, barèges, muslinés, organdies, tarlatans, and Chinese Batiste were alone wearable during the late insupportable heat". If you had lost a relation within the year, you could go to Jay's, or The London General Mourning Warehouse as it was then called, and get "Muslin Dresses for Half-Mourning. The extreme heat of the season has given an extraordinary impetus to the sale of PRINTED MUSLINS". In a world without refrigerators, it was also useful to be told of Carson's Meat Preservers, by which meat could be cured in twelve or fifteen minutes and "all taints avoided, even in the hottest weather", or of "Lemon and Kali, a cooling beverage" advertised by a chemist in Cornhill as "of inestimable value to those whose duties oblige them to perambulate the crowded streets of large towns in hot weather".

But crowds, even out of doors, were a thing to avoid. An article in the *Illustrated London News* describes the "languid limbs, and lazy lounging gait of people who passed . . . in the street, or crowded to the Serpentine". Indoors it was far worse;

evening parties were too hot to attend, even though the doors were taken right off their hinges, and morning concerts were a sea of waving fans, an undulation of fainting ladies.

The theatres were half empty. Macready's season at the Princess Theatre, where he had been playing *King Lear* and a new play called *The King of the Commons*, finished on this Friday 19th June. "Acted King James better than usual, wishing my last night at the Princess's to leave a pleasing impression— as I think it did. Called for and very warmly received" he noted in his diary, adding a sarcastic note about the poor receipts at the Haymarket and Drury Lane that week. If the theatres were empty, the open-air pleasure gardens, Vauxhall, Surrey Gardens and Cremorne, were crowded every night with people watching the fireworks and the balloons which floated about in the night sky. The river steamers, cutting their way up and down the crowded Thames, were packed with people trying to get some cool breezes.

Those who had the money and the time even for these modest diversions were the best off. It was a grim time for those who had to work indoors. At Wolverhampton, where on the 18th the temperature was 96° in the shade, the works had to be stopped because the workmen could not support the unprecedented heat. In London, work went languidly on in stifling warehouses, and those with business in the City felt the pavements burning through the soles of their boots as they went to and fro, and were thankful when a passing water-cart gave an illusion of freshness to the dusty street.

One of those whose business took them into the City in these suffocating days was Haydon. After a day out borrowing money from a silk manufacturer friend in Spital Square, he records "Terrifically hot today". He was back there a week later, dining with a friend who had promised to lend him £1,000, but who now had to admit that the money was not forthcoming. The disappointment was sharp, and Haydon did what he rarely did—drank too much, and felt the results for days afterwards. He could not work much; his days were spent in sitting staring at his half-finished picture, or "harassing about to no purpose in the heat". One morning he made a great bonfire in the courtyard of his house and spent all day, in that tropical weather, burning great masses of letters and documents. At night he could not sleep, and this increased his nervous irritability. His family wanted him to see a doctor, but he refused. He had always suffered in hot weather and had a passion for fresh air; his favourite wind was an east-north-easterly in February, and he was always flinging open windows, in his own and other people's houses. Heat made him feel as though there were too much blood in his brain, which must somehow be relieved.

On this day, Friday 19th June, Haydon wrote nothing at all in his diary, not even his usual prayer at the beginning of the day, for help in getting through it.

Browning was writing early that morning—one more letter to Elizabeth Barrett, the last before their meeting next day. At that early hour it was cool, and looked like rain—a relief in one way, but a worry in another. On this Friday he was due to join a river party to Greenwich given by the Procters for Gräfin Hahn-Hahn. It had been arranged that if it was raining heavily on Friday the party should be put off to the next day, Saturday, and Browning was anxious about that, not because he cared in the least whether the party to Greenwich came off or not, but because if he had to go to it on Saturday, that might interfere with his visit to Miss Barrett that day. However on the Friday morning he had still had no word about the party being put off. He was due to meet the Procters in Central London and go down to Greenwich with them and the rest of the party. He was rather bored with the whole idea of it, and embarrassed too at not having succeeded in reading *Gräfin Faustina* before he met its authoress again. Though he had bought the book the night before, he had not had time to "get it up" in a couple of hours. By the time he had to end his letter and go off from New Cross to meet the Procters, the day was already getting hotter.

Browning was always being invited to parties to meet Gräfin Hahn-Hahn. Not only was there this Greenwich trip, and the party at the Carlyles' next Wednesday, but he had already met her on at least two occasions. The first was at a ball at the Procters' at the beginning of June. That had been a glorious evening for Browning, though not because of his meeting with the Gräfin. He had had a letter that morning from Elizabeth Barrett promising definitely to marry him before the end of the summer; and so he danced all evening at the Procters', feeling "altogether happy", and did not get home till four o'clock "with the birds singing loud and the day bright and broad". He used to walk home from these late parties, all along the interminable Kent Road to the New Cross Turnpike where he came in sight of the open country, and took the first turn to the right after the turnpike, past a quickset hedge and so among trees and gardens and little green hills to his parents' odd house which looked like a "crooked, hasty and rash goose-pie".

Besides Gräfin Hahn-Hahn, Browning had met many friends and acquaintances at the Procters' ball: Thackeray and Edwin Landseer, Chorley the music critic of the *Athenaeum*, the ubiquitous Mrs Jameson, Macready and Milnes, who was "unusually cordial", thought Macready. Not so Browning—or at any rate Macready thought not: Browning was probably too much absorbed in his euphoric mood to have thoughts to spare for Macready, but the actor wrote furiously in his diary "Browning . . . did not speak to me—the *puppy!*"

These two men had been friends for years, but had quarrelled drastically three years earlier over the production of Browning's play *A Blot in the 'Scutcheon* when Macready was manager of Drury Lane. Macready was the most in fault, but his temperament was far more resentful than Browning's, and ever since the quarrel he had tended to describe Browning in his diary as "a wretched insect". Tactful hosts like John Kenyon now took care not to invite the two men to dinner the same night; but a ball with a lot of guests was different. In any case, Macready was so difficult that there was no way of making sure one had not invited him at the same time as some deadly enemy, temporary or permanent. It was only a month ago that he had had a tremendous row with Forster, editor of the *Daily News*, which had embroiled Dickens, Maclise and Stanfield,

and though there had been an apology by Forster and a recon-
ciliation, the patching up was rather temporary.

Macready may have been a difficult guest, but everyone was
eager to have him at their parties. He was now the undeniable
head of his profession, the great tragic actor of the day; a man
not easily understood—overbearing but full of self-reproach,
austere socially but passionate on the stage, scholarly, hyper-
critical, laborious and of an iron courage and will. Many people
hated and feared him, mimicked him, recoiled from his suspicions and raw nerves. But his family and home life was happy,
and his close friends loved and admired him. Dickens and Forster
were warmly faithful, in spite of quarrels. Dickens dedicated
Nicholas Nickleby to him—a slightly ambiguous tribute, when
one thinks of the stage manner and appearance of that great
tragic actor Mr Vincent Crummles; he is supposed to have been
modelled on the actor Davenport, but must have reminded
many readers of Macready. But Dickens and Macready, and
their families, remained excellent friends. So did the Carlyles
and the Macreadys; Mrs Carlyle was godmother to one of the
Macready children, went to their Christmas parties to see
Dickens and Forster conjuring and Thackeray dancing—and to
be made to dance herself by Forster—and thought Macready's
shyness in private life rather touching. "Poor dear William! . . .
to see a man who is exhibiting himself every night on a stage,
blushing like a young girl in a private room is a beautiful
phenomenon for me!" Still more surprisingly Carlyle, who
thought that acting was a profession fit only for slaves, had a
very high opinion of Macready, "a man of scrupulous veracity,
correctness, integrity, a kind of *Grandisonian* style of magna-
nimity, both in substance and manner, visible in all his conduct.
. . . I greatly esteem the man". Mary Russell Mitford, though
she had nearly as much cause as Browning had to quarrel with
Macready the actor-manager, thought highly of Macready the
man. "Very fascinating . . . of the most polished and delightful
manners, and with no fault but the jealousy and unreasonable-
ness which seems to me the natural growth of the green-
room", and she went on to describe one great secret of Macready's power: "I have a physical pleasure in the sound of Mr

Macready's voice, whether talking, reading or acting (except when he rants). It seems to me very exquisite music, with something instrumental and vibrating in the sound, like certain notes of the violoncello". Macready's voice was endlessly imitated; admiringly copied by friends like Forster, brutally mimicked by stage enemies. It must have been an extraordinary sound, echoing and re-echoing through English and American theatres in a hundred unconscious imitations all through the nineteenth century, as Sir John Gielgud's voice does through the twentieth-century theatres.

It was therefore not surprising that, in spite of all quarrels and awkwardnesses, Macready was invited to the Procters' ball. Procter and Macready had known each other for many years; Macready had put on Procter's play *Mirandola*, and there had been the usual row and breach, but it had been made up, and they met frequently all through the 1830's and 1840's. The Procters in any case would not have bothered much about Browning's feelings if he and Macready met at their ball. In 1846 Browning was invited out a great deal, but less as a poet than as a useful conversable bachelor, a good dancer, a good-looking very well-dressed young man, small, pale, with waving hair worn very long like most men's at that time. For a man who had already published some of his finest work, and had a just confidence in his powers, this purely social acceptance was a sore point. This had come out in connection with the other party, besides the Procters' ball, to which Browning had recently been invited to meet Gräfin Hahn-Hahn.

This was a breakfast party given by Mrs Jameson in the middle of June. Browning told Elizabeth Barrett that he was invited to meet "this and the other notable"; but Mrs Jameson told Miss Barrett that Browning himself was the "celebrity" of the occasion who had been specially invited to meet Gräfin Hahn-Hahn, and related how, though gracefully effacing himself, he had charmed the whole company. Miss Barrett of course passed this on to Browning (perhaps unconsciously embellishing Mrs Jameson's account a little, in the light of her own admiring love for Browning).

Browning remembered about this as he sat writing his letter

to Elizabeth Barrett on this morning of Friday 19th June,
before he went off to the Procters' Greenwich party—all the
more because Mrs Jameson was also going to be at the party.
"Something you said on Mrs Jameson's authority amused me"
he wrote "—the encomium on my grace in sitting still to see
the play and not jumping onto the stage to act too—as if it
were not the best privilege one finds in being 'known' never so
little, that it dispenses one from having to make oneself
known". It was a sensitive point. Mrs Jameson might call him
a "celebrity", or Miss Barrett might say she had; but he did
not, for instance, get a mention in the list of well-known
English people whom she had met that Gräfin Hahn-Hahn sent
to Germany a few days later.

It was not a very congenial set of people that went to Greenwich that day. Mrs Jameson was always a helpful element at a
party; but Browning was abstracted at this time, Gräfin Hahn-
Hahn was a figure to attract rather too much attention in a
public place, and though Procter was a mild dreamy drooping
little man, his wife was anything but mild. Procter, who wrote
under the name of Barry Cornwall but earned his living as a
Commissioner in Lunacy, had been at Harrow with Byron and
knew all the writers of the day. Browning's *Colombe's Birthday*
was dedicated to him, and so was *Vanity Fair*, which Thackeray
had started to write in this spring. Procter was a sympathetic
host but Mrs Procter, "Our Lady of Bitterness", was not at all
easy to please, and particularly disapproved of what she considered Browning's idleness.

Nor did the day turn out any cooler, as had been hoped.
"London June 19th Wind this day at noon N.E., light airs and
sultry weather" reported *The Times* Ship News. The sweltering
Thames at Greenwich, awash with London's drains and refuse,
imparted no coolness. It was almost possible to believe *Punch*'s
tall stories about the Irish rivers which were simmering in the
heat so that salmon could be fished out ready boiled. *Punch* was
making the most of the heat wave; it was full of pictures of
ragged children playing in the splash of water-carts, and of the
fountains in Trafalgar Square (one of *Punch*'s favourite targets
just then) being turned into a public shower-bath. Most topical

of all was the cartoon of the two Front Benches in the House of Commons, each with a figure on it; the caption was— "*Lord John.* 'If it's too hot there, Sir Robert, I'll change places' ".

On this Friday evening Peel and Lord John Russell were both in their places on the Front Benches, and the physical and mental heat in the House was indeed fierce. Peel spoke to clear himself of Bentinck's and Disraeli's charges that he had betrayed his chief Canning over Catholic Emancipation in the 1820's. He pointed out that Disraeli had relied on a *Times* report of a speech by Peel which no other paper had confirmed, and that even *The Times* reporter had admitted that he couldn't hear Peel very well on that occasion. Peel's speech this night was punctuated by "Loud and continued cheering", "Hear, Hear, and great cheering", "Prolonged cheers and laughter". He ended by suggesting that Disraeli's paraded veneration for the memory of Canning was simply assumed to wound a political opponent, and that thereby he was "desecrating feelings which are in themselves entitled to esteem and respect". Bentinck and Disraeli refused to withdraw and returned to the charge; Lord John Russell, in a chilly speech, admitted that Peel had cleared himself of this particular charge, but suggested that he had been unfair to Canning.

But the feeling of the House was overwhelmingly with Peel. Greville, who had been in bed with gout but had hobbled down to the House to be present on this exciting occasion, said that Bentinck's reply was ill-judged and against the feeling of the House, that he and Disraeli cut a miserable figure, and that the attempt to ruin Peel's character "failed and recoiled on the heads of his accusers and . . . has gathered round him feelings of sympathy which will find a loud and general echo in the country".

Greville was a sound judge of the movements of public opinion. A widespread personal sympathy for Peel, cutting across party affiliations, became evident in the next few days, and was curiously reflected from the development of Haydon's affairs. There were a few captious and not entirely satisfied observers, like Macready who wrote in his diary next day "Read in the papers Sir R. Peel's defence of himself against the attacks of Bentinck and Disraeli, in which I think he turned to shame their venomed and virulent abuse. His *not supporting* Canning I thought wrong, and think so still; it seemed to me then a false step, and I think it has had, as I have watched him, an influence on his whole life". But that was not the general feeling, which was expressed in the House by Roebuck, a Radical like Macready, who spoke of "his strong feeling of gratitude to the right honourable baronet, and his supereminent carelessness and contempt for the right honourable baronet's opponents".

Peel had had a personal triumph, but as the *Daily News* said in its leader on his speech, though his vindication against Bentinck's and Disraeli's charges was fully proved, it had nothing to do with the case. The whole storm had blown up during the debate on the Irish Coercion Bill, which Peel was pressing through Parliament simultaneously with the Corn Bill. The Corn Bill was now with the House of Lords; the third reading of the Irish Coercion Bill was due next week in the House of Commons; it was then that the final test would come.

On Saturday 20th June Haydon wrote only one sentence in his diary. "O God, bless us all through the evils of this day. Amen".

This prayer often appeared in his journal during these weeks. Sometimes it was the only entry for the day. When he wrote at any length, it was often about the picture he was painting, *Alfred and the First British Jury*. The idea of its composition had come to him in April, during his disastrous exhibition at the Egyptian Hall. He had woken at four in the morning, with his head full of a conception of the picture. "Is it the whisper of an Evil or a good spirit?" he asked himself then; he concluded that it was a good spirit. The picture was rubbed in; one day he worked six hours at it and "advanced Alfred gloriously"; another day his mind suddenly fired up with the idea of a new background for it—he "dashed at it, and at dinner it was enormously improved". Even while he was out trying to pacify his creditors, his mind would dwell on the picture, and when he got home again he would "dash about like an inspired devil" to make the alteration in the background that he had thought of while he was out. He looked up costume details at the British Museum and then put in the figure of a Saxon lord; masses of drapery were inserted; a model, the white-haired old pawnbroker Rochfort, was found for the head of a kneeling figure—he was to come for a sitting at nine o'clock this very Saturday morning. The head of King Alfred himself remained to finish.

Haydon's method was to fix the composition of a picture, make an oil sketch, and from this, roughly sketch in with umber onto the canvas the outline of the whole picture. After this he did each principal figure in turn from a model, finishing as he went along. He ground his own colours, and set up his palette every day before breakfast. He generally painted mounted on steps, because of his short sight and the huge size of his canvases. He wore three pairs of large round concave spectacles one on top of the other; when actually painting he would push them all up on his forehead and paint with the naked eye, peering close at the canvas; then he would pull down one pair of glasses, look at the model, get down from the steps, walk away from the picture studying it first through one, then two, then three pairs of glasses; then, with one pair on, look at the reflection of his picture in the looking-glass at the side of the studio, then climb onto his steps and start painting again with no glasses on. But the studio was small—it was the front drawing-room of the house, the back one was his cast and colour room—and he could never get far enough away really to see the effect of the whole picture, and his defective eyesight produced the errors of proportion—particularly the shortness of leg—which give a fatally ludicrous look to so many of his heroic figures.

Haydon had an inexplicable sense of urgency about *Alfred and the First British Jury*. Neither this picture nor any of the series had been commissioned; he would have the utmost difficulty in finding buyers for them if he finished them, and any price he did succeed in getting for them was already mortgaged to his creditors. There was no reason to hasten their conclusion, but he felt tied to a desperate time-table. One section of the picture must be finished by the end of June. There was something crucial about the month of June. "Oh Lord! carry me through the next and the dangerous month" he had written on 31st May, and on 1st June "O God I begin this month, June, in fear and submission. Thy will but not mine be done. Carry me through in spite of all appearances and realities of danger for Jesus Christ's sake". The smell of danger hung about his studio as he struggled on through the blazing month of June in causeless haste: "never mind, so long as I get them done. The great thing is to get them done"; "if I can but finish the left-hand corner and Alfred's head by 30th June, I'll do"; "nothing coming in, all received, no orders of any description, one large Picture painting, and three more getting ready, and

Alfred's head to do. In God alone I trust, in humility. Amen".
Repeatedly he called on God to let nothing on earth stop the
completion of his six pictures. On the day before he sent his
papers to Elizabeth Barrett for safe keeping, he was still
writing "I will finish my six, under the blessing of God". But
today, 20th June, he wrote nothing in his diary but "O God,
bless us all through the evils of this day. Amen".

On this Saturday morning Elizabeth Barrett drove with her
sister Arabel to pay a call in St John's Wood. The Marylebone
and Paddington area across which she drove was now solidly
built up. By 1846 the district north of Oxford Street, south and
south-west of Regent's Park, was covered with handsome new
terraces and squares for the prosperous professional class who
now preferred this part of London to any other. It contained
pockets of slum—there was one just off Portman Square. The
sewers under Cavendish, Manchester and Bryanston Squares
were in a very shaky state, clogged and collapsing. The streets,
not yet all paved, were full of dust in this hot dry June. But it
looked a glossy prosperous district, full of shining carriages,
and in it lived many of the most successful writers and painters
of the day. The Procters lived in Harley Street, the painter
Turner in a gloomy dilapidated house in Queen Anne Street,
Miss Barrett herself in Wimpole Street, her cousin John
Kenyon in York Place, as the northern half of Baker Street was
then called. Dickens had a charming roomy house, with two
triple-windowed bays running up two stories, and a spacious
garden behind a high brick wall, in the angle of Devonshire
Terrace and the New Road, as the Marylebone Road then was.
The painter John Martin lived in Allsop Terrace, just the
other side of the New Road, and a little further west Macready
had a fine Regency house, behind a free-standing screen of
Ionic pillars, in Clarence Terrace. It alone, of these houses, is
still there. A bank has replaced Turner's house, a block
of flats Miss Barrett's, an office Charles Dickens'.

In 1846 lawyers like Serjeant Talfourd, editors like Forster,
were still apt to live a little further east, nearer the scene of their

labours. Talfourd had a house in Russell Square, Forster lived in the handsome pilastered house in Lincoln's Inn Fields whose dark roomy staircases and antechambers Dickens described as Mr Tulkinghorn's in *Bleak House*. This, like Macready's house, still stands.

But the growth of London in the 1840's was westward. By 1846 Bayswater was wholly built up as far as Stanhope Gate, though there were still some open fields west of there and north of the Bayswater Road, then the Uxbridge Road. All this newly built area drained into the Serpentine, and such was the effect that people still could catch a lethal fever if they took an evening stroll by its waters.

This was Haydon's neighbourhood. His house was in Burwood Place, a little street running from the Edgware Road (then still called Connaught Terrace at its southern end) to Norfolk Crescent. The house, which has also vanished now, was four-storied with iron railings round the area and pretty little balconies at each of the tall first-floor windows. It was on the south side of the street on the corner of the Edgware Road, overlooking a stream of traffic which sometimes included Queen Victoria on her way from Buckingham Palace to Paddington Station. It was one of the noisiest situations in London, but when Haydon was painting he became so absorbed in his work that nothing penetrated to his consciousness of all the uproar of carts, carriages, barking dogs, street cries, banging door knockers.

West of the new Bayswater terraces, Notting Hill was still fields, with just a fringe of houses along the north side of the Uxbridge Road and along Moscow Road. Then you came to leafy Campden Hill, and Holland House with its great green oblong of park, and so south to the village of Kensington, at whose western end Leigh Hunt lived in a pretty but sadly smelly house in Edwardes Square, while at its eastern end Thackeray had just moved into a bow-windowed little house in Young Street. South from there were fields and lanes and market gardens, and a few new streets and terraces in Brompton and the King's Private Road, until you reached the village of Chelsea, and the Carlyles' house in Great Cheyne Row, and

Saturday 20th June

Turner's secret and poorly-furnished hide-out in Cremorne Road. If you wanted to get from the Carlyles' to New Cross, where Browning lived, you would have to take a river boat from the Cadogan Steam Boat Pier a few yards east from the Carlyles' house along Cheyne Walk, or have a long ride or drive, due east, crossing the river at Vauxhall Bridge, through built-up Kennington and Walworth to where the fringes of the Rotherhithe and Deptford dockland faded out into open fields. Except for Mrs Jameson, far away to the westward in the distant village of Ealing, Browning lived the furthest from the centre of London of any of this group of friends and acquaintances. Only the rich banker Samuel Rogers and the well-to-do Member of Parliament Monckton Milnes had houses right in the centre, in St James's Place and Pall Mall, which in 1846 was still where the Establishment lived.

Miss Barrett's drive across Marylebone that morning was for a call at 24A Grove End Road, where her friend the blind scholar Hugh Stuart Boyd lived. When she got there, she did not go upstairs to see her sixty-five-year-old friend, who lived as a recluse, never going downstairs, never even moving from his chair. He and Elizabeth Barrett had not met for seven years, not since her serious illness began, and the close intellectual friendship which they had once enjoyed made it all the more difficult to begin again after so long an interval. They had kept up a correspondence, not so frequent as once it had been, but still an exchange of ideas—but these too now seemed more a barrier than a link to Miss Barrett; her literary tastes had moved on, his had stayed fixed in a past age.

Arabel Barrett went upstairs to see Mr Boyd, tell him that Elizabeth was there, and arrange for a visit next week. Elizabeth Barrett stayed downstairs and thought about her old friend, his prodigious memory, his incapacity for affection, his slow child-like mind, and how he sat there alone all day and every day, and yet was cheerful in his deliberate isolation. He said over to himself the countless passages of Greek poetry that he knew by heart, and thought how great a poet Ossian was, and what miserable reptiles those critics were who tried to impugn his authenticity, and how all the new poets since

Pope had utterly degenerate taste and no ear for the sacred monotony of the only correct metres. "As for you and Tennyson, he never heard of you . . . he never guesses at the way of modern literature" she told Browning in a letter next day.

The implication that Tennyson and Browning were the rising poets of whom every cultivated person would have heard in 1846 perhaps needs some qualification. Elizabeth Barrett's special interest in modern poetry, as well as her special interest in one of the two modern poets, made her a not quite objective witness.

Tennyson had published nothing since his two-volume *Poems* in 1842, which had been received with moderate approval by the critics, but had sold steadily ever since. His name had been much in the public eye during the winter of 1845–6, when he had been granted his Civil List pension—Milnes, Carlyle and Rogers had all had a hand in procuring it for him from Peel, though Arthur Hallam's father was the prime instigator—and when Bulwer Lytton, angry that the pension had not been given to Sheridan Knowles, had attacked Tennyson in *The New Timon* as "School-Miss Alfred" and provoked Tennyson's annihilating retort on "The padded man—that wears the stays" and his "dandy pathos".

Public opinion was mostly on Tennyson's side in this squabble. His reputation in 1846 was not, like Browning's, confined to a few discerning critics. His fellow authors admired his work— Carlyle, Dickens and Rogers gave him unstinted praise, and Wordsworth called him the first of living poets—and so did the general cultivated public. Already in 1844 undergraduates at Oxford had held a debate on the proposition that Tennyson was a greater poet than Wordsworth, and the younger man had been considered a possible candidate for the Laureateship which was awarded to the older one. Apart from a few traditionalists like Hugh Stuart Boyd—or like Haydon, who thought Tennyson's work obscure and affected—he was now accepted as a genius by all those who read poetry at all. Mrs Carlyle called him so in a letter recommending his 1842 Poems, but added "the *vulgar* public have not yet recognised him for such", and this is borne out by Milnes' protest, as late as 1845, that his constituents would never have heard of Tennyson as a poet. He was not yet a name to the whole nation, as in his later years. His position was summed up by Richard Hengist Horne and Elizabeth Barrett in the essay on him which they wrote in collaboration for *A New Spirit of the Age.* "The name of Alfred Tennyson is pressing slowly, calmly, but surely—with certain recognition but no loud shouts of greeting—from the lips of the discerners of poets . . . along the lips of the less informed public, to its own place in the starry house of names. . . . This poet's public is certainly awake to him, although you would not think so".

The essay concluded by saying that "beyond a very small circle he is never to be met". The writers were here perhaps revealing their own, rather than Tennyson's, social boundaries; the circle in which he moved when he came to London was not really as small as all that. He went to Samuel Rogers' and Monckton Milnes' breakfast parties; Mrs Carlyle found him in the audience when Dickens and Forster and their friends were performing Ben Jonson; Browning met him at a public dinner. But the friends with whom Tennyson spent most time in London were Thackeray, Moxon, Aubrey de Vere, Coventry Patmore, Macready, Carlyle. He strode about the London streets at night with Patmore, who would be sympathetically silent during Tennyson's gloomy moods, or with Carlyle, who made the sleeping streets of Chelsea resound with his denunciations against the Government or against the "acrid putrescence" of the stucco houses, the "black jumble" of the suburbs where there used to be pleasant fields. Dickens was a friend too, and Tennyson was godfather to Dickens' fourth son who was christened that spring. Dickens, like all Tennyson's friends, wanted to organize his life for him, to extricate him from his gloomy indecision, and tried to get him to join the Dickens family party when they left for Switzerland this June. Tennyson would not go. He told Elizabeth Barrett's brother George, whom he met one day in the Inns of Court, that if he went with Dickens they would be bound to quarrel over Dickens' sentimentality, and break up their friendship; it was safer to decline the invitation. So he stayed behind in London, and mooned about in a haze of short sight, depression and tobacco smoke.

"A large-featured, dim-eyed, bronze-coloured, shaggy-headed man is Alfred" said Carlyle of Tennyson, and added that he was "one of the powerfullest *smokers* I have ever worked along with". Tennyson, who was over six feet tall, seems to have struck his contemporaries as a man of quite exceptional height. Mrs Carlyle—who thought him handsome and let him smoke for hours in her drawing-room—describes him as so tall that his head touched the ceiling like a caryatid, and nothing but capital letters sufficed Browning—himself very short—to describe his fellow poet, "a LONG, hazy kind of a man".

Browning's references to Tennyson in 1846 show him inclined to envy Tennyson but struggling against the inclination. He deeply admired *The Two Voices* and *Locksley Hall*, he knew Tennyson was a true poet, but in letters to Elizabeth Barrett he could not resist dwelling on Tennyson's excessive subservience to the critics, glancing at the Civil List pension which Tennyson got "for nothing", making fun of him acting with Count d'Orsay as godfather to Dickens' son. He saw Tennyson as naïf, vacillating, hardly able to take care of himself—but "the genius you see, too". In later years the two poets were understanding friends, but this was a difficult stage in both men's careers.

Tennyson on his side was not always perfectly generous about Browning's poetry; his and Mrs Carlyle's are the cruellest and most memorable of all the innumerable gibes against *Sordello*. Browning's reputation as a poet was not mounting in 1846, like Tennyson's; it was less than it had been in the 1830's, before *Sordello* was published, although from 1841 to 1846 he had been publishing, in the successive numbers of *Bells and Pomegranates*, many of what now seem his most accessible poems—*Home Thoughts From Abroad*, *The Pied Piper*, *How They Brought the Good News from Ghent to Aix*—as well as some of his finest, *The Lost Leader*, *The Bishop Orders His Tomb in St Praxed's*.

Although even the cultivated public did not yet understand

Browning, some judicious critics already knew better. Carlyle, Forster, Landor, expected great things from him; Dickens saw genius in him, and an individual force such as no other living poet could match. And Browning had the confidence and strength of mind to wait till time should do justice to him— that ability to wait which Elizabeth Barrett had recommended so strongly and so vainly in her letters to Haydon.

The latest number of *Bells and Pomegranates*, containing *Luria* and *A Soul's Tragedy*, had been published only two months before this June morning on which Miss Barrett sat in Boyd's house and thought about modern poetry and how it was treated by the public. Forster had given *Luria* and *A Soul's Tragedy* a fairly kind review in *The Examiner*, and Carlyle and Kenyon had praised them. But Browning's father still had to pay the cost of publishing his son's poetry. Moxon, who published Tennyson's and Browning's poetry, and Miss Barrett's too, reported in the summer of 1846 that he had sold 1,500 copies of Tennyson's 1842 Poems in the last year and would have to bring out a fourth edition; Miss Barrett's 1844 Poems were selling very well and would soon be out of print; but for Browning's poems there were only vague reassurances that they were "going off regularly", "selling and likely to sell", that a second edition of *Luria* would perhaps be called for eventually. The sonnet which Walter Savage Landor had written that spring about Browning's poetry, and which began—

> "There is delight in singing, though none hear
>   Beside the singer",

was a rather back-handed compliment to a poet whose public had hardly yet been found.

Miss Barrett drove back in good time from her morning visit to Boyd, because Browning was coming to see her that afternoon. He brought her flowers from the New Cross garden, roses in full bloom and Madonna lilies in bud; he was not quite sure if these would open, but by the evening all but two were in full blow in the stifling heat of the second-floor room in Wimpole Street, its window shaded by a painted blind and choked by the ivy clambering up from the window-box to cover all the lower panes. This darkened window shed a green dusk over the room, which was crowded with furniture: rows of crimson bookshelves topped by busts of poets, a bed, a sofa, a chest of drawers, a wash-stand, a wardrobe, a large round table, an armchair—it must have been difficult to thread one's way through the crowding furniture, and not to tread on Flush as he backed under a chair to yap at one's umbrella. On the sofa lay Miss Barrett, and Browning sat in the armchair and tried to put into words the religion of his love for her, its adamantine doctrine and its luminous revelation.

There is no portrait of Elizabeth Barrett at this period, nor any contemporary description of her appearance except Miss Mitford's report that she had lost her bright complexion and looked more than her forty years. A couple of years earlier, at Haydon's request, she had written a self-portrait for him; she told him that she was very small, five foot one inch tall; that nobody agreed about the colour of her eyes which had been called black, grey, hazel, blue, but which she herself considered to be "dark-green-brown—grounded with brown, and green otherwise"; that she had not much of a nose, but, to make up for it, her mouth was decidedly too large. Her hair and complexion were dark, her face small, and her voice quiet.

It is a sensible objective description; I wonder how much idea of her it gave to Haydon, who never had seen and never was to see her. The image of Mrs Browning that we all know comes from a later picture, but the elements of it must have been present in 1846—two thick curtains of dark ringlets falling from a centre parting, and, looking out from between them, the taut face of an Egyptian cat goddess, with heavy eyes and small strong bones.

Next morning, Sunday, Haydon wrote in his diary "Slept horribly. Prayed in sorrow and got up in agitation".

In the morning he set out to walk to Hampstead where he was to dine with Commissioner Joshua Evans and his wife. He was to discuss a picture of *Byron Musing on a Distant View of Harrow* which he had offered to paint for Commissioner Evans. He had been planning this picture for nearly a year; he had asked Leigh Hunt for details of Byron's appearance and dress, and Mrs Hunt for a full-length silhouette of the poet. He had made a preliminary sketch for the picture, and also a sketch for the distant view of Harrow which was visible from the garden of the Evans' house at Golders Hill; this was to be the background of the picture.

Haydon's elder son Frank walked part of the way with him to Hampstead. This Sunday was the Summer Solstice, the longest day of the year, and it was again fiercely hot. As they walked across Regent's Park, Haydon complained very much about the intense heat, and said how badly he had slept all night. As he lay awake he had realized how it was that people committed suicide. He could imagine throwing himself off the Monument—the idea of dashing his head to pieces was a pleasure, a relief.

It was no new idea to him. These same fields on the way to Hampstead where he was now walking were specially haunted for him with the thought of death. Here he had walked nearly thirty years before with Keats, and he had come to believe that Keats had tremulously recited the *Ode to a Nightingale* to him, and that together they had been "half in love with easeful death". As the Ode was not written till May 1819, and the two men had quarrelled the previous month about Haydon's insistent money demands, after which there was a coolness between them, Haydon's memory of the Ode recital was perhaps a little touched up. But in his imagination, at any rate, Keats, suicide, and Kilburn Meadows were linked together. Two years afterwards he had walked alone in the Meadows thinking of Keats, of whose death in Rome he had just heard, and of another friend recently killed in a duel; and he had had a revelation of life's insignificance, of the radiant peace and calmness of a brighter world. In the next few days, anxious about money and tormented by frustrated passion, he had come near to killing himself. In the years that followed he often walked in Kilburn Meadows in the evening after a hard day's work in his studio. He enjoyed the fresh air of the hay fields in the evening light, but he often indulged his imagination in melancholy visions in which he actually seemed to hear the wild cry of a suicide and to see a blood-bedabbled corpse on the grass.

His buoyant spirits, which so often shot to the surface again when deeply plunged in difficulties and distresses, occasionally sank when a trouble no worse than many previous ones flowed over him. In 1833, when he was again arrested for debt, "After a day and night of torture, leaving my family and children bewildered, I recovered my faculties after very nearly putting an end to myself in the night"; in 1842, "If the falls of Niagara were near, I would go over them shouting to put an end to this horror of living". But always in a few hours or a few days he recovered his faculties, wondered at his impulse to self-destruction, put it down to bad digestion or bad air, decided it was an aberration of the brain under physical causes for which his true self had no responsibility. In between these moments of self-destructive impulse, his normal attitude to suicide was one of rather defiant confidence—"In such humours Men shoot themselves—but not me".

But he was always fascinated by suicide stories of other men. Writing of a forger who killed himself with prussic acid, he said "There is something self-willed and grand about that defiance of an unknown HEREAFTER! Don't you think that Cato was more of a hero than Napoleon by putting an end to himself? I suspect I do". His diaries are full of references to the suicides of Castlereagh and Romilly, and their immediate causes. Only six months before this June morning of 1846, Haydon had dashed down in his diary "Good heavens! Gurwood has cut his throat! The Man who headed the forlorn hope at Ciudad Rodrigo! the rigid Soldier, the iron-nerved Hero! had not morale to resist the relaxation of nerve brought on by his own over-anxiety about the Duke's Dispatches. Where is the responsibility of a Man with mind so easily affected by body?" Other men shot themselves in such humours—but not Haydon. But next day his diary has "Poor Colonel Gurwood—what security has any man?"

Now, on this hot morning's walk across Regent's Park, he talked to his son Frank of throwing himself off the Monument. Frank Haydon was now a clerk in the Record Office. He had been at Cambridge and had been intended for the Church, but according to his father he had lost his nerve at the idea of preaching, and so Haydon had got Sir Robert Peel to give his son a clerkship. Frank Haydon was a nervous sceptical youth; forty years later he killed himself. "He was our first child, and I overwhelmed him with eager interest, which broke him down" said Haydon in explanation of his son's temperament; he expected all his children to have his own energetic spirits. Secretly Frank Haydon hated and despised his father. Haydon's selfishness, his inviolable conviction of his own greatness and irresistible charm, maddened his son. Frank Haydon suffered miseries of embarrassment from his father's dogmatism and showing off, and years later he revenged himself by writing vicious footnotes to the more pious and pompous sentences in his father's diary.

He was, however, frightened this morning by Haydon's talk of suicide. He tried to persuade his father not to dwell on such ideas, and presently Haydon calmed down to some extent, and began to talk of his terrible shortage of money, and to say how much he loathed the idea of another imprisonment for debt. Frank Haydon asked him if he had written to his sister Mrs Havilland to try and borrow some money. Haydon said he had written, but his sister had never answered his letter.

When they got to the Avenue Road bridge, Frank Haydon turned back. He meant to go and see the family doctor and consult him about his father's state of mind. When he got home, he mentioned this to Mrs Haydon, but she laughed at the idea that her husband could be thinking of killing himself, so Frank Haydon gave up the idea of calling in the doctor.

Haydon walked on to the village of Hampstead through the burning heat. North of Regent's Park the way to Golders Hill was almost all through open fields, with a few scattered farms and large houses, such as Belsize House in its great park. West across the fields ran the new Birmingham Railway from Euston. This was the area, beginning to be devastated by the railway and its accompanying streets and warehouses, that Dickens was just about to start describing so vividly in *Dombey and Son*, the first words of which were written at Lausanne six days after this hot Sunday morning. The tentacles of Camden Town were stretching out along the railway into the fields, which were rutted with cart-wheel tracks and defaced with heaps of bricks and streaks of lime. Cow-houses, and summer-houses, and the foundations of new little streets of dwellings for the railway workers, were all jumbled together on the edge of the open country, and the jangling Sunday church bells and the roar and rattle of the trains jarred the baking dusty fields as Haydon walked on to Hampstead.

While Haydon was walking out of the northern fringe of London, at its southern verge Browning was sitting on the grass in the garden at New Cross, and was conscious of the immensity of the whole round earth under him, and saw it as an image of the love that now supported all his life. At the same time Elizabeth Barrett was sitting on the drawing-room window seat in Wimpole Street, writing to him while he was thinking of her. She had her feet up on the window seat and was writing on her knee, leaning against the frame of the open window. In that shady street it seemed to her perhaps a little cooler than yesterday, but still very hot. Presently Flush, whom she had left behind upstairs, thumped at the drawing-room door to be let in, and she had to get up and open the door, and then he nearly knocked her down by leaping up at her the moment she opened the door. She went back to her letter-writing, and

71

Sunday 21st June

Flush jumped up onto the window seat and lay down by her feet. They were all alone in the house, all the family had gone to church. "How did you get home? how are you, dearest?" she wrote to Browning, thinking of their afternoon together yesterday. "The Saturday's visit is the worst of all to come to an end, as always I feel. In the first place stands Sunday, like a wall without a door in it! no letter!", and then there were Monday and Tuesday and Wednesday before they could see each other again.

A mile to the south of where she sat in her window-seat, a group of people well known to her and Browning had met for a breakfast party in a house in St James's Place. The dining-room windows, wide open on this sultry morning, overlooked a small garden with a gate leading into the Green Park, where Sunday crowds were strolling on the undulating lawns in the grateful shade of the big trees.

"How can you go and dine with Rogers this hot weather? He has been dead these thirty-two years and cannot be expected to keep". Everybody made these cadaverous jokes about the breakfast party's host, the banker, poet and art collector Samuel Rogers. There must have been something exceptionally corpse-like about his appearance, a silvery phosphorescence of decay. "He ought to have been buried long ago" said Mrs Carlyle, and Haydon noted in his diary that Rogers "always puts me in mind of a man who had laid in a Necessary for a month, and had just been washed for the night. To see him standing behind a beauty was no joke". They said it to his face as well as behind his back. "Why, as you can afford it, don't you set up your hearse?" Lord Alvanley asked him—a double dig at Rogers who, wealthy as he was, used to walk home on foot through the rain from the grandest parties, wearing galoshes. When Rogers told Sydney Smith that a wren had looked at him with a curious eye, Sydney Smith replied "Why, I wonder? If it had been a carrion crow, one could have understood it"; and when Rogers told Ward that a watering-place where he had stayed was so full that he could not find a bed, Ward's answer was "Dear me, was there no room in the churchyard?"

It is not easy now to see why Samuel Rogers' appearance
was so notoriously repugnant, how he could have been described
as the ugliest man in Europe, perhaps in the world. The Richmond crayon of him in the National Portrait Gallery must
have been even more flattering than Richmond portraits usually
were, for it shows an elegant old man with a straight-featured
well-proportioned face. Other portraits are less kind, but none
of them suggests a really repulsive appearance. But already in
1818 Byron had written brutally about Rogers' leaden gummy
eyes, his mummy-like carcass; S. C. Hall said he had a drooping
eye, a thick underlip, and a large head out of proportion to the
rest of him; and Carlyle struck off a famous and not unkindly
sketch of him as "a half-frozen old sardonic Whig-Gentleman!
no hair at all, but one of the whitest bare scalps, blue eyes,
shrewd, sad and cruel; toothless horseshoe mouth drawn up to
the very nose; slow-croaking, sarcastic insight, perfect breed-
ing". The final word, as so often, was Sydney Smith's, who
recommended Rogers, when he sat for his portrait, to be drawn
saying his prayers, with his face hidden in his hands.

Rogers gave as good as he got. His sharp tongue was much
feared, all the more perhaps because he never raised his voice,
but spoke quietly and deliberately, with an old-fashioned formality, referring to even his dead friends as "Mr Pitt", "Mr
Sheridan", and deploring modern accentuations of words—
"cóntemplate", "bálcony"—as very offensive. "They tell me
I say ill-natured things. I have a very weak voice; if I did not
say ill-natured things no one would hear what I said" he explained with his customary subdued malice. He was caustic
and severe, rather than rude, and often as generous in deed as
he was sharp in word. Fanny Kemble said that he had the kind-
est heart and the unkindest tongue of anyone she knew, and
Sydney Smith, whose witticisms both to and about Rogers
were the most cutting of all, nevertheless said that he knew no
one kinder, more fun, with better manners or more integrity,
and that if he had to choose which Englishman he would most
willingly stumble on when travelling abroad, it would be
Rogers. Tennyson said that Rogers was "often bitter, but very
kindly at heart" and added surprisingly "we have often talked

of death till I have seen the tears roll down his cheeks". They had had a disagreement when Rogers took exception to something Tennyson said, and told him he was trying to be smart, but that had not prevented Rogers from helping to get Tennyson his Civil List pension, and Tennyson was grateful. Elizabeth Barrett said of Rogers "he makes an epigram on a man, and gives him a thousand pounds; and the deed is the truer expression of his own nature".

He was on the whole a good friend to Haydon, who often appealed to him for money or for commissions. Rogers, whose walls were crowded with masterpieces, was readier to give Haydon money than to buy his pictures. He took tickets in the raffles by which Haydon managed to dispose of some of his unsaleable pictures, but he only actually commissioned one small painting of Napoleon. When the Cartoon Competition for the House of Lords frescoes took place, Rogers was one of the judges; Haydon was not awarded a prize—Rogers knew good painting when he saw it.

His house was full of treasures, some of the best of them in the dining-room where his breakfast party was now assembled. In this crimson-walled room there was a Poussin landscape, a Tintoretto sketch for the Scuola di San Marco, a Rembrandt self-portrait, a Rubens copy of the Mantegna *Triumph of Julius Caesar*, a Velazquez, a Bonington, and the emotional *Ecce Homo* by Guido Reni which is now in the National Gallery. There was a terra-cotta bust of Pope by Roubiliac, the marble version of which was in Sir Robert Peel's collection at Drayton. There was a mahogany sideboard carved by Chantrey, and on the chimney piece there were busts of Roman emperors. Rogers was a collector of great flair and skill who had been buying steadily and with discrimination all through his long life. He collected pictures, he collected people; his breakfast parties had been famous for forty years. He was now eighty-two, and he was still giving them.

The party on this morning of 21st June consisted of Gräfin Hahn-Hahn, Oberst Bystram, Mrs Jameson and Milnes. Rogers liked to have at least three people at his breakfast parties, but not more than six or eight, because the party must not be large enough to break up into groups; the conversation must be general, but there must be no loud noisy talking and laughing, and no monologues. The parties began at ten o'clock and generally went on till about one. The food was simple— tea or coffee, brown bread and very fresh country butter, and strawberries. "There was not too much of anything, not even too much welcome; yet no lack of it" said Procter.

On this occasion Gräfin Hahn-Hahn held forth on modern literature. Rogers was not a literary fossil like Hugh Stuart Boyd—he had encouraged and invited to his house many young and little-known writers. But he was suspicious of German writers; he liked conversation, not exhortation, at his breakfast table; and he did not think highly of female intelligence. Women had to be beautiful, like Caroline Norton, or at least sensible, like Mrs Jameson, to be acceptable at Rogers' parties. Laying down the law was permitted even less to them than to the male guests. So when Gräfin Hahn-Hahn had been talking for some time about modern literature, Rogers suddenly stopped her with the question "Did you ever read Addison?"

It was exceedingly improbable that Gräfin Hahn-Hahn had ever read Addison, or would have admired him if she had. Rogers could not have devised a more deflating question. Addison, archetype of the "prudish English", with his formidable impervious responsibility and rectitude, was not the man for Faustina.

There was usually a manœuvring among Rogers' guests to be the last to leave, as those who went first left their reputations behind them; Rogers would cut them up for the benefit of the remaining guests. After Gräfin Hahn-Hahn and Oberst Bystram had quitted Rogers' breakfast party, he remarked to Milnes "Those are the two ugliest adulterers I have ever had in this house".

Haydon came back from Hampstead at five o'clock that evening. He was to have dined with his Hampstead friends, but had not felt up to it, so he came home for dinner. While the Haydons were at table, Leopold Martin, son of the painter John Martin, was shown in. Haydon had sent a desperate appeal for money

Sunday 21st June

to John Martin that morning, and Leopold had been sent round by his father to Burwood Place to offer help. Leopold Martin, an intensely respectable character who was easily shocked by anything at all uncommon, reported to his father that he found Haydon at a dinner-table "on which, together with many choice things, were French and other costly wines, and many items of luxury usually found but on the tables of the wealthy". He considered that his father's benevolent aid would be quite out of place.

During dinner Haydon got up from the table and turned a picture to the wall; its glass was reflecting the light and dazzling him unbearably. He looked feverish and ill, and seemed to be lost in thought. He said very little all evening, except to ask his wife to go to Brixton next morning to call on Coulton, editor of *Britannia* and an old friend of the Haydons. Mrs Haydon thought it rather an odd suggestion, but she agreed to go. Presently Haydon went up to his bedroom, but not to bed; he was writing for hours, and they heard him walking restlessly to and fro at intervals all through the short hot night.

The thermometer stood at 90 degrees in the shade in London
next day, Monday the 22nd, and the sky was cloudless all day.
All over the country that day, people were writing to each
other to complain of the heat. Wordsworth wrote about it from
Westmorland to Crabb Robinson; Mrs Grote, wife of the
historian, wrote from Buckinghamshire about it to Varnhagen
von Ense. Milnes had written to her about his German protégée;
"Countess Hahn-Hahn must not leave England without having
seen you; tell me how I can bring her and you together" he had
asked. But Mrs Grote was installed in her ugly but comfortable
house at Burnham, and was not inclined to come up to London.
Writing on the 22nd, she told Varnhagen "I offered him full
powers to conduct this famous lady hither, but cannot go up to
London myself, because the weather has been, for nearly four
entire weeks, so hot (viz 83° Fahrenheit) as to make it impossible for me to undergo any such unwholesome fatigue".
Milnes could have brought Gräfin Hahn-Hahn down to Burnham, she had no objection to the heat; speaking through the
mouth of her heroine Faustina, she said "I fancy the sun has a
feeling for me, for I was born on his fête day, the 22nd of
June".

Browning had at last succeeded in reading *Faustina* and was
writing about it to Elizabeth Barrett this morning. He was not
impressed by the heroine's ardent temperament and the troubles
it caused. "Think of unhappy Countess Faustina with her
'irresistible longings', and give her as much of your commiseration as she ought to get" he suggested to Miss Barrett.
But he was thinking chiefly about Elizabeth Barrett's account
of herself in her Sunday letter, picturing her sitting on the
drawing-room window-seat and wishing he could go and stand
in Wimpole Street and look up at her, and watch her as she went

out on a visit which he knew she was to pay this afternoon. In her second-floor room, behind the lowered blind, the lilies which he had brought her on Saturday were now full blown, drawn open by the heat.

Peel was writing letters too that day—one to Carlyle, in answer to his letter of the 18th, thanking him for the copy of *Cromwell* and explaining in his stately prose that "whatever may have been the pressure of my public engagements, it has not been so overwhelming as to prevent me from being familiar with your exertions in another department of labour, as incessant and severe as that which I have undergone". This was as near as he would go to a reference to Carlyle's offered sympathy over the attacks on him; it was a polite rather than a warm reply. But he wrote another letter that day in which, through all the protocol of loyal humility, he showed more of his heart. "Sir Robert Peel presents his humble duty to your Majesty, and assures your Majesty that he is penetrated with a deep sense of your Majesty's great kindness and your Majesty's generous sympathy with himself and Lady Peel. Sir Robert Peel firmly believes that the recent attack made upon him was the result of a foul conspiracy concocted by Mr Disraeli and Lord George Bentinck, in the hope and belief that from the lapse of time or want of leisure in Sir Robert Peel to collect materials for his defence, or the destruction of documents and papers, the means of complete refutation might be wanting. . . . He hopes, however, he had sufficient proof to demonstrate the falseness of the accusation, and the malignant motives of the accusers. He is deeply grateful to your Majesty and to the Prince for the kind interest you have manifested during the progress of this arduous struggle, which now he trusts is approaching to a successful termination".

Another arduous struggle was that day reaching a different kind of termination. While Peel was writing, Haydon was writing a letter to him. "Life is insupportable. Accept my gratitude for *always* feeling for me in adversity. I hope I have earned for my dear wife security from want. God bless you".

The 22nd was a significant anniversary day for Haydon. On this day twenty-five years earlier—on 22nd June 1821—he had been arrested for debt for the first time. He was then working on his picture *The Raising of Lazarus*, with the painter Bewick for his model. The sheriff's officer who came to arrest him was so terrified at being left alone in the studio with the resurrected corpse on the great canvas—the unfocused eyes, deeply sunken in their sockets, gazing out of the gaunt face through the parted folds of the shroud—that he refused to arrest Haydon, and rushed out of the studio. Haydon had then spent a long, long harassed day freeing himself from his creditors, giving a little money to a yet more unfortunate friend, attending a glittering reception, and meditating on the unjust social system that hanged a poor thief from St Giles but allowed rapacious attorneys every protection, imprisoned the upright John Hunt but crowned the venal Castlereagh with honours; and on the rewards and punishments of the next world that would put all these injustices right. But he concluded "Is it not more than probable that J. Hunt, the poor boy in St Giles, Lord Castlereagh and myself, the bailiff and the poor attorney will be equally subjects of commiseration, pardoned, made happy?" A year after that, Castlereagh cut his throat.

On this morning twenty-five years after his first arrest for debt, Haydon came down early in the morning and went into his studio and wrote letters till half-past eight, when he rang his bell and arranged for a messenger to take a letter to the Duke of Sutherland at one o'clock that day, but not to wait for an answer. Then he went out and walked to Oxford Street, went into the shop of a gun-maker called Riviere and bought a pistol. When he got back to the house, he had breakfast alone, and went back into his studio, locking the door. He wrote page after page of letters and messages; at some time during that night and morning he wrote a will of nineteen clauses; letters to his wife and each of his three children, to Peel, to Sir George Cockburn, to Talfourd; his "Last Thoughts"; and the final entry in his diary.

> "God forgive—me—Amen.
> Finis
> of
> B. R. Haydon.
> 'Stretch me no longer on this tough world'—Lear.
> End—
> XXVI Volume".

He arranged the studio, with a portrait of his wife on an easel facing the great unfinished canvas of *Alfred and the First British Jury*. On a table by the picture he put his diary, open at the last page, the letters he had written, his watch, and a Prayer Book open at the Gospel for the Sixth Sunday after Epiphany—"For there shall arise false Christs, and false prophets, and shall shew great signs and wonders; insomuch that (if it were possible) they shall deceive the very elect".

While he was preparing, at ten o'clock, Mrs Haydon passed the door of the studio on her way upstairs to get ready to go out. She tried the locked door as she passed, and Haydon called out loudly and hurriedly "Who's there?"

"It is only me" Mrs Haydon answered "I am just going up to dress before going to Brixton".

"Oh very well" said Haydon from behind the locked door, and as she turned to go on upstairs he called "God bless you. I will see you presently".

A few minutes later he followed her upstairs to her room, and repeated to her the message which he wanted her to give to Coulton, the man she was going to see in Brixton. He seemed as if he were sorry for having spoken roughly when she tried the door of the studio; he had something to say, but he did not say it, only waited a little and then kissed her and went back to his studio.

It was now half past ten, and he sat down to write one more page, with a confused echo of the Gospel about the false prophets who shall deceive even the elect.

> "Last Thoughts of B. R. Haydon. ½ past 10.
> No man should use certain evil for probable good, however great the object.

Evil is the prerogative of the Deity.
I create good, I create, *I* the Lord do these things.

Wellington never used evil, if the good was not certain; Napoleon had no such scruples and I fear the Glitter of his Genius rather dazzled me—but had I been encouraged, nothing but good would have come from me; because when encouraged, I paid every body. God Forgive the evil for the sake of the good. Amen".

At a quarter to eleven he had finished writing. He took the pistol he had bought that morning, and standing by his big picture, put the pistol to his head and pulled the trigger. The wound was not a mortal one—the bullet was deflected by the skull. Haydon was able to reload the pistol, but then he dropped it on the floor, took up a razor and, staggering about the room, cut his throat twice with long gashes and fell dead in front of his picture.

At half past four that Monday afternoon, Miss Barrett drove
with Mrs Jameson to St James's Place to see Samuel Rogers'
pictures. Mrs Jameson, who had published a catalogue of
Rogers' collection, had the entrée to the house and had arranged
to take Miss Barrett and show her round. Miss Barrett had had
hopes that Mrs Jameson might invite Browning to come too,
but though this would have been a joy, it might have been an
embarrassment too, as Mrs Jameson did not know how often
Browning saw Elizabeth Barrett, still less that they were engaged. It was therefore perhaps just as well that Browning was
not included in the party. In fact, the two women went round
the house alone, though at the last moment there had been a
possibility that Rogers might be there and show them round,
an idea which alarmed Miss Barrett. "But we did not see him"
she told Browning "and I suppose the Antinous on the staircase
is not at all like him. Grand it is, in its serene beauty".

Mrs Jameson was kind and competent in explaining the
pictures to Miss Barrett. These two women were now very
good friends, though Miss Barrett's first impression of Mrs
Jameson when they met in 1844 had been rather startled. Mrs
Jameson's appearance at this time of her life generally put
people off at first. As a young woman she had been fine-looking
—white-skinned, red-haired, blue-eyed, with a plump pretty
figure and beautiful hands and arms. But the difficulties of her
life gave her in middle age a formidable appearance which
repelled people when they met her first. Carlyle, meeting her at
dinner, took an instant aversion to her—"a little, hard, broad,
red-haired, freckled, fierce-eyed, square-mouthed woman;
shrewd, harsh, cockneyish-irrational: it was from the first
moment apparent that, without mutual loss, we might 'adieu
and wave our lily hands' "—and he continued for a time to refer

to her in his letters in inverted commas as "the celebrated
Mrs Jameson", a label which seems to have particularly irritated him. Nor was Elizabeth Barrett more attracted by her
first sight of Mrs Jameson—"she is very light, has the lightest
of eyes, the lightest of complexions; no eyebrows, and what
looked to me like very pale red hair, and thin lips of no colour
at all . . . the expression is acute rather than soft" and the eyes
were like cold blue steel.

But Elizabeth Barrett, even at first, was not really put off
by Mrs Jameson's appearance, and very soon both loved and
admired her. So did the Carlyles, to whom before long she
became an habitual visitor in spite of Carlyle's initial prejudice.
So did Browning, who warmed to her specially because of her
admiration for Miss Barrett, while Mrs Jameson told both
Miss Barrett and her German friend Ottilie von Goethe that
she liked Browning very much, and admired his poetry. So
did Samuel Rogers, who wrote to her with affection and
often invited her to his breakfast parties. She knew a great
many people in literary London, and was constantly invited
out.

She had not reached this position as of right, or without hard
work and fortitude. She was an Irish woman who had had to
earn her living as a governess as soon as she was grown up.
In 1821 she met and became briefly engaged to a barrister
called Robert Jameson, four years younger than she was. The
engagement was broken off, but he persisted in his determination to marry her and in 1825 she gave way and they were
married. The marriage was a failure from the start. The couple
—the cold inconsiderate husband and his puzzled wife—lived
in London for some years, during which time she took to
writing, and published anonymously her very successful book
Diary of an Ennuyée. In 1829 Jameson was appointed Puisne
Judge of Dominica in the West Indies, but Mrs Jameson did
not accompany him to his post. She stayed at home writing
books, and visited Germany. Later Jameson was transferred
to Canada and in 1836 Mrs Jameson made one more effort to
make their marriage work, and went out to join him.

When the couple were apart, Jameson wrote the most

affectionate and appealing letters to his wife, referring to her "high fame among your German admirers" which made him "sometimes despond for your poor American savage". But although he wrote affectionately he never answered any of her questions on practical matters, or made any arrangements for her welcome or comfort when she did come to Canada at his pressing request. During their separation he wrote to her twice, she to him eleven times. He wrote in jest that "it was his intention to marry again immediately". She replied "My dear Robert, jesting apart, I wish it only depended on me to give you that power. You might perhaps be happy with another woman—a union such as ours is, and has ever been, is a real mockery of the laws of God and man". This confirms her confidences to others, that their marriage had never been consummated. The unspecified conditions which she made for returning to him may have been connected with this. She had already written to offer him a separation, and to implore him either to decide for it or distinctly to tell her to join him—which he did. On the way to Toronto she wrote to her family "If I could believe all that Jameson writes, I might suppose I was going to an Elysium; but the puzzling thing is, to reconcile his words and his actions, what he is, and what he seems; he is quite past my comprehension". When she finally arrived in Toronto, she got the coldest of welcomes, and by 1838 they had agreed to separate. But Mrs Jameson knew her world well enough to be aware that everyone would blame the wife for leaving a husband, however difficult, without some proof of her side of the story. She asked Robert Jameson for a letter specifying that it was with his full consent and acquiescence that she left him to go back and live in England, and exonerating her from any blame or reproach in the matter. He produced the letter, stating that she carried with her "his most perfect respect and esteem" as well as his undying affection. Their separation arose from no wish of his own but he was "compelled to believe" that it was "best calculated for her happiness" and therefore he could not but approve it.

On paper Robert Jameson, like others of his contemporaries, was an admirable husband. Probably Mrs Jameson herself never quite understood what had gone wrong. In the travel book which she afterwards wrote about Canada, she refers with puzzled pain to the mystery of love, in face of which the unprepared personality was too often "blinded, astonished, and frightened, and ignorant". She told her mother and other friends that hers had been a marriage in name alone, and to Elizabeth Barrett she told an odd, not quite believable, story about how Robert Jameson had never forgiven her for breaking off their first engagement, and had told her on her wedding night that he had married her only to revenge himself. This story is made suspect by the fact that a similar story was told of the Byron marriage, and that Mrs Jameson was a close friend of Lady Byron, that patron saint of injured wives. Mrs Jameson was in Lady Byron's secrets, and may unconsciously have made the incident her own. In the eighteen-thirties and forties the endlessly discussed matrimonial affairs of the Byrons became a sort of textbook case to which all symptoms of diseased marriages were referred.

The odious Samuel Carter Hall, original of Mr Pecksniff, speculated about the Jameson marriage with a knowing unction which makes it perfectly clear from what model Dickens got some of the most repulsive parts of Pecksniff, but does perhaps explain something in the development of Mrs Jameson's character. She was, said S. C. Hall, "such a woman as a man might have loved to adoration", and she would never have gone in for the Rights of Women if she had made a success of her private life. "Of the cares and duties of maternity she knew nothing; while those of a wife she was unable to discharge. I by no means infer that she was disqualified by nature for either; on the contrary I consider she was well-fitted for both; but I believe that if she had been a mother, or, in the ordinary sense of the term, a wife, she would not have been found in the ranks of the 'strong-minded' ".

Mrs Jameson was a defender of Women's Rights, and tried to convince Elizabeth Barrett to support them too, but without much success. Mrs Jameson herself was a sensible rather than a rabid feminist. In her *Memoirs and Essays*, which had just been published in this month of June 1846, there was one essay on *Women's Mission and Women's Position* which made the shrewd observation that it was not much use talking about Women's Mission to be the angel of the home when the majority of all working and middle class girls and women had to go out to work, if their families were not to starve, and therefore had no chance of acquiring the household skills which were supposed to distinguish them as ministering angels.

She knew what she was talking about. When she finally separated from her husband, he legally contracted to pay her £300 a year, but he did not pay it; nor did he leave her anything in his will when he finally drank himself to death. Mrs Jameson supported herself and her mother and sisters, and adopted and educated a niece, on the proceeds of her books and articles, and very hard she had to work to do it. She wrote on Shakespeare's heroines, she wrote travel books and articles about Canada and Italy and Germany, she wrote guide-books to famous British art-collections, she wrote sketches of famous men and women, she wrote an article on *The Relative Social Position of Mothers and Governesses* which now throws a very hard glare on the realities behind *Agnes Grey*. Her thought was sensible, realistic, firm; she wrote with sympathy, with no great imagination or distinction of style, or insight; but she was clear-headed and fair—she would have made an excellent Civil Servant.

She did not allow the collapse of her marriage to wreck her life. She wrote, she studied, she travelled, she sight-saw. It was an industrious, conscientious life, with little self-pity. She filled the emotional gap in her life by warm friendships with one or two other women—Lady Byron, Ottilie von Goethe; but she had many affectionate friends, men as well as women, young and old, and was liked and respected—she fitted in, she was a bringer-together, an arranger, a kind reliable discreet friend, and a much-sought-after guest for dinners and breakfasts in the chief literary houses in London. If it still seems odd that this art critic, of no great scholarship or distinction of mind, separated from her husband and living in a remote suburb with a widowed mother and several sisters, should have been such a favourite guest, the explanation may perhaps be that she was a very good listener. It is easy to forget how urgently necessary a receptive audience must have been at those parties where Carlyle, Milnes, Rogers and Macaulay—the most inundating of them all—were performing. A sensible well-informed woman like Mrs Jameson, astringent enough not to be insipid, clever enough to understand but not clever enough to compete, must have been a godsend.

This was the woman who now took Elizabeth Barrett round Rogers' house. Miss Barrett was given a short lecture about the collection, how it had been chosen to illustrate the graceful and the elevated, to exemplify harmony, elegance, simplicity and pathos not turning into real pain. Was Mrs Jameson thinking of the Guido Reni when she made this last point? She would, she declared, choose this collection above any other known to her as a means of educating the eye and mind in art appreciation, something which had to be learnt, and did not come by nature. It certainly needed to be learnt by Miss Barrett, who had seen hardly any painting and was mainly interested in the subjects and literary associations of pictures.

They looked into the dining-room, where Mrs Jameson had breakfasted the morning before with Gräfin Hahn-Hahn. Miss Barrett observed the Guido Reni without much excitement, and merely noted the Tintoretto sketch of the *Miracle of Saint Mark* which Mrs Jameson thought was so spirited, so glowing, so richly coloured. Miss Barrett admired the Rembrandt self-portrait, "such a rugged, dark, deep, subterraneous face . . . yet inspired", and was carried away by the Michelangelo terra-cotta statuette of Lorenzo di Medici, a model for the San Lorenzo figure—"the blind eyes looking . . . seeing . . . as if in scorn of all clay! And the union of energy and meditation in the whole attitude!" A touch of lecture notes about this last sentence, perhaps—she was retailing it all to Browning afterwards. But there is a quite personal reaction in her description of the Roubiliac bust of Pope, "a too expressive, miserable face—drawn with disease and bitter thoughts, and very painful, I felt, to look at", and in her disapproval of the marble busts on the chimney-piece, "beautiful busts, white with marble, . . . and representing—now, whom, of gods and men, would you

87

select for your Lares . . . to help your digestion and social merriment? . . . Caligula and Nero in childhood!''

They went upstairs, past the colossal white marble statue of Antinous and the reproduction of part of Haydon's beloved Elgin Marbles which ran round the staircase, and into the drawing-room. Miss Barrett was flagging; she listened as attentively as she could to Mrs Jameson's explanation about the Rubens copy of the Mantegna *Triumph of Julius Caesar*, which she was to understand as being "a kind of double original, the blended reflection of two master minds, the antipodes of each other and here meeting midway. It is as wonderful as a psychological curiosity, as it is beautiful as a work of art". All that Miss Barrett retained of this was that Mrs Jameson had called Rubens' picture a *version*, not a copy, and that she had also said that the Raphael *Virgin and Child* in the same room was "divine" but "worn and faded to a shadow of Raphael's genius". The superlative Titian *Noli Me Tangere* in the same room, now one of the glories of the National Gallery, gets a mention but no description in Miss Barrett's letter.

The library was the third show room in Rogers' house, and here there were drawings by Raphael and Michelangelo and some books and documents which did arouse Miss Barrett's enthusiasm. There were letters from Byron and Fox and signatures of Johnson, Sterne, Gray and Burke on contracts for their works, but the one which excited Miss Barrett most was Milton's agreement for the sale of *Paradise Lost*. She told Browning "Almost I could have run my head against the wall, I felt, with bewilderment—and Mrs Jameson must have been edified, I have thought since, through my intense stupidity".

It must in fact have been rather annoying for Mrs Jameson that in that house of treasures—pictures by Veronese, Velazquez, Watteau, the *Knight in Armour* which Rogers thought was a Giorgione and which is now in the National Gallery, the Reynolds *Strawberry Girl*, miniatures by Fouquet and Holbein, Greek vases, Roman bronzes—Miss Barrett seemed specially interested in a small picture by Benjamin Robert Haydon. Mrs Jameson did not have a high opinion of Haydon as a painter. She had once gone to his studio with Lady Byron for Haydon to do a sketch of Lady Byron to insert into his vast picture of the *Meeting of the Anti-Slavery Convention*. She criticized Haydon's drawing, there was a sharp exchange of words, and Haydon was so unnerved that the resulting portrait of Lady Byron was poor even in his own estimation. Mrs Jameson conceded, however, that Haydon's *Napoleon Musing at St Helena* in the Rogers collection was among his best work.

Haydon painted twenty-three versions of his *Napoleon Musing at St Helena*. Rogers' version was the fourth. He had called at Haydon's studio, seen the third version, which Haydon was doing for the Duke of Sutherland, and told him that when Talleyrand and the Duchesse de Dino had seen the second version, at Sir Robert Peel's house at Drayton, they had said Haydon had made Napoleon too fat. Haydon had some warrant for his idea of Napoleon's size in his St Helena days; Haydon's sister had seen Napoleon at Plymouth in August 1815 on his way to St Helena, and had reported that he had "a large stomach, though not otherwise fat". However, Haydon offered to do a more svelte version of Napoleon for Rogers, who replied without great enthusiasm commissioning a 2 feet 6 inches by 2 feet version of Napoleon for thirty guineas.

Haydon's little picture of Napoleon was a curious and compelling image. The Emperor, fined down according to specification but with practically no neck and with Haydon's inevitable defect of disproportionately short legs, is seen from three-quarter back, arms crossed, standing on the edge of a cliff gazing out to sea. Only his cheek and chin and the edge of one eye are visible, but the uniform—cocked hat, cut-away coat with epaulettes, white breeches and knee-boots—is carefully rendered; Haydon took a lot of trouble to get the details right. On a stone in the foreground at the edge of the cliff there is an inscription, "Ainsi passe la Gloire—Austerlitz, Jena . . . Wagram, Waterloo". Beyond stretches the ocean, under a heavy sky with a dull glow of light along the horizon which casts Napoleon's shadow back onto the turfy cliff.

The figure is unsuccessful, but there is something memorable about the desolation of the great stretch of empty sea and the unbroken horizon and the lonely seagulls wheeling far below.

Wordsworth thought so; he wrote a sonnet about the picture.
Tactfully explaining that he was leaving it to others to praise
the technical skill of colour and drawing in the picture, he concentrated on the

> "signs
> Of thought, that give the true poetic thrill,—
> That unincumber'd whole of blank and still—
> Sky without cloud—ocean without a wave—
> And the one Man, that labour'd to enslave
> The world, sole standing high on the bare hill,
> Back turn'd—arms folded, the unapparent face
> Tinged (we may fancy) in this dreary place
> With light reflected from the invisible sun,
> Set—like his fortunes! but not set for aye
> Like them—the unguilty Power pursues his way
> And before *Him* doth dawn perpetual run".

The obsessive interest in the painting's subject which informed the painter's hand communicates itself, through the
noble unmoved justice of Wordsworth's mind, to us. The
figure on the cliff edge cast an intense shadow on all the length
of Haydon's life. Even at ten years old he was reading lives of
Napoleon and other ambitious men; his son Frederic thought
he had read every word about Napoleon that had ever been
published. On the only expedition he ever made to France, in
June 1814, he went to Rambouillet and penetrated to the private
closet of Napoleon, then in Elba, and lost himself in dreams of
the Emperor, his brain in a blaze, plotting the conquest of the
world. He had a medal and a bronze statuette of Napoleon in
his bedroom. He encouraged his son Harry—who died before
he was four years old—to have a passion for Napoleon's
memory, and the little boy had a collection of two hundred
prints of Napoleon which he was always looking over, and used
to stand gazing at his father's picture of *Napoleon Musing at
St Helena*. He was his father's favourite child. The whole
length of Haydon's diaries is full of anecdotes and reflections on
Napoleon—admiring reflections, disapproving reflections, an
obsessive return again and again to the man who was too great

for mere scruple, who dared to seize the critical moment. Napoleon was the greatest of all the Daemons that crowded Haydon's imagination.

His friends fed his obsession. Miss Mitford said that the century had produced only two men, Napoleon Bonaparte and Benjamin Robert Haydon. S. C. Hall told him—"Haydon, if you had a little less vanity and a little more pride, you would have been the great man of your age"; only the last six words really penetrated Haydon's mind and he replied "Delightful! What more could you say of Alexander or Napoleon?"

Elizabeth Barrett had contributed her share. During the period of her most frequent exchange of letters with Haydon, no subject had been more discussed between them than the contrast between Napoleon and Wellington. He sent her a copy of *Napoleon Musing at St Helena* to see, and this started a discussion. In the correspondence Haydon seems to have taken the side of Wellington, provoking Miss Barrett—who had written poems in praise of Napoleon—to declare that, though it might have been expedient, it was unjust to have exiled the Emperor to that waste island lost in the ocean, and that Wellington, who might have intervened, was ungenerous to do nothing to help his fallen foe. Napoleon was her hero, a man of gigantic faults but with a mind large enough to comprehend the world which his arms were stretched to seize.

In writing so, Elizabeth Barrett may have done Haydon more harm than all the good her wise counsels of moderation on other subjects can have done him. Napoleon was his temptation. All through the last years of his life he struggled against it. He collected unflattering anecdotes about Napoleon to record in his diary, but somehow as he wrote them down, they always became tinged with admiration of the Emperor's fascination, his audacity, his understanding of human nature, his military genius. "Napoleon's Coach broke down on his return from Elba. Well, it is glorious to be able to fight a *last* battle". Constantly he compared his own actions to Napoleon's: "Napoleon could have done no more in the time", "Let 'em wait, as Napoleon said", "Napoleon suffered the same thing"; he was of the Napoleon species, he told himself.

Monday 22nd June

Miss Barrett, as she looked at Haydon's picture of Napoleon in Samuel Rogers' library, had a renewed—a very recent—memory of Haydon's obsession with his hero. The letter she had had from him last Thursday, when he sent her his pictures and journals for safe-keeping, had talked of Napoleon, of glory and of fame. She had rather lost touch with Haydon until the letters came last week, and now, just after hearing from him about Napoleon, she was seeing his picture of the Emperor. She had no particular wish to start corresponding again with Haydon, but her thoughts were with him on this Monday afternoon.

When Haydon left his wife in her room and went back to his studio, their daughter Mary went into her mother's room and stayed with her while she was dressing. At about a quarter to eleven they heard what sounded like a shot, but troops were exercising in Hyde Park that morning and they decided it must have been the troops that they heard firing. Within five minutes they heard a heavy fall in the room below them, and thought Haydon was moving his pictures about and letting a corner fall suddenly, as he often did.

Mrs Haydon left for Brixton soon after eleven. Mary walked part of the way with her and then came back to the house. She was worried about her father's despondency, and at a quarter past twelve she went and knocked at the studio door, and getting no reply, opened the door and went in. The room was rather dark and quite silent except for the loud ticking of the watch on the table. Haydon was not sitting at the table where she expected to see him, and she looked to see if he was standing back in the further corner of the room to study his picture. He was not there either, and now she saw that he was lying on the floor. She thought he had lain down on the floor to study the foreground of his picture, and she spoke to him. When he did not answer, she went up and leaned over him and spoke to him again, but softly, so as not to disturb him too abruptly. He seemed to be lying in an odd position, huddled together, and she began to have a horrible idea that he had fallen down in a fit. She stepped right up to him and stooped over, her foot slipping as she did so, and touched his head, which was very cold, and his cheeks quite white, his eyes fixed. There seemed to be a pool of red paint on the floor, and in it she saw a razor in a case, another razor lying loose, and a pistol. Then she realized what had happened, and that her foot had slipped in her father's blood, in which his body was lying.

Mary Haydon screamed out, and her scream was heard by the cook Mary Hackett, who ran upstairs and looked into the studio and saw the body. Mary Haydon rushed out across the road to get the family doctor, but he was out; a neighbouring surgeon was sent for, and Mary Haydon threw herself into a cab to go to Brixton and fetch her mother. On the way there she crossed with Mrs Haydon who was bringing their friend Coulton back to Burwood Place to transact some business with Haydon.

So it was without preparation that Mrs Haydon heard the news when she entered the house. Coulton took charge, went upstairs to the studio and saw the body and the letters, and the will appointing him, Talfourd and Darling as executors. He took the letters addressed to Peel, Sir George Cockburn and Talfourd and went to deliver them himself. A surgeon arrived and examined the body and reported that Haydon had died from haemorrhage from the wounds in his throat. Mrs Haydon's son by her first marriage, Orlando Hyman, who was a don at Wadham College, Oxford, was sent for. The nervous Frank Haydon was little help in such a crisis, and Frederic Haydon, the second son, was at the other side of the world. He was a midshipman in H.M.S. *Grecian*, which on this 22nd June was in harbour at Rio de Janeiro.

This son, unlike Frank, admired his father; he had the same sort of argumentative confident temperament, and understood his father's aspirations. But he was in low spirits that Monday morning because of an unpleasant experience at a cemetery the day before, when he had seen bodies being dragged and hurled out of the hospital dead-cart into a pit. The taste of earth stayed in his mouth for months afterwards, he said. Next day he was walking the deck of the *Grecian* in the forenoon watch when he was seized with a wave of inexplicable grief, a presentiment of evil, so strong that he recorded it in his journal. His account of all this was written many years later, but the contemporary entry in his journal shows that it was not all hindsight, since it was not till weeks later that he heard that his father had killed himself that morning.

The miserable confusion of the house in Burwood Place that afternoon was seen by two inopportune visitors. The painter John Martin had not been quite reassured by his son's account of the Haydon household the evening before. He was an old friend of Haydon's, had shared his struggle against the Royal Academy, knew what it was like to be desperate for money, to be full of huge conceptions but paralysed by ingratitude and neglect. And he had had a grim warning against ignoring signs of desperation in a friend. In 1838 his nephew Richard, who had lived with him for nine years and whose sudden outburst of incoherent fear had been little regarded, cut his throat with a razor in John Martin's house. When John Martin heard his son Leopold's account of how Haydon had seemed on Sunday evening, he decided to see for himself, and on Monday afternoon he took Leopold round to see Haydon. Many years later Leopold Martin wrote a prim description of what they found when they got to Burwood Place. "To our utter dismay we found the house in the most frightful disorder. The poor wife was weeping, seemingly in deep anxiety and distress, her condition being truly both painful and shocking to witness".

Mrs Haydon is an enigmatic figure. When Haydon married her in 1821, she was a twenty-eight-year-old widow with two small sons. She was a beauty, with dark glossy hair, dark eyes with very fine eyebrows, a brilliantly rosy complexion, full curving lips, and a lovely line of cheek-bone. She was perhaps a Jewess; Hazlitt and Miss Mitford both thought she was the perfect realization of Rebecca in Scott's *Ivanhoe*. She and Haydon were very much in love when they married, and she did him a lot of good—her fun and fondling made him relax and laugh and enjoy himself. On Haydon's side the passion lasted all his life; when he records in his diary the pleasures of their love he is just as rapturous in 1844 as in 1821, and he continued to compare all the pretty women he met unfavourably with her. On her side, illness, money worries, the births of eight children and the deaths of five of them, turned her into someone different. She led a very retired life, almost always at home looking after the children, hardly going out to meet Haydon's friends and acquaintances, though some of those that knew her liked her very much—Wordsworth, for instance, and Miss Mitford who thought she had "exceedingly sweet and captivating manners". But hope and illusion had been gradually ground out of her, she could not join in her husband's irrepressible belief that Providence would extricate them from their difficulties. She no longer shared Haydon's still violent physical passion, though she had grown more possessive about his companionship, of which he did not give her so very much, even at home; he spent all day in his studio, and was apt to read at meals. Her high spirits had given way to irritability and occasional hysteria, though she could still muster a rather pathetically bright and playful enjoyment of the few parties and family excursions that came her way. When on the tenth anniversary of his wedding day Haydon surveyed their marriage, it seemed to him to be on the whole a success; the first excitements were over, they had gone through many difficulties over their children and their financial affairs, but they were still happy and faithful in a settled way—and he concluded with his favourite quotation from *Paradise Lost*—"Hail wedded love!"

But eighteen months later began one of the oddest chapters in Haydon's extraordinary life, and the part that Mrs Haydon played in it showed that there were dangerous and vindictive qualities in this retiring and domesticated woman. In February 1833 Haydon met the three lovely Sheridan sisters, Lady Seymour, Mrs Blackwood and Mrs Norton, and was at once captivated by their beauty. At first he was almost more enchanted by Lady Seymour—the Eglinton Tournament's Queen of Beauty—than by Mrs Norton, while still thinking his own wife as beautiful as either; he had visions of a Mohamedan paradise in which he could enjoy all three of them. Mrs Haydon passed a wretched spring of jealousy, anxiety and illness; she was pregnant, and their child Alfred was ill—he died in May; a daughter was born a month later and Haydon insisted on giving her the Christian names of Lady Seymour and Mrs Norton. By July Haydon, now quite infatuated by Mrs Norton's intellectual brilliance and her dark glittering beauty, was constantly calling on her, embarrassed by the force of his feelings and unable to keep away, and finally declaring his passion to her.

The progress of his infatuation was interrupted by his arrest for debt at the end of July, and in August Mrs Norton left London and they did not meet again till the following February. All through the winter Haydon continued to think fondly of Mrs Norton, and when Lady Blessington told him malicious stories about her, he resented it. Mrs Norton kept him at a distance after his avowal, and he only succeeded in renewing their friendship by means of moral blackmail—in May 1834 he persuaded her to sit as his model for a picture of Cassandra which, he said, would save his family from ruin. He construed her consent into an avowal that she returned his passion, although, with his usual astonishing mixture of candour and self-deception, he recorded in his diary that she had kept him aloof for a year, that she would not admit to loving him, and that she told her servants he was a bore. Still more extraordinary, he told his wife every detail of his feelings for Mrs Norton, almost as though they were a disease which he had involuntarily caught and about which his wife ought to sympathize; at the same time protesting that he had remained faithful and innocent, that he loved his wife as much as ever, and that he thought her just as beautiful as Mrs Norton.

Mary Haydon suffered tortures of jealousy, and made some hysterical scenes, and some desperate attempts to hold her husband by reproaches, by flattery of his beauty and genius, by referring to her own conquests. It was a wretched time for her, as another of their children, Harry, was dying—he died in May 1834, and Haydon added to his wife's misery by reproaching her for neglecting the child. Throughout that summer Mrs Haydon kept a jealous watch; Haydon found that she had been "accidentally" reading his diary, which was still full of adoring references to Caroline Norton.

But Mrs. Norton was getting bored with Haydon's infatuation, kept cancelling appointments to sit for him, and by September had gone away from London without giving him any news of herself or her plans. Haydon now began to convince himself that she was an artful woman who had led him on and tried to keep him in her power, to suspect her relations with Lord Melbourne, to believe and pass on to others spiteful stories about her, and to regard her as a fallen woman, intriguing and hypocritical, though he still admired her beauty. By January 1835 he had convinced himself that Mrs Norton had made a deliberate onslaught on his domestic happiness. Although all her actions, which he himself records, indicate that it was she who dismissed him, he was now persuaded that a secret invitation, intelligible only to him, underlay all her words and looks of dismissal.

In the winter of 1835 to 1836 there was a rapprochement, and Mrs Norton sat to Haydon again. He was again enraptured, and Mary Haydon, unable to bear this renewed danger which had seemed to be past, took action against her rival. When Haydon was recurring to this time in his journal eighteen months later, he said that Mrs Norton made advances to him which made him resolve to sever their relations, but there is nothing about this in his diary at the time. Mrs Haydon may have delivered some sort of ultimatum to him, but the decisive action which she took was less direct.

At this time the picturesque and mendacious Edward Trelawney was meeting Mrs Norton at a good many London parties, and on one occasion he called on Haydon when Mrs Norton was sitting to him. He talked to Mary Haydon, and referred to Mrs Norton in rather unflattering terms. There is nothing in the diary at the time to suggest that Haydon himself had any suspicions about Trelawney and Mrs Norton; but four years later he recorded that the couple had tried to use his studio as "a room for intrigue and assignation" but that he had virtuously refused to permit this. This was supposed to have taken place in December 1835.

At Easter 1836 Caroline Norton finally quarrelled with her husband and left his house, and Norton instantly started looking round among Caroline's admirers for someone whom he could cite as co-respondent in the divorce action which he was determined to bring against his wife. Trelawney was for some time one of the most likely choices, till Melbourne's wealth and political importance caused him to be finally selected as the victim. A cousin of Haydon's was in the confidence of Norton's solicitor, so a channel was available to Mary Haydon through which information against Trelawney and Mrs Norton could be poured. Some action she certainly took, both to convince Haydon himself of Mrs Norton's obliquity, and to blacken her reputation with others. From the moment when Norton's intention of bringing a divorce action against his wife was announced, Haydon's references to "Caroline", as he now familiarly and contemptuously calls her in his diary, are violently abusive and hostile, repeating the most scurrilous rumours against her, and repulsive physical details which his wife had told him, alleging that she had had them from Mrs Norton herself. In 1841 he recorded in his diary that he was convinced, and could prove, that his wife had brought on Mrs Norton's "trial and exposure"—that is, her husband's action against Lord Melbourne, in which Melbourne and Mrs Norton were acquitted; but Haydon never accepted this verdict. A month later he recorded an accidental meeting between his wife and Mrs Norton and added "Mary ruined her, and she knows it".

Haydon's bent for turning everything into a dramatic incident makes him an unreliable witness in this matter. The idea that the famous Mrs Norton had been ruined by his wife in revenge for Mrs Norton's attempted seduction of him would be an agreeable tribute to his charms and importance, and he may have invented, as he certainly exaggerated, the whole story, which is interesting chiefly for the smoky light it casts on the figure of Mary Haydon. Of Caroline Norton it tells us little; the Haydons saw her through the distorting medium of their own preoccupations. In spite of all Haydon's dark sayings about her depravity, his references to her as a Messalina and a dreadful whore, his promise of horrid revelations, there is no real evidence, on his own showing, that she ever did more than amuse herself with his goggle-eyed adoration. But all the rest of his life he maintained that she had heartlessly attempted to seduce him. Years afterwards he told Elizabeth Barrett, who passed it on to Browning, that Mrs Norton had made advances to him. Browning's comment—"the telling *that*, if it were true, is nearly as bad as inventing it. That poor woman is the hack-block of a certain class of redoubtable braggarts—there are such stories by the *dozen* in circulation. All may have been misconception"—is the best comment on the whole strange and unpleasing episode.

Throughout the time of his infatuation with Mrs Norton, Haydon continued to make love to his wife, to admire her beauty and goodness, to rely on her affection. Their marriage was a true one, perhaps the most genuine thing in Haydon's life. Mary Haydon was a realist; Haydon's fine words and protestations did not mean much to her, she loved what was really there—the energy, the courage, the vigorous passion, the bright eyes, the well-poised head. During the Mrs Norton crisis, Mary Haydon kept a diary; Haydon read it and, melted by her misery, wrote an extremely high-flown protestation of fidelity. "I do not believe one word of all this fine stuff puff" wrote Mary Haydon below. Haydon, descending rapidly from his high horse, wrote below that "You do, you little black-eyed hussy".

"I do not believe one word of all this fine stuff puff"—that had come to be Mrs Haydon's attitude to her husband in his rhetorical vein. In the ten years that followed the Caroline Norton episode, she had much illness and increasing financial difficulties as the Haydons' comparative prosperity in the 1830's, when Haydon had several large and lucrative commissions, gave way to the failures of the 1840's. Their life was to be always like that; her husband would always be making speeches and writing to the newspapers, declaiming, protesting, denouncing; behind it all would go on their real life of meals and bed, debts and pawnbrokers, walks in the fields and occasional trips to the seaside. When her son Frank came home from the walk to Hampstead with his father on the last day of his life, and told Mrs Haydon about Haydon's talk of suicide, she laughed at the idea and told Frank to put it out of his mind. But a month earlier she had written a melancholy little poem to her son Frederic, the midshipman, telling him to stay in the distant sunny isles, not to come back to the toils and cares of England; she longed to join him, to escape, to get away from the life "where each morn is expected with Fear".

*　　*　　*

"Are we going to have a storm tonight? It lightens, it lightens"
wrote Elizabeth Barrett to Browning that evening at the end
of her letter describing her visit in the afternoon to Samuel
Rogers' pictures. It had been brilliantly clear and as hot as
ever all day, but at ten o'clock lightning flashes on the horizon
to the east and north were seen from the centre of London. The
flashes grew brighter, the thunder began to be heard, and by
midnight it was crashing and rattling overhead, and the much-
needed rain was falling heavily. It was a wild storm of rain and
wind. A woman running along a London street to shelter from
the torrential downpour fell and broke her leg, and lay un-
noticed in the lashing rain till she was found and carried to
hospital, where her leg had to be amputated. In St Clement's
Lane the fierce wind blew down a chimney pot—it fell on a
twenty-two-year-old girl and fractured her skull. The wind
veered round to the south-west, the glass fell, and all over
England the damp cool freshness of the rain spread at last.

"We regret to state that Mr B. R. Haydon, the historical painter, died suddenly at his residence in Burwood-place, yesterday morning. The unfortunate gentleman was in his usual health on the previous evening, and it is believed that his decease was hastened by pecuniary embarrassment".

This paragraph in *The Times* of Tuesday 23rd June caught the eye of Elizabeth Barrett's brother Alfred at Paddington Station that morning; he copied it out and sent it by post to his sister. Browning saw it too that morning, and after some hesitation wrote to Elizabeth Barrett to tell her. He thought she might not have had the news yet; he knew she did not see a newspaper in the mornings. If she had not yet heard, his letter might seem brutal, but he could not write without mentioning such a tragedy at all. He thought more of the effect on Miss Barrett than of the news itself; he knew Haydon very slightly, had not much admired what he had heard about him, and now deduced from the wording of *The Times* announcement that Haydon must have killed himself. It was the shock to Elizabeth Barrett that mattered to Browning, especially after the storm the previous night—storms always made her ill. But perhaps she would not feel it as much as he feared; she and Haydon had never actually met, after all—she might regard him as a mere acquaintance.

Elizabeth Barrett felt a good deal more than that. From the moment when she first learned the news, when she got her brother's letter, she was overcome with sadness, and with a feeling of guilt too—could she have averted Haydon's suicide if she had offered to lend him money? She had assumed, when Haydon sent her his pictures and journals for safe-keeping, that it was just one of his usual recurring financial crises. Everybody had warned her that lending money to Haydon was like dropping it into a hole in the ground, and at that particular moment she had no money of her own in hand, and would have had to apply to her father for a loan—which would not have been granted. But all these excuses seemed poor enough now. "*Would* it have availed, to have dropped something into that 'hole in the ground'? Oh, to imagine *that*! Yet a little would have been as nothing!—and he did not ask even for a little—and I should have been ashamed to have offered but a little. Yet I cannot turn the thought away—*that I did not offer*".

She was sure that Haydon had killed himself on a sudden insane impulse. He could not have been meditating suicide when he wrote the letters she had had from him last week, though she could see now that there was a note of desperate feeling in them. "Oh that a man so high hearted and highly endowed . . . a bold man, who has thrown down gauntlet after gauntlet in the face of the world—that such a man should go mad for a few paltry pounds! For he was *mad* if he killed himself! of that I am as sure as if I knew it. If he killed himself, he was mad first".

She got her brother Henry to go round to Burwood Place that afternoon, telling him to make a general inquiry after the family. Frank Haydon came to the door and said that "Mr Haydon was dead, and that his family were quite as well as could be expected".

The news of Haydon's suicide spread round London. One of the first to react to it was the Prime Minister. Haydon's farewell letter had been left at Downing Street by Coulton on the Monday afternoon; Peel endorsed it—"Last letter from Haydon. It must have been written a few minutes before he deprived himself of life. Observe the word 'wife' had been originally written 'widow', and been altered by him". Peel wrote at once to Coulton, saying how painfully shocked he was to hear the news, and enclosing a cheque for £200 from the Royal Bounty Fund for the immediate relief of Haydon's family. He added that when a subscription was opened he would contribute to that from his private purse.

Wellington's reaction was different. On the morning after Haydon's death, as soon as he saw the news in *The Times*, he

sent a servant round to Burwood Place to recover his hat, which
Haydon had borrowed for painting the Duke's portrait.

Some of those who knew Haydon were not entirely surprised
at the news. Macready, reading the announcement in the paper,
noted in his diary—"It is most sad—most dreadful for the
surviving relations, but it is a termination of a life that does
not surprise me". The painter Frith said that Haydon's death
"distressed, if it scarcely surprised, all who knew him". Turner,
however, was not distressed. Maclise, who heard the news at
the Athenaeum, saw Turner there reading the newspaper and
went up to him and said—

"I have just heard of Haydon's suicide. Is it not awful?"

Turner, without looking up from his newspaper, said "Why
did he stab his mother?"

"Great heaven, you don't mean——"

"Yes, he stabbed his mother".

That was all Turner would say; the toothless eccentric old
man would not even now forgive Haydon's attacks on his old
school—though hardly his *alma* mater—the Royal Academy.

If some of Haydon's friends were not surprised, others were
utterly astonished. "I had been completely upset by the terrible
shock of poor Haydon's death" wrote Miss Mitford from her
Berkshire cottage. "He was a friend of five and thirty years
or more; has sometimes written me three or four letters in a
week; and was so brilliant, so animated, so full of life, so young
in mind and manner, that the death itself, set aside the frightful
manner of it, had something that took me by surprise—like
the death of a young bride. . . . He was an excellent husband,
excellent father, excellent friend! I am certain that he calculated
upon the interest which this deplorable event would excite for
his wife and family, and that that feeling mingled with the
weariness of a long hopeless struggle, in prompting him to this
fatal act . . . Sir Robert has behaved very nobly . . . I am told
that few events of our times have made so great a sensation as
this tragedy of real life".

Another friend of Haydon's of thirty years' standing, Leigh
Hunt, who had gone out of town to cure a cough among the
meadows and lime trees of the village of Wimbledon, read

the news of Haydon's death as he sat in his lodgings. Leigh Hunt had launched Haydon's campaign against the Royal Academy by publishing an article of his in the *Examiner*; Haydon had visited Hunt in prison, and had argued with him over every possible subject except religion and Napoleon, two topics on which the two men felt so strongly and so differently that it was' safer to keep off them. Now in 1846 Leigh Hunt was almost as short of money as Haydon, but it did not worry him—nothing worried him, the picturesque old man with his open shirt collar and his loose flowing dressing-gown, and his delicate elusive face—bright darting eyes, a dark complexion, a marmot nose, a cleft chin and plentiful greyish-black hair falling on his shoulders. He was writing a long, long letter to Forster, full of his claims to a Civil List pension which Forster was trying to get for him, and at noon he broke off to read the newspaper. "I have just read of poor Haydon! how dreadful! how *astonishing*! for he is one of the last men of whom I should have expected such a thing. I looked upon him as one who turned disappointment itself to a kind of self-glory,—but see how we may be mistaken. Poor fellow! but then, poor family! That is the worst".

The news spread and spread. Dickens heard it in Switzerland, and wrote about it in the little study of his house in Lausanne, overlooking the lake and the shifting colours of the great mountains beyond, which changed from red to grey to purple to black, and sometimes seemed so near and sometimes lost in mist. The garden below was full of roses, and the country round was all vineyards and pastures full of hay, and green lanes with birds singing in the trees, and after the great storm the weather was cooler, with a stir of air, though the sunshine still poured down on the blue glittering lake. Dickens was sympathetic about Haydon's death, but he was not so much moved as to lose his sense of proportion, that critical toughness which was later to make him use Haydon, combined with Leigh Hunt, as' his model for the self-indulgent Harold Skimpole in *Bleak House*. He said that he was greatly shocked by Haydon's death and thought the account of the inquest "one of the most affecting pieces of fact I have ever heard". But he added "All his life he had utterly mistaken his vocation. No amount of sympathy with him, and sorrow for him in his manly pursuit of a wrong idea for many years—until, by dint of his perseverance and courage it almost began to seem a right one—ought to prevent one from saying that he most unquestionably was a very bad painter, and that his pictures could not be expected to sell or to succeed. I went to that very exhibition at the Egyptian Hall, of which he writes so touchingly in his Diary. And I assure you that when I saw his account of the number of visitors he had had in one of the papers, my amazement was—not that there were so few, but that there were so many. There was one picture, Nero entertaining himself with a Musical Performance while Rome was burning—quite marvellous in its badness. It was difficult to look at it with a composed and decent face. There is no doubt, on the other hand, that in the theory of his art, he was very clever, and in his general tone of thought a very superior man and I must say that having written so well on art, and having suffered so much in a hopeless attempt to elevate it, I think he was (as his widow is) a very good subject for a pension. I little thought that I should ever live to praise Peel. But D'Israeli and that Dunghill Lord have so disgusted me, that I feel inclined to champion him—and should have done so, even if he hadn't shown a striving artist such delicate attention and compassion as he showed to Haydon".

Sir Robert Peel's kindness to Haydon, at a moment when he was being so ruthlessly harried himself by Disraeli and Lord George Bentinck, caught public attention almost as much as Haydon's suicide itself. The newspapers were full of it. "All honour to his name; be his political destiny what it may, the glory of this one act—which he little dreamed the world would ever hear of—is a set-off against a score of party-victories and a hundred arena-defeats" proclaimed S. C. Hall's *Art Union Monthly Journal*, with an unctuous incomprehension both of Peel's standard of values and of how Haydon would have felt at having any part of this—his last clap of thunder—stolen from him. The Coroner at the inquest on Haydon spent more time on Peel than on Haydon in his summing up. "I cannot fail . . . to remark on the munificent act of Sir Robert Peel towards the unfortunate deceased. I think it must speak to the heart of a great many thousand persons, that whilst others were, so to speak, attempting to destroy his mind, and amidst a pressure of public business almost unparalleled, Sir Robert Peel had not forgotten the sufferings of others".

There were some persons, however, to whose hearts Haydon's death spoke a special urgent message. Holman Hunt said that when Haydon killed himself, the tragedy and the failure that caused it increased the anxiety of all the friends of young painters. Not long after, a surgeon in Chelsea committed suicide, and a witness at the inquest on him testified that "he had frequently read the late Mr Haydon's case; and all his talk was of self-destruction". A watchmaker at Plymouth who was heavily in debt killed himself by taking prussic acid, and left a letter to his wife, and papers containing the extracts from Haydon's diary which had been printed in the newspapers, with pencil marks against them. He had spoken of Haydon to his wife, and in his farewell letter to her he said that something would be done for her and the children if he were out of the way.

The inquest on Haydon was held at half past nine on the morn-
ing of Wednesday 24th June at the Norfolk Arms Tavern in
Burwood Place, only three doors away from Haydon's house.
The Coroner was Dr Thomas Wakley, M.P., founder of *The
Lancet*, a man whom Haydon had particularly despised. When
Wakley made fun of Wordsworth's poetry in a speech on the
Copyright Bill in the House of Commons in 1842, Haydon
wrote in his Diary—"The greatest infliction on the pride of
any Poet would be that his poetry was relished by a Coroner,
who sees Human Nature only through the medium of cut
throats, stomach pumps and Arsenic".

The Coroner went first to Haydon's house and inspected the
body. Then a jury of fifteen was sworn in and went in their turn
to see the body. They came back "apparently much affected".
Haydon's body had been lying in its pool of blood in the studio
for nearly forty-eight hours, and there was more blood smeared
about the room and splashed on the big canvas of *Alfred and the
First British Jury*.

The first witness at the inquest was Haydon's daughter
Mary, who was led into the court by the family doctor, Bryant.
The *Daily News* reporter, wringing the last ounce of drama out
of the situation, described her as "only sixteen years of age
and extremely handsome", but she was in fact twenty-two. She
seems to have been a good-looking shy pious girl. The Coroner
was kind and encouraging to her, and offered her a chair. She
told the story of how she had found her father's body, and in
answer to a question, she went on—"I saw my father last alive
about 10 o'clock on Monday morning. He then looked agitated
—more so than usual. I have never before known him to make
any attempt on his life".

The Coroner. "Had your father been under medical treatment lately?"

Mary Haydon. "No, Sir".

The Coroner. "Had he complained of his head in any way of late?"

Mary Haydon. "Yes. It was very unusual for him to do so; but on Sunday night last he did complain, and during the last two or three days I recollect to have seen him frequently put his hand up to his head".

The Coroner. "Did your father usually sleep well?"

Mary Haydon. "He has not done so for the last three months".

The Coroner. "And did he not seek medical advice?"

Mary Haydon. "No, Sir. He did not seem to think that necessary. He was always in the habit of taking his own medicine".

The Coroner (to the Jury). "Bless me, how extraordinary it is that persons will so neglect themselves. The number of lives annually sacrificed through a neglect of symptoms of this sort is perfectly monstrous". (To the Witness.) "Do you know that your father's rest has been much disturbed of late?"

Mary Haydon. "I do. He slept in a room by himself, over the servants' bedroom, and I have heard them say that my father was very restless early in the morning of late".

The Coroner. "Has he complained of a burning pain across his temples, or of any deficiency of sight?"

Mary Haydon. "No, Sir". She added "My father was a man of very temperate habits".

The Coroner. "Have you observed anything very remarkable in his manner of late?"

Mary Haydon. "I have noticed that he had a very different expression of countenance during the last three days. He was very silent during the whole of that period, and apparently absent in his mind. I cannot say that he tried to avoid meeting the members of his family more than usual".

She was then asked about the weapons with which her father had killed himself, and about the doctors called in after his death, and her own and her mother's movements that morning. That was the end of her testimony. The direction of the Coroner's questioning of her was obvious—he was building up a picture of insanity due to brain disease. Mary Haydon, a truthful unsophisticated girl, did not quite see what he was driving at.

The next witness was the Haydons' cook Mary Hackett, but she had nothing much to contribute except an account of how she ran up and saw the body when she heard Mary Haydon's scream of discovery. She had only been with the family a fortnight, and though she thought the master was "rather odd in his way", she could not say whether there had been anything unusual in his manner when she last saw him, because she had not known him long enough to know what his usual manner was.

Haydon's stepson, the Reverend Orlando Hyman, was the next witness. He was a clever well-read man who got a scholarship to Oxford when he was sixteen, and became a Fellow of Wadham. Stepfather and stepson had not always got on well, though Haydon considered himself a model stepfather, and in fact the cost of his stepson's education—which he bore entirely, as what little money came from Mrs Haydon's first husband was lost in an attorney's bankruptcy—had added to his financial difficulties. Orlando Hyman was seven years old when his mother remarried, quite old enough to resent it; and by the time he had got his fellowship at Oxford and had begun to see through his stepfather's intellectual pretensions, relations between them were bad enough to embroil his mother and his half-brother Frank—who sided entirely with him. In the last few years there had been less friction, but when he came to give evidence at the inquest on his stepfather, he was obviously picking his words very carefully indeed.

He began his evidence by saying that he had last seen Haydon on Saturday. "I very rarely saw much of him. On Saturday I observed a very great alteration in his countenance. All his family observed the same change, but thinking that it arose from the unfortunate circumstances in which he was placed, we were thrown off our guard, and did not pay so much attention to it. The deceased seldom said much to me, and never complained to me; but my mother has frequently mentioned to me that he complained to her. He was eccentric from his youth".

The Coroner. "I knew him well thirty years ago, and then I remember he was very eccentric occasionally".

Hyman. "Yes, Sir; and he has latterly become more so".

The Coroner. "He was, I believe, a man of very temperate habits?"

Hyman. "He was a man of marked sobriety, and led the most regular life possible".

The Coroner. "Do you know, Sir, was the deceased in the habit of keeping a diary, in which he noted down the principal circumstances which occurred to him?"

Hyman. "He was, Sir".

The Coroner. "Have you read any portion of that diary of late?"

Hyman. "I have looked into it several times lately, from the fact of its having been left open, which was a somewhat unusual occurrence".

The Coroner then produced the diary and gave it to Hyman, saying "As I do not wish the private circumstances of deceased's family to be unnecessarily exposed, I would rather you would look it through, and mark such passages for reading as, without giving the family pain, might enable the jury to form a correct conclusion as to the state of the deceased's mind at the period of his death. I have glanced through it myself and I observe a note from Sir Robert Peel attached to one of the entries which I should like to have read. If the jury are not satisfied with the arrangement I propose, they can of course inspect the diary for themselves, but I do not wish that the deceased's circumstances should be unnecessarily paraded before the public".

The jury made no objection to the arrangement, so Orlando Hyman retired to mark passages in the diary to read out. Meanwhile the Haydons' housemaid Elizabeth Western gave evidence, but nothing new came out. Neither Mrs Haydon nor Frank Haydon gave evidence.

The coroner now asked whether Hyman was ready to give extracts from the diary. Hyman said he was; he thought he had better start with the April entries about the failure of the exhibition at the Egyptian Hall, on which his stepfather had built so many hopes.

Wednesday 24th June

The Coroner. "Very well, let it be so. He seems to have made all the entries which I have observed with great care and minuteness".

Hyman. "Yes, Sir. He was very much attached to his diary, and the volume I hold in my hand is the twenty-sixth which he had completed. All the greater incidents of his life are carefully registered in these volumes".

The Coroner. "Poor fellow! I trust the reporters whom I see present will be careful in noting the extracts to be read from this diary, not to give publicity to names which may occur, or anything else calculated to give pain to the family of the deceased".

This was no doubt said particularly to protect the Duke of Beaufort and Lord Brougham who, unlike Peel, had not responded to Haydon's last appeals for money, as he had recorded in the diary on 16th June. The caution must have been necessary; *The Times,* the *Morning Chronicle,* the *Daily News,* the *Morning Post,* the *Standard,* practically the whole London press printed three-column verbatim reports of the inquest next day.

Hyman read out Haydon's hectic fluctuating account of the progress of his exhibition and the fatal competition from the circus dwarf—"They rush by thousands to see Thumb. They push, they fight, they scream, they faint, they cry help and murder. . . . I would not have believed it of the English people". This made a strong impression; it was to be referred to again and·again in leading articles and cartoons. He read the entry for 16th April: "My situation is now of more extreme peril than even when I began Solomon thirty three years ago!"

There was a break while the doctor who had examined Haydon's body gave evidence of the cause of death, and the pistol and bullet were handed to the jury. Haydon's letters to his wife, to his sons Frank and Frederic and to his daughter, were read·out to the Court by the Coroner's Deputy. Then the reading of the diary extracts went on: "Tom Thumb had 12,000 last week; B. R. Haydon 133½", "my brain got a little confused, as I foresaw ruin, misery and a Prison!", "my necessities are dreadful, owing to my failure at the Hall. In God alone I trust, to bring me through next week safe and capable of paying my way. O God, it is hard, this struggle of forty-two years".

Two references to kind acts, from two very different men, were the only relief to this mounting wail of despair read out by Hyman. One was Peel's response to Haydon's appeal; the other, from a man whose financial circumstances were by now as desperate as Haydon's, was a letter that perhaps gave Haydon more real comfort than Peel's prompt £50.

"I must speak to you of your picture. I went to the private view and admired exceedingly *Aristides*. It is Raffaelesque, and your sketch of the *French Revolution* digne de Michel Angelo. This is my candid opinion . . . Au revoir soon

Believe me yours faithfully

Count d'Orsay".

The resplendent dandy was not quite so magnificent now— his complexion a little worn, his figure a little thickened, his debts enormous, but he still had an easy good nature when it cost him nothing.

Hyman went on reading the diary extracts: "18th June. O God bless me through the Evils of this day. Amen. Great anxiety"; "21st June. Slept horribly. Prayed in sorrow and got up in agitation"; "22nd June. God forgive—me—Amen. Finis of B. R. Haydon".

The inquest had now lasted over three hours. Now the Coroner had to sum up. He did not make much of a job of it. He said he "felt the case to be too distressing for remark"; it was clear that Haydon had killed himself; the jury would have to decide on his frame of mind at the time. The Coroner's eloquence was reserved for Peel's munificence at such a critical moment in his own career.

The jury found that "the deceased, Benjamin Robert Haydon, died from the effects of wounds inflicted by himself, and that the said Benjamin Robert Haydon was in an unsound state of mind when he committed the act".

Was Haydon insane when he killed himself? He is often referred to by modern writers, perhaps too positively, as a manic depressive. Elizabeth Barrett was certain he must have been mad when he committed suicide, and her opinion was shared by most of the public comment at the time. "Of his insanity, we cannot entertain a doubt" said the *Art Union Monthly Journal*. But some of those who knew Haydon personally, not just by correspondence as Miss Barrett did, thought otherwise. His pupil Bewick declared that there never was a greater mistake than to say that Haydon was insane. The barrister Talfourd, one of Haydon's executors, told Browning he did not think Haydon was mad though "of a mad vanity, of course". Miss Mitford thought that Haydon had killed himself with a quite cold-blooded motive—in the calculation that so desperate an act would ensure that his wife and family were provided for.

The doctors who examined Haydon's brain after his death both thought that the post-mortem showed conclusively the existence of disease in the brain. One thought that the irritation of the brain was long-standing, the other that the inflammation was comparatively recent. "There were innumerable bloody points through the brain".

Haydon himself had a curious interest in disease of the brain and its connection with suicide. Five years before he killed himself, he wrote in his diary "It may be laid down 'that self destruction is the physical mode of relieving a diseased brain', because the first impression on a brain diseased, or diseased for a Time, is the necessity of this horrid crime". In one of the passages in which he dwelt on the suicides of Castlereagh and Romilly he considered that in both cases it was due to excess of blood on the brain; both recovered their reason the moment they had cut their throats and the blood began to flow. Then in the last days of 1845 another well-known man cut his throat. "Romilly, Castlereagh and Gurwood!" wrote Haydon in his diary. His son Frederic thought Gurwood's suicide affected Haydon more than the failure of his exhibition. As the heat of the summer came on, the idea of a pressure, a congestion in the brain, that had to be relieved, began to grow on him. Three years earlier he had said proudly "I believe I am meant to try the experiment how much a human brain can bear without insanity" but in June 1846 he wrote more humbly to Elizabeth Barrett that he hoped his brain would not turn. Those "innumerable bloody points through the brain" were pushing him towards a drastic relief.

In the book which Frederic Haydon made up out of his father's diary and correspondence, two drawings are reproduced. One—which is now in the National Portrait Gallery— is a head and shoulders of a classically beautiful young man, with fair curls falling on his shoulders, a very high forehead, heavy straight black eyebrows, large dreaming eyes, a Grecian nose, a firm mouth with a thin but curved upper lip, a dimpled strong forward-jutting chin, a noble neck. Across it is written "A vile caricature of B. R. Haydon by Mr Keats". This perhaps refers to a profile above the main head; the latter may be Haydon's more flattering version of his appearance to offset Keats' "vile caricature" profile of him. The two young men were obviously pulling the sheet of drawings to and fro, and teasing each other with their scribbles.

The second drawing is definitely by Haydon himself. It shows a face very like the first one thirty years later. It is a head of a man with fair curls falling on his shoulders, though now the hair has receded from the high forehead, which is heavily lined. The eyebrows are as straight and black as ever, the Grecian nose now has more of a hook (more like Haydon's real one), there is the same forward-jutting chin, though the dimple has gone; the same narrow curved upper lip, but now the mouth is just open to reveal the teeth in a disquieting snarl. The bright eyes are not now in a quiet dream, but are staring at some torturing vision, rolling in a panic beyond the reach of reassurance. The caption of this drawing is *A Study from memory of an expression*

115

in insanity. Was Haydon remembering a face he had seen in a looking-glass one day?

He was quite capable of noting an expression which he could subsequently use in a picture, even at a moment of extreme tension. He did drawings of his own children when they were dying or in fits. Once when he called on Eastlake's brother and found him in a paroxysm of asthma, he wrapped him in a blanket, carried him off in a cab to his studio, and painted a study of his head while he was still in paroxysm. When he saw a child killed in the street, he did what he could to help the child's mother and then went home and made a study of her glaring suffocated look of horror. He was a painter before all, and had often used his own face as a model. But would he have given the drawing such a title afterwards—*A Study from memory of an expression in insanity*? It may have been Frederic Haydon's title.

There is a counterpart to Keats' drawing of Haydon—a profile drawing by Haydon of Keats. Both were done in November 1816 soon after Haydon and Keats first met. If one looks at Haydon through the eyes of Keats, one sees a rarer creature than a conventional eye can discern. Keats outgrew Haydon, and came to feel that he could foretell exactly what Haydon would say about poetry or painting; Haydon treated him shabbily over money; but Keats' unique mind had recognized something in Haydon that was akin—not akin in intellect or talent, but in intensity. After their first evening of fiery talk Keats wrote a sonnet hailing Haydon as one of the great spirits on earth, who would give the world another heart and other pulses. He sent his great sonnet on the Elgin Marbles to Haydon, with another acknowledging Haydon's right to them, as the man who had taught his country to worship the beauty of the Marbles. They discussed and admired each other's work, they joked and ragged, they shared walks and parties. Sometimes it seemed to Keats that Haydon was the only man he knew in the world who truly understood what it felt like to be a creative artist—"the turmoil and anxiety, the sacrifice of all that is called comfort, the readiness to measure time by what is done, and to die in six hours, could plans be brought to

116

conclusions; the looking on the sun, the moon, the stars, earth and its contents, as materials to form greater things". When Haydon wrote a cutting letter to Keats' friend Bailey, Keats was not surprised or shocked; he made Haydon's strange character the starting-point for his most wonderful speculations on genius and imagination.

In one of his letters to Haydon, Keats quoted the lines from *Love's Labour's Lost* about Fame being "registered upon our brazen tombs" and went on: "I pray God that our brazen Tombs be nigh neighbours". When Haydon was going through old letters for the Autobiography which he started writing in 1841, this expression of Keats' struck a note which kept echoing through his mind. He quoted it twice in letters to his friend Seymour Kirkup in Rome, planning a visit to Italy where he perhaps would end his days and be buried beside Keats in Rome. Against the original sentence about the neighbour tombs in Keats' letter, he wrote "I wonder if they will be".

"Alas! no" wrote another hand against Haydon's own note; the hand of Monckton Milnes. In 1846 Milnes' *Life, Letters and Literary Remains of John Keats* was still two years away from publication, but he had been collecting material for it for years past, and during the winter of 1845–6 he and Haydon had been in correspondence about the Keats letters in Haydon's possession. Haydon wanted justice done to Keats' memory; he also wanted his own good influence on Keats, and Leigh Hunt's bad influence, to be made quite clear. Copies of Keats' letters and anecdotes about him were passed over to Milnes, at first through the publisher Moxon. Eventually, in May 1846, Milnes and Haydon met to discuss the forthcoming biography, and Haydon afterwards wrote to send Milnes another Keats' letter cut out of his diary. He ended "Mr Haydon begs to express his great pleasure in becoming known to Mr Milnes, whose poetry he has so much admired—he only fears he talked too much about himself".

Milnes endorsed this letter "Haydon had put an end to his own life before my book was ready". When the book did appear, it contained a sympathetic unexaggerated tribute to Haydon. "Surely such a man should not have been left to perish" he wrote—one of the best epitaphs for the tomb that was to have been a brazen one with Fame registered upon it.

Keats left one lasting trace on Haydon's mind. "I have enjoyed Shakespeare more with Keats than with any other human creature" wrote Haydon in his diary when Keats died. Of all Shakespeare's plays, *King Lear* had always haunted Haydon's imagination the most; on the very first page of his diary, describing a visit to Dover in 1808, he mused about Lear and Cordelia. In 1817 when Haydon and Keats saw most of each other, Keats' mind, too, was full of *King Lear* and above all of the scene where Edgar persuades Gloucester he is on the edge of Dover Cliff. Keats felt that the "cliff of Poesy" was towering over him, the sound of the sea whispered in his ears; he hung suspended, the world below and its inhabitants dwarfed to the size of mice. The letter to Haydon with the reference to the "brazen tombs", which Haydon looked up in 1841 and gave to Milnes in May 1846, is full of *King Lear* quotations and images. Keats' profound understanding of

> "the fierce dispute
> Betwixt Hell torment and impassion'd clay"

sank indelibly into Haydon's imagination. His diary is full of quotations from the play, and from all through it, as though he knew it nearly by heart. Two lines from it were used again and again to point his onslaughts on power and corruption—"Take physic, pomp." and "An ounce of civet, good apothecary". He included *Lear Bidding Defiance to the Storm* in a list of possible subjects for pictures. He compared his friends to characters in the play—Charles Lamb was the Fool, Fanny Brantling was Cordelia.

Anyone living in London and going to the theatre in the 1820's and 1830's was bound to feel a special revived impact from *King Lear*. All through the long years of George III's insanity it had been banned from the stage; plays about mad kings were too near the bone. When George III died in 1820 and it became possible to revive the play, Drury Lane and Covent Garden raced to put it on first. Covent Garden won, with a cast which had Junius Brutus Booth as Lear and the twenty-six-year-old Macready as Edmund. This was still the Nahum Tate version of *King Lear* with Edgar marrying Cordelia at the end. Thirteen years later Macready was playing Lear himself, and he played it at intervals all through the 'thirties, restoring the proper text including the part of the Fool which was normally cut then. In February 1839 he played it at Covent Garden before Queen Victoria and, republican that he was, hurled Lear's prayer for the "poor naked wretches", the "houseless heads and unfed sides" straight at the Royal Box with meaning emphasis. The Hungry Forties were beginning, and Lear's voice seemed to echo through them. "O Do-nothing Pomp; quit thy down-cushions; expose thyself to learn what wretches feel, and how to cure it" thundered Carlyle in *Past and Present*, scarcely remembering that he was quoting.

In this June 1846, Macready was acting Lear again at the Princess Theatre, but "very languidly and not at all possessed with the character", he thought. His conception of Lear was a vigorous one; he thought Garrick, Kemble and Kean all concentrated on the feebleness instead of the vigour of old age when playing Lear. He himself saw Lear as a strong energetic old man, able to ride, hunt, rush about in a storm, kill the man who was hanging Cordelia; hearty and blithe in his good moments, vast in imagination and range of thought, huge in grief, no trembling tottering old dotard.

Haydon once went to see Macready as Lear, but came away after the first act, saying he could not stand any more of it. His conception of Lear was very different from Macready's. It was the sweetness and pathos of Lear's madness, his flashes of insight, that moved Haydon. Lear at the beginning of the play, "imperious and wanton", made him feel only contempt; it was in his madness that he seemed so wonderful to Haydon. He analysed Lear's madness in a long passage very early in his diary, comparing it with the madness of Orlando Furioso. It was opposite this passage that Frederic Haydon, in his extracts from his father's diary, placed the drawing *A Study from memory of an expression in insanity*.

King Lear was another of Haydon's avatars. Haydon, like Lear, felt himself to be a victim of ingratitude; called upon the

119

gods to vindicate him; was royal by nature, and had been betrayed. If one looks at Haydon with the eyes of Regan, one can see truer points of likeness. Haydon, too, had ever but slenderly known himself, was an entire egoist, saw himself as a special kind of man set apart, whom the rain ought not to wet, at whose bidding the thunder would cease. But he had not the authority in his countenance that men would fain call master; he had none of Lear's late humility and compassion, and he did not fear madness—he played with, he almost welcomed, the idea that his troubles might drive him mad. This was the last of all the heroic parts that he played. In his last hours, he renounced the Napoleon rôle—"I fear the Glitter of his Genius rather dazzled me"—but he could not die simply as himself. All his life was lived under the inspiration of heroes—the towering over-life-size figures that he painted—and his last act was meant to be a picture too, a picture with a motto.

"Finis
of
B. R. Haydon.
'Stretch me no longer on this tough world'. Lear.
End—
XXVI Volume".

When Mrs Carlyle wrote to invite Browning to meet Gräfin
Hahn-Hahn on Wednesday 24th June, she also wrote to her
friend Geraldine Jewsbury in Manchester, expressing mis-
givings about the forthcoming party—and at the same time
tantalizing her whipping-boy friend a little by dwelling on a
gathering of interesting writers at which Miss Jewsbury was
not to be present. Geraldine Jewsbury wrote back to condole
with Mrs Carlyle on the unsatisfactory state she was in after
her recent visit to Lady Harriet Baring, and to insist that she
needed a rest with real friends in the north. She went on "It is
such a plague to make new friends, or else I guess you would
make something of 'Hahn-Hahn'. She must have known sorrow! I feel very interested about her, although I have not read
a line of her books. I had the *Countess Faustina* ordered the
other day, but it is not come yet! I fancy, after all, the world has
sense to know realities when it actually sees them . . . and that
'Hahn-Hahn' and the Baron, being really respectable and
neither feeling nor seeming ashamed of themselves, it makes no
fuss! I think it is a very good sign of the times, for people just
as high in rank have been tabooed, and her being an authoress
hardly explains the charitable solecism! Do tell me something
about her; her experience and history would be worth all the
novels—and she could write—if she would speak a word to
women good for them to hear. But Carlyle putting up with her
is the most wonderful thing possible; I thought he was of a
real Scotch strictness in those matters, and could not stand
'George Sandism' in theory, let alone practice. . . . If your
breakfast comes off on Wednesday you'll not thank me for
hindering you! I know what it is to give parties myself, with a
small establishment! Your breakfast tempts me terribly. I

should like to be there, and no doubt there would be many of the same opinion".

Miss Jewsbury might well be surprised at Gräfin Hahn-Hahn being received in Carlyle's house. He had recently taken to detesting "George Sandism" with particular violence, because he thought Mrs Carlyle admired George Sand too much, and he blamed Geraldine Jewsbury's influence for that. George Sand's books, he said furiously, were "distinguished by nothing better than a lax treatment of the sexual relation", and the only thing to be said for Roman Catholicism was that it might be a sort of barrier against the still worse evils of "George Sandism". Carlyle was feeling even more fractious and unsettled than usual this June, because he had just finished his work on the second edition of *Cromwell* and he was always particularly difficult when he had no work on hand. "Having twice escaped alive from these detestable Dust-Abysses, let me beg to consider this my small act of Homage to the Memory of a Hero as finished" he had written a month earlier in the Preface to the second edition of *Cromwell*, and now that he was free from the dust abysses, he did not know what to do with himself. He was bored, bilious and restless, and exasperated his wife by vague talk of giving up the Cheyne Row house and going to live in Scotland in seclusion for his "few remaining years".

Mrs Carlyle had other troubles, which made the effort of giving a party an unwelcome extra burden. The heat wave had made her ill, and though by the 24th it was cooler—the great storm of Monday night had brought down the temperature—she still felt the effects of the long weeks of fierce heat. The dust abysses of *Cromwell* had affected her too. "The Cromwell-turmoil is again subsiding and the second edition will be out in a few weeks. '*Thanks* God!' and now I hope we shall really be done with that man! if he had been my husband's own Father he could not have gone thro' more hardship for him! We have lived 'in the valley of the shadow' of Cromwell now, as of Death, for some three years". But there was another substantial shadow across the Carlyles' lives in these days— the shadow of Lady Harriet Baring, Carlyle's friend and now

122

theoretically Mrs Carlyle's friend too—Mrs Carlyle had only recently come back from a stay with the Barings at Addiscombe, in the country near Croydon. A luxurious stay, but she had been very glad to get back to Chelsea; "there was much to be put straight on my return *morally* as well as *materially*".

However she was committed to giving the party for Gräfin Hahn-Hahn. There were two ways by which the guests could make their way to Cheyne Row that Wednesday—apart from going there by carriage, as the Gräfin probably did. You could go by river steamer to the Cadogan Steam Boat Pier close to Battersea Bridge—the old wooden bridge with its peaked centre and thick clustering piers, iron railing and gas lamps— and walk from there a few yards along the dusty tree-shaded Cheyne Walk, unembanked and with nothing but a wooden rail between it and the mud and ooze of the foreshore. Or you could take a horse bus from Piccadilly, down Sloane Street and along the King's Road, where you got off at Cook's Ground and went down a zig-zag lane between cottage gardens with ramshackle wooden palings, and so emerged at the north end of Cheyne Row.

The Carlyles' house at Number 5 was a red-brick three-storied house in a terrace built in 1708. When they took it, it seemed to them immensely spacious, with more rooms and cupboards than they would ever need; but when one visits it now, one is surprised to find what a dark little house it is, in spite of its handsome tall sash windows. It perhaps was lighter then, for there were no houses opposite, only a row of lime trees and a high brick wall, beyond which to the west lay gardens and scattered buildings. There were open hayfields and lines of trees beyond their own little garden at the back, too. Within, although the panelled walls darkened the rooms, there was a shine of high polish on the furniture; Mrs Carlyle was a notable housewife, and kept her single servant well up to the mark over cleaning and scouring and polishing, while she herself made curtains and chair-covers, darned stair-carpets, painted wardrobes which she had bought second-hand. Everything was very tidy in the house—no books or papers were lying about in the rooms where guests were received.

Wednesday 24th June

On arrival they were shown into the parlour, the ground-floor room overlooking the street which was Mrs Carlyle's drawing-room, since at this time the main first-floor room was Carlyle's study. The parlour represented successive layers of Mrs Carlyle's life; the mahogany chairs with horse-hair seats came from her father's house at Haddington, the round table from the remote farmhouse where she and Carlyle had lived in Scotland, the piano and the curtains had recently arrived from Templand when her mother died. There was a sofa, and a prie-dieu chair on which Mrs Carlyle generally sat, and a tub chair for Carlyle, and a bust of Shelley by Mrs Leigh Hunt, and a Dürer print. Nothing was new, or brightly coloured, or luxurious-looking; it was all neat and subdued, solid, lived-in.

There was nothing brightly coloured about the hostess, either. She had a sickly face, dun pale, and silky black hair parted in the middle and smoothed down each side of her face in front of her ears, and then turned under and knotted at the back of her head. Her nose was retroussé, her cheeks sunken; the life of her face was in her large lustrous black eyes under straight dark brows. She was a slight wiry woman of five foot four, well though economically dressed. Not a woman to ignore, to under-rate, to relax with—not a woman to trust, perhaps not a woman to like, but one never to forget. "Clever, witty, calm, cool, unsmiling, unsparing, a *raconteuse* unparalleled, a manner inimitable, a behaviour scrupulous, and a power invincible—a combination rare and strange exists in that plain, keen, unattractive and yet unescapable woman" said the American actress Charlotte Cushman who saw Mrs Carlyle this summer.

The guests—Gräfin Hahn-Hahn, Browning, the German writer Amely Bölte, probably Mrs Jameson—assembled early for this party which was variously described as a breakfast and a dinner. The normal middle-class dinner hour then was six o'clock, but the Carlyles dined at any time—two, three, four, five-thirty, seven—according to their current fancies about the effect of their diet on their insomnia or their dyspepsia. Carlyle liked dinner to begin with soup; after that, for a dinner party, there would be some kind of fowl—but boiled; it had to be boiled, not roast, to suit Carlyle—stewed mutton or beef or just possibly roast mutton, and a pudding. Potatoes might accompany the meat, but certainly no green vegetables, and there would be no salads and no fruit. It is not surprising that the Carlyles both suffered so terribly from constipation. The drink at the party would be sherry, or perhaps some fine Cambridge ale, with port, and a glass of brandy and water, after the meal.

The party had adjourned for this meal to the small dining-room at the back of the house, overlooking the garden. This was the best-furnished room in the house, with an oval mahogany dining table, more of the handsome dining-room chairs from Haddington, a fine ebony-inlaid sideboard, a rosewood clock on a bracket, and a dwarf armchair which had been Jane Welsh Carlyle's as a child. At most of the Carlyles' dinner parties, it was the overwhelming conversation of the host that people remembered most distinctly; but we do not know what Carlyle said at the dinner table on this occasion. The reporters are Amely Bölte and Browning, and what they reported relates to Gräfin Hahn-Hahn.

Amely Bölte wrote to Varnhagen von Ense about the meeting between her compatriot and the Carlyles. She related the sensation that the Gräfin's arrival in London with such a companion as Bystram had created everywhere. "She herself seemed not to have the slightest idea of the existing prejudice against her, and asked quite naïvely why George Sand would not be well received in London?" If only we could hear Carlyle's reply to that! We know so much about Carlyle's talk—it was the wonder of his age, one of the three things in Europe that impressed Emerson most; a flood, a war-chant, a cavalry charge of splendid sentences, spurring on into a thunder of denunciation or exhortation, slackening for mimicry or anecdote or kindly reflection, rearing up into loud body-shaking contemptuous laughter, but hardly ever stopping. Even his writing often sounds as though he were taking dictation from his own conversation, and using the devices of typography to indicate vocal changes—capital letters for the heavy ironic emphasis, italic for the sudden boom on a key word, question-marks for a lift in the voice. Probably an accomplished actor today who knew the Annandale accent could take, for instance, the first paragraph in that chapter in Carlyle's *French Revolution* which is called *September in Argonne* and produce from it something which would sound very like one of Carlyle's great crashing monologues, so clearly has he marked in it the rhythm and dynamics of the speaking voice.

His observations at dinner on George Sand can have been none the calmer for Amely Bölte's contributions to the discussion. Mrs Carlyle reported two days later that Fraulein Bölte had "returned from Germany all agog with *something* that she calls '*the new ideas*'—above all quite rabid against marriage. Varnhagen, Bettina, all the Thinkers of Germany she says have arrived at the conclusion that *marriage* is a highly *immoral* Institution as well as a dreadfully disagreeable one".

It is therefore all the more astonishing, and to the credit of both parties, that Carlyle liked Gräfin Hahn-Hahn. He liked her for her lack of affectation, for "a certain simplicity and sincerity about her expression", so Amely Bölte reported to Varnhagen. He did not admire her books, and could see no point in them. It was not her admiration of him which won his approval, either, for she seemed never to have heard of him before. He simply thought she was sincere, and liked her for that.

She was less successful with Browning. That morning she must have assiduously read her *Morning Chronicle*, the only paper which gave a detailed account of Haydon's suicide in advance of the inquest reports, which did not appear till the Thursday papers. Browning distastefully told Miss Barrett in a letter written on Wednesday evening—"Countess Hahn-Hahn said across Carlyle's table that poor H. had attempted to shoot himself and then chosen another method—too successful. Horrible indeed——".

George Sand, loose talk about marriage, the suicide of a painter, such topics were bound to launch Carlyle on an avalanche of denunciation. Browning got it in the garden after dinner, where they had retired for Carlyle to smoke. The garden was no more than a little stone-flagged back yard leading to a grass plot with gooseberry bushes and rose bushes, wall-flowers and jasmine, a cherry tree and a walnut, ending in a wall beyond which lay bushes and fields and the distant chimney pots of houses behind a line of trees. Here Carlyle paced up and down and poured forth the flood of ideas suggested to him by all these decadent Southern ideas of novelists and painters—decadent *Italian* ideas, they obviously were, since all the true vigour and energy came from the Northmen, the Germanic peoples. Nothing good could come from Italy—if it was good, it could not really be Italian in the mind of Carlyle, who could start a chapter of *Past and Present* with the thundering invocation "Brave Sea-captain, Norse Sea-king, Columbus, my hero, royallest Sea-king of all!" Now he was telling Browning, between huge whiffs of his 20-inch churchwarden pipe, that Iceland was the only foreign country he wanted to visit, Iceland the true cradle of the Northmen and their virtues; all that was worth a Northman's caring to see was there, not in Italy. Modern Italy's abasement was a direct judgment of God. "Here is a nation in whose breast arise men who *could* doubt, examine the new problems of the Reformation etc— trim the balance at intervals, and throw overboard the accumulation of falsehood—all other nations around, less favoured, are doing it laboriously for themselves ... now is the time for the acumen of the Bembos, the Bentivoglios and so forth ... and these and their like, one and all, turn round, decline the trouble, say 'these things *may* be true, or they may not, meantime let us go on verse-making, painting, music-scoring'— to which the nation accedes as if relieved of a trouble—upon which God bids the Germans go in and possess them; pluck their fruits and feel their sun after their own hard work".

You can hear it crashing out—"verse-making, painting, music-scoring"—with Carlyle giving each word a good bite before letting it go, as David Masson reported. Carlyle was a Philistine about painting, a despiser of artists—"airtists", he pronounced them. "I can make nothing of airtists, nor of their work either" he said flatly to two painters. He is not likely to have felt much sympathy for Haydon when Gräfin Hahn-Hahn produced her grisly details about his suicide at the dinner table. But one strong bent of mind was the same in both men. They were both Hero-Worshippers, and one particular hero had a special call to both of them. Only a week before this, Haydon had written in his diary "Let my imagination keep Columbus before my mind for ever. Amen". Columbus was another avatar—the hero who heard a Voice in the roaring of the Atlantic waves, telling him to persevere. Haydon had turned to Columbus for inspiration in 1841, before he could have read the great passage in *Past and Present* (published in 1843). Did he ever read it? He began with a prejudice against Carlyle for his obscurity, but once he had overcome this, he warmly admired Carlyle's work, and is known to have read and re-read *The French Revolution* in the last year of his life. When, in the week before he killed himself, he exhorted his imagination to keep Columbus before his mind for ever, was he re-echoing Carlyle's *bravura* invocation in *Past and Present*?——

"Brave Sea-captain, Norse Sea-king, Columbus, my hero, royallest Sea-king of all! it is no friendly environment this of thine, in the waste deep waters; around thee mutinous discouraged souls, behind thee disgrace and ruin, before thee the unpenetrated veil of Night. Brother, these wild water-mountains, bounding from their deep bases (ten miles deep, I am told), are not entirely there on thy behalf! Meseems *they* have other work than floating thee forward: and the huge Winds, that sweep from Ursa Major to the Tropics and Equators, dancing their giant-waltz through the Kingdoms of Chaos and Immensity, they care little about filling rightly or filling wrongly the small shoulder-of-mutton sails in this cockle-skiff of thine! Thou art not among articulate-speaking friends, my brother; thou art among immeasurable dumb monsters, tumbling, howling wide as the world here. Secret, far off, invisible to all hearts but thine, there lies a help in them: see how thou wilt get at that. Patiently thou wilt wait till the mad Southwester spend itself, saving thyself by dexterous science of defence, the while: valiantly, with swift decision, wilt thou strike in, when the favouring East, the Possible, springs up. Mutiny of man thou wilt sternly repress; weakness, despondency, thou wilt cheerily encourage: thou wilt swallow

THOMAS CARLYLE by John Linnell, 1844

JANE WELSH CARLYLE
by Karl Hartmann, 1850

SAMUEL ROGERS, MRS NORTON (*on right*) AND MRS PHIPPS
by Frank Stone, *c.* 1845

RICHARD MONCKTON MILNES
by Caroline Smith, 1848

NAPOLEON MUSING AT ST HELENA by B.R. Haydon

WELLINGTON MUSING ON THE FIELD OF WATERLOO by B.R. Haydon

'A VILE CARICATURE OF B.R. HAYDON BY MR KEATS':
a page of drawings by Keats and Haydon

MACREADY AS KING LEAR with Helen Faucit as Cordelia

PARLOUR OF THE CARLYLES' HOUSE IN CHEYNE ROW

ANNA JAMESON by John Gibson

WILLIAM WORDSWORTH ON
HELVELLYN by B.R. Haydon, 1843

THOMAS NOON TALFOURD
by H.W. Pickersgill

CURTIUS LEAPING INTO THE GULF by B.R. Haydon

down complaint, how much wilt thou swallow down! There shall be a depth of Silence in thee, deeper than this Sea, which is but ten miles deep! a Silence unsoundable; known to God only. Thou shalt be a Great Man. Yes, my World-Soldier, thou of the World Marine-service,—thou wilt have to be *greater* than this tumultuous unmeasured World here round thee is: thou, in thy strong soul, as with wrestler's arms, shalt embrace it, harness it down; and make it bear thee on,—to new Americas, or whither God wills!"

"Thou shalt be a Great Man": that was the voice in the storm that Haydon heard, but not the icy mid-Atlantic voice that said the mountainous waves "have other work than floating thee forward", that the ocean winds cared little about filling his sails. Haydon's ship went down; nor did Carlyle's own barque drive on with quite the majesty that he invoked. No man was less given than he was to "swallowing down complaint", no man praised Silence in longer more deafening monologues, no man was less likely to strike in valiantly, with swift decision, about anything. "We have been enquiring all about for houses in the country—without, it seems to me, much chance or even *much intention* of a practical result" wrote Mrs Carlyle this week to her cousin. "This perpetual talk of moving takes away all one's pleasure (such as it was) in Chelsea—I feel myself no longer in a *home* but in a *tent* to be struck any day that the commanding officer is sufficiently bilious".

Haydon's last letter to his wife, read aloud at the inquest on him, contained this sentence—"I hope Sir Robert Peel will consider I have earned a pension for thee", and in his will he recurred three times to the thought of public provision for his family.

"14. I return my gratitude to Sir Robert Peel, always a kind friend in emergencies. I hope he will consider the talents and virtue of my son Frank, and Sir George Cockburn will not forget my son Frederic. . . .

"16. I have done my duty to the Art—educated the greatest Artists of the day—Eastlake, the Landseers and Lance, and I hope advanced the whole feeling of the Country. I hope my dear friend Sir Robert Peel will not forget my Widow and family. . . .

"19. . . . God Almighty forgive us all. I die in peace with all men, and pray Him not to punish for the sake of the Father the innocent Widow and children he leaves behind. I ask her Pardon and my children's for this additional pang, but it will be the last, and released from the burden of my Ambition, they will be happier and suffer less".

The appeal was not unheeded by the Prime Minister. Appeals to him for money seldom were; cold as his manner was, his charity was not. On a list drawn up by a begging-letter writer of the day, his name figures with those of Queen Adelaide and Charles Dickens as the people most likely to respond to an appeal for a fiver. Peel had already sent £200 to Haydon's executors, but that was Treasury money, not his own. In this week he also gave £100 of his own money to the public subscription for Haydon's family, gave Frank Haydon a better-paid post in the Customs as landing-waiter, and recommended Mrs Haydon for a Civil List pension of £50 a year, to which

Lady Peel added another £25 a year from official sources at her disposal.

The Prime Minister had other things to think about during this week than the finances of the Haydons. On the evening of Thursday 25th June, the House of Commons was engaged on the second reading of the Irish Coercion Bill. In the middle of the debate, a message arrived from the House of Lords and the Speaker told the House "I have to acquaint you that the House of Lords have agreed to the Corn Importation Bill and to the Customs Duties Bill, without any amendments". The announcement was greeted with loud cheering. The long battle was over; the Corn Laws had been repealed at last.

But the business of the House had to go on, and the debate on the Irish Coercion Bill was resumed. The last speech was made by Cobden, who said that, though he would vote against the Bill, he repudiated the suggestion made by Lord George Bentinck that the coming division would be Peel's punishment for treachery over the Corn Laws. "He apprehended that there would be no doubt, at all events in the public mind, that the measure which the right hon. baronet had been passing this session was about the most popular that any minister could have introduced. . . . Whatever hon. members opposite might say, the right hon. baronet would carry with him out of office the esteem and respect of as large a number of the population as had ever been done by any minister that was ever known. . . . He was not misinterpreting the feelings of the people of the country or those of the working classes, when he tended to him his heartfelt thanks for his untiring perseverance, for his un-swerving firmness and for the great ability with which he had now for six months conducted the most magnificent reform ever effected in the country through this House of Parliament". (Loud cheers.)

The House then divided. When Members returned from the lobbies, there was a pause, and then a whisper went round, and then it was announced that the Government had been defeated by a majority of 73. Some accounts say that this announcement too was received with loud cheers, others that it was received in a dead silence of apathy and misgiving. But when a colleague muttered the numbers into the Prime Minister's ear, he did not reply, or even turn his head.

There was a Cabinet meeting on Friday morning, at which Peel persuaded his colleagues that a dissolution of Parliament would be useless and that the only course for the Government was to resign. At two o'clock he wrote to the Queen, who was at Osborne, asking permission to call on her next day.

On Saturday afternoon he went down to the Isle of Wight to see the Queen; he dined with her and stayed the night. Prince Albert, in his memorandum on the Prime Minister's interview with the Queen, reported that he seemed much relieved to be laying down the crushing burdens of office which, he said, he could not have supported much longer. The relief was not shared by the Queen. Her feelings were now very different from what they had been seven years before when Peel first waited on her as prospective Prime Minister. Then she had thought him stiff, unsympathetic, quite insolent in his insistence on her changing the Ladies of her Household with the change of Government. Now she was very sorry to part with him. "The Queen seizes this opportunity . . . of expressing her *deep* concern at losing his services, which she regrets as much for the Country as for herself and the Prince. In whatever position Sir Robert may be, we shall ever look on him as a kind and true friend, and ever have the greatest esteem and regard for him as a Minister and as a private individual".

On Monday 29th Wellington in the House of Lords and Peel in the Commons announced the resignation of the Government. The House of Commons was packed, with peers and ambassadors filling every seat in the galleries. Private business for the day being concluded, the House waited tensely for Peel to arrive. At last he walked in—"colder, dryer, more introverted than ever, yet to a close gaze showing the fullest working of a smothered volcano of emotions. He was out of breath with walking and sat down on the Treasury Bench . . . as he would be fully himself before he rose" reported the Bishop of Oxford. Presently he rose, amid breathless silence, and began his farewell speech. He said that he had no complaints to make. He had changed his mind, and for that change he was punished by expulsion from the House, but that was better than continuing without a full assurance of the confidence of the House.

This was expected to be said; but he then startled the House by saying that the credit for the Repeal of the Corn Laws was not his—"the name which ought to be chiefly associated with the success of these measures is the name of Richard Cobden".

Finally he returned to himself and to what would be said of him by his own party and by his opponents, honourable and dishonourable. But it was not of these that he spoke last of all, in his famous peroration. "It may be that I shall leave a name sometimes remembered with expressions of goodwill in the abodes of those whose lot it is to labour, and to earn their bread by the sweat of their brow, when they shall recruit their exhausted strength with abundant and untaxed food, the sweeter because it is no longer leavened by a sense of injustice".

Some of the more sophisticated people in Peel's own world were not much impressed by his farewell. Greville said that though Peel fell with great éclat and in a halo of popularity, his speech, especially the panegyric on Cobden and his "clap-trap about cheap bread in the peroration", gave great offence all round. Samuel Wilberforce, Bishop of Oxford, who unlike Greville had actually been present when the speech was given, was more sympathetic, but still with an element of doubt. "It was very fine: very effective: really almost solemn: to fall at such a moment. He spoke as if it were his last political scene: as if he felt that between alienated friends and unwon foes he could have no party again; and could only as a shrewd bystander observe and advise others. There was but one point in the speech which I thought doubtful: the apostrophe to 'Richard Cobden'. I think it was wrong, though there is very much to be said for it".

Macready, who understood the operation of public feeling by emotion—it was his job—had no doubts about the speech. "30th June. Read the paper, not losing one word of Sir R. Peel's interesting speech. His laying down office was a proud minute, far prouder than its assumption. With Sterne, one might say 'Oh how I envied him his feelings!'"

When Peel and Wellington came out of the House at five

o'clock that Monday evening, the streets were crowded with people who rushed forward enthusiastically, rapturously, cheering. Peel's feelings were, the *Daily News* reported, "deeply affected". Wellington acknowledged the cheering by "his usual military salute". The week before, when he had left the House of Lords in the early morning after the passing of the Corn Importation Bill, a crowd had cheered him. "God bless you, Duke" a workman had shouted. "For heaven's sake, people, let me get on my horse" was all the reply he had got from the Duke.

Miss Barrett, unlike Macready, did not read the papers during these days, and had no thoughts to spare for Peel's defeat when she wrote to Browning on Friday. It was another action of Peel's that held her attention. "I have not had the heart to look at the newspapers, but hear that Sir Robert Peel has provided liberally for the present distresses of the poor Haydons. And do you know, the more I think the more I am inclined to conclude that the money-distress was merely an additional irritation, and that the despair leading to the revolt against life, had its root in disappointed ambition. The world did not recognize his genius, and he punished the world by withdrawing the light. If he had not that thought in him, I am wrong. The cartoon business and his being refused employment in the Houses of Parliament . . . *that* was bitter: and then came his opposition with Tom Thumb and the dwarf's triumph. . . . He was a man, you see, who carried his whole being and sensibility on the outside of him; nay, worse than *so*, since in the thoughts and opinions of the world. All the audacity and bravery and self-exultation which drew on him so much ridicule, were an agony in disguise—he could not live without reputation, and he wrestled for it, struggled for it, *kicked* for it, forgetting grace of attitude in the pang. When all was vain, he went mad and died. Poor Haydon! He measures things differently now! and let *us* now be right and just in our ad-measurement of what he was—for, with all his weaknesses, he was certainly not *far* from being a great man".

She wrote to other friends about it during these days—to

old blind Boyd, excusing herself for not going to see him as she had promised, since she had been too much shaken by the news to be well enough to go out; to a friend from the Barretts' Herefordshire past, to whom she spoke of the shock and the total surprise that Haydon's death had been, since even his last letters had given her no notion that there was anything to fear. She lamented the potential greatness that had been in Haydon, the largeness of his conceptions which his hand was not capable of carrying out in paint; but she added "As it is, he lived on the *slope* of greatness and could not be steadfast and calm. His life was one long agony of self-assertion. Poor, poor Haydon! See how the world treats those who try too openly for its gratitude! 'Tom Thumb for ever' over the heads of the giants".

Her thought had hardened a little since she first heard the news. She had thought over and over Haydon's motives, and had ceased to reproach herself for not offering him money, it was not there that the danger had lain. It was the idea of Browning's strength that made her realize Haydon's weakness. Everything, even Haydon's ghastly death, was now only a springboard from which she and Browning could dive deeper into each other's hearts. She wrote to him "It is hope and help, to be able to look away from all such thoughts to *you*, dearest beloved, who do not partake of the faults and feeblenesses of these lower geniuses. . . . You are above all these clouds—your element is otherwise—men are not your taskmasters that you should turn to them for recompense". She ends her letter with a reference to the weather, but with a special meaning. Winds and wet weather foretold the autumn, and before the autumn cold started she must make up her mind to marry Browning and go away with him to Italy, or they would have to wait another year.

So in these cool days at the end of the week, Browning's letters were full of insistence on the change in the weather. They were sitting by a fire at New Cross, there was a piercing cold north wind; he sent her some brown autumn-looking leaves in his Friday's letter. It rained fitfully that day, but Miss Barrett was able to go out in the carriage to Hampstead, and lean out through the carriage window to pick a sprig of wild-rose leaves from the hedge; she sent it to Browning in her answering letter, green leaves for brown, with a certain wilful defiance—autumn was not so near as all that, the wind was not in the north, only north-west. Browning wrote back on Saturday insisting "my brown leaves might be sent to you by myriads for all that, for all the light laugh,—all roses fast going, lilies going . . . autumnal hollyhocks in full blow".

"Gather ye rosebuds while ye may"—the reference is unmistakable:

> "Then be not coy, but use your time,
> And while you may, go marry".

Browning had schooled himself to patience and waiting on Elizabeth Barrett's will, but it was not easy. Early in that month he had been driven into telling her that every day that passed before their marriage·day was "one the more of hardly endurable anxiety and irritation, to say the least; and the thought of another year's intervention of hope deferred—altogether intolerable!" It was a sultry electric summer to him.

To Peel, who went straight down to his country house at Drayton, it was a silent summer calm after the great storm. Later that week he wrote to a friend—"Lady Peel and I are here quite alone—in the loveliest weather—feasting on solitude and repose, and I have every disposition to forgive my enemies for having conferred on me the blessing of the loss of power".

Even the fall of the Government did not crowd Haydon's
suicide out of the newspapers, which went on commenting and
drawing morals. *The Times* had a resounding article on 26th
June, chastising the abjection of public taste which neglected
high-minded paintings in order to gape at a disgusting dwarf.
Macready, a careful reader of the newspapers, wrote in his
diary "was interested by the leading article, and by one on
Haydon—poor man!—with which I could not agree. I am
sorry for his infirmities, but they could not, like Leigh Hunt's,
lead to anything but embarrassment and suffering. Am *I*
better? Alas! I have very much to reproach myself with".

The obituary notices on Haydon were very often combined
with a review of his *Lectures on Painting and Design*, the second
series of which had been published in the spring. "The sad
and terrible close of the author's career gives a most melancholy interest to this volume" begins a typical article in the
Examiner, which goes on to praise Haydon's lectures, in four
full columns, for much that is true and valuable on art, but to
blame them for some inaccuracies and prejudices. The writer
expressed what seems to have been a general opinion even
then, that Haydon was a better writer than painter, classing
him with Goethe and Hazlitt as in "the highest class of appreciators and reasoners on art" and deciding that he would have
made an admirable Professor of the Arts of Design, most
inspiring to his pupils. A reading of Haydon's published lectures bears out this judgment. One can understand that they
were a popular success. They were calculated to hold an
audience's attention, with their mixture óf technical information
about bones and muscles, tempera and encaustic, of generaliza-
tions on aesthetics, and of vivid amusing biographical sketches
and anecdotes of contemporary painters, whose work he often

praised with affection and discrimination. The lectures show a cultivated mind, wide reading, many interests; they also show occasional wildness, exaggeration, heavy irony, overplaying of his hand, but less than might have been expected from him. He himself sometimes had a perception that he had chosen the wrong art, that his powers could have made him a successful writer instead of an unsuccessful painter, that his books were in a way dearer to him than his prints.

Even in a book review, the writer of the *Examiner* article (possibly Forster) could not keep off the topic of Tom Thumb, the aspect of Haydon's tragedy that had most struck the public imagination. "We went to see the picture of *Aristides* (in some respects a fine work) and with difficulty forced our way up the stairs crowded with Tom Thumb's visitors into poor Haydon's empty room (not a human being was in it)". George Cruikshank took up the theme in two widely-discussed etchings for the *Comic Almanack*. One was called *Born a Genius* and showed a garret with a starving artist crouching before an unfinished painting; the other was called *Born a Dwarf* and showed an over-dressed pigmy on a sofa in a luxurious room, with bags of money at his feet.

A group of Haydon's friends and patrons did not wait for the Press to point out to them the action they should take. On Tuesday 30th June there was a meeting at the Serjeants' Inn chambers of Thomas Noon Talfourd, one of Haydon's executors, to set on foot a public subscription for the Haydon family. Lord Morpeth presided; Haydon had painted his portrait in his huge *Reform Banquet* picture, and showered him with begging letters and petitions—"amiable creature, accomplished and refined", "his smile is exceedingly good" recorded Haydon. There were others there who had sat to Haydon in the past, and bought pictures from him—Byron's friend Sir John Hobhouse, the Rev. George Croly, William Jerdan the editor of the *Literary Gazette*, the antiquary William Richard Hamilton. And there was Count d'Orsay, who had already squandered the fortune of his wife, stepdaughter of his mistress Lady Blessington, and who now had to keep boar-hounds in the courtyard of Gore House to keep his and Lady Blessington's creditors at bay—a curious figure to find at this meeting to raise money for the widow of a ruined man.

The meeting passed a resolution of regret—"That without presuming to offer any judgment as to the place which Mr Haydon will ultimately fill in the annals of his art, or any opinion on the controversies in which he was sometimes engaged, this meeting feels that the efforts of his genius, and the circumstances of misfortune which obstructed them, justify an expression of public sympathy with his widow and daughter. That such expression would be most fitly conveyed by securing a permanent provision to his widow and daughter, left wholly destitute by his death; and that a public subscription be opened for that purpose".

Serjeant Talfourd read out a letter from Sir Robert Peel, regretting that pressure of public business prevented him from attending the meeting, saying that Mrs Haydon had been awarded a Civil List pension of £50 a year, and offering £100 from his private purse towards the subscription. Before the meeting closed, the subscription already amounted to more than £400.

The newspapers fully reported the meeting and urged the public to subscribe. Over the next two months the subscription mounted, finally reaching £2,000. A hope had been expressed at the meeting that "the differences which had existed between Mr Haydon and many of his professional contemporaries would not prevent them from aiding to alleviate the distress of the widow and daughter of a talented and able, though an eccentric and unfortunate artist". The Royal Academy took the hint, and sent £50. Other contributors were Mary Russell Mitford, who sent a subscription to Serjeant Talfourd, and Dickens, who wrote to Forster from Switzerland "I am very sorry to hear of Haydon's death. If any subscription be proposed, put me down for five pounds". And Wordsworth wrote to his publisher Moxon "Would you be so kind as to pay for me five Pounds to the Haydon subscription. Poor Fellow! what a shocking end to come to".

Wordsworth had already been appealed to by Orlando Hyman, almost as soon as Haydon was dead, for help in raising money for Mrs Haydon. On Wednesday 1st July, the day after the meeting at Talfourd's, Wordsworth was writing a reply to a letter of Hyman's which had taken some time to reach him, having been misaddressed. "I should be happy" Wordsworth wrote "to promote the interests of my lamented Friend's family as far as lies in my power; but I cannot hope to do much, because almost all of those Persons to whom I could apply are themselves disposed, I have no doubt, to come forward, having seen more of Mr Haydon than my own opportunities, for some years past, have allowed me to do. I will not however omit my best endeavours to promote the subscription as soon as it is set on foot. . . . Every one must acknowledge that Mr Haydon had no common claim as an Artist upon the gratitude of the Country, both for what he executed himself, and for the zealous pains which he took to teach and incite others to aim at a style of art, both in its subjects and execution, of much higher character than was the general practice. Pray present my most sincere condolence to the afflicted Widow, and best wishes for her future comfort and peace".

The freezing banality of Wordsworth's letter-writing style is exaggerated in a letter of condolence; the official expression of sympathy sounds as inadequate as the perfunctory "Poor Fellow! what a shocking end to come to". Wordsworth never said more than he really felt, which disconcerted many of his contemporaries; "Wordsworth does more to unidealise himself than any man I know" said John Kenyon sadly. Perhaps a very faint warmth does percolate through the last sentence of Wordsworth's letter, his message to Mrs Haydon. He had always felt a special sympathy for her, revealed by many inquiries and messages to her in his thirty-year-long correspondence with Haydon.

Haydon and Wordsworth first met in 1809 at Sir George Beaumont's house. By the end of 1815 they knew each other well enough for Wordsworth to send Haydon a sonnet which was a support and inspiration to him all his life.

"High is our calling, Friend!—Creative Art
(Whether the instrument of words she use,

Or pencil pregnant with ethereal hues)
Demands the service of a mind and heart,
Though sensitive, yet, in their weakest part
Heroically fashioned—to infuse
Faith in the whispers of the lonely Muse,
While the whole world seems adverse to desert.
And, oh! when Nature sinks, as oft she may,
Through long-lived pressure of obscure distress,
Still to be strenuous for the bright reward,
And in the soul admit of no decay,
Brook no continuance of weak-mindedness—
Great is the glory, for the strife is hard!"

If all Haydon's life had been spread out before Wordsworth as he wrote this sonnet, he could have said nothing more prophetically relevant. Haydon learnt everything of the long-lived pressure of distress, the hard strife; he kept the conviction of a mind heroically fashioned, he listened with full belief to the whispers of his muse, and in some sort he lived up to Wordsworth's exhortation—there was no decay in his soul; it charred, perhaps, but it never rotted. From the moment that he received Wordsworth's sonnet, he felt a blaze of joy and dedication; he told Sir George Beaumont that the sonnet supported and inspired him whenever he suspected that his enemies were right about his genius and aspirations; in the last years of his life, he was still cheering himself with repetitions of the line "While the whole world seems adverse to desert".

If Wordsworth gave Haydon immortality by writing a sonnet to him, Haydon has given posterity a better idea of what Wordsworth looked like than any other portrait painter has done. He left a life-mask, two oil paintings and several drawings of Wordsworth, and a figure of his friend as a worshipper in the crowd in his *Christ's Entry into Jerusalem*. He told Wordsworth that he was putting him into the picture as a believer: "I cannot quote your ideas, therefore I must do so with your face". He took a lot of trouble over this figure; Wordsworth sat to him three times for it, he got the poet to have a cast made of his hands and sent to London, and he made one other preparation which it is very unlikely the poet knew about. Among Haydon's drawings in the British Museum there is a study of a figure seen both full face and profile—a bald, thick-set, slightly paunchy male nude, with one hand on the breast. The face is only slightly indicated, but there is a detailed separate study of an ear. The caption, in Haydon's handwriting, is *Study for Wordsworth in Jerusalem*. Haydon always made nude studies of any figure in his pictures, and then draped the figure afterwards. This one was not, we may be certain, drawn from life; but it would make an interesting variation on the portraits of Wordsworth generally used to illustrate biographies of him.

The climax of Haydon's early acquaintanceship with Wordsworth was the famous "immortal dinner" when, with the half-finished *Christ's Entry into Jerusalem* towering over the heads of the guests, Haydon entertained in his studio Wordsworth, Charles Lamb, Keats and the fatuous Comptroller of the Stamp Office. In the 1820's and 1830's, Haydon's admiration for Wordsworth was rather cooled by what he felt to be the poet's egoism, orthodoxy and puritanical spirit, and he recorded some malicious and very funny anecdotes about Wordsworth in his diary. Wordsworth on his side remained steadily, temperately, friendly; telling an American correspondent that Haydon was "a great enthusiast, possessed also of a most active intellect; but he wants that submission and steady good sense which are absolutely necessary for the adequate development of power in that art to which he is attached".

They drew together again in the last years of Haydon's life. In 1840 Wordsworth wrote another sonnet on a picture of Haydon's, this time on *Wellington Musing at Waterloo*; he wrote eight letters in three weeks with various versions and amendments of it. Haydon responded by asking Wordsworth to be godfather to his second son who, though born in 1827, was not christened till September 1840, when he received the names Frederic Wordsworth. In June 1842 Haydon began his admirable portrait of Wordsworth on Helvellyn which is now in the National Portrait Gallery, and they had some pleasant sittings, talking over old days and old friends. Haydon measured

Wordsworth, and found he was exactly 5 feet 9⅞ inches tall; he also did a drawing of him with and without his false teeth.

Wordsworth said of the engraving from this picture "I think myself it is the best likeness, that is the most characteristic, which has been done of me". The old man stands with crossed arms and bent head, against a stormy background of cloud and rock. It is not a poetic face; it is the "benevolent wolf" of Milnes' description of Wordsworth, or better still, the likeness in Carlyle's testy retort to Duffy—"No, not at all; he was a man quite other than that; a man of an immense head and great jaws like a crocodile's". Haydon has succeeded in conveying what he described to Miss Mitford as Wordsworth's "dull eyes, with that look of internal vision I never saw in any other face".

It was this picture that brought Haydon and Elizabeth Barrett together. Her sisters saw the unfinished portrait in his studio, and when Haydon heard from them how much their invalid sister would like to see it, he sent it round to her. Miss Barrett was enthralled; she wrote a poorish sonnet (inspiring sonnets was one of Haydon's most undeniable gifts) about the cloudy background and the thoughtful poet-priest, ending—

> "A noble vision free
> Our Haydon's hand has flung out from the mist!
> No portrait this, with Academic air!
> This is the poet and his poetry".

She sent the sonnet to Haydon, who sent it to Wordsworth, who wrote kindly back with a few suggestions for tidying up the sonnet, which Miss Barrett did not adopt. The sonnet was published in the *Athenaeum*. Later Haydon collected the portrait from Miss Barrett, but lent her instead another one which he had done of Wordsworth—the seated full-length *Wordsworth on Helvellyn* which is now at Dove Cottage.

Haydon's renewed cordiality for Wordsworth was chilled by Wordsworth's acceptance of a Civil List pension in 1842 and then the Poet Laureateship in 1843, and by his action in attending a Court Ball and a Levée in consequence of his appointment. The fuss that Wordsworth's friends and admirers made about this incident only becomes intelligible when one realizes what a burning question State patronage of literature was in the mid 'forties. The award of Tennyson's Civil List pension had brought into play Carlyle, Milnes and Rogers, and had resulted in the public fracas between Tennyson and Bulwer. Equally public had been Harriet Martineau's announcement that she was refusing a Civil List pension on the grounds that the offer had been made privately by the Prime Minister and not by Parliament and that therefore she would be "robbing the people who did not make laws for themselves". Opinion ranged all the way from Miss Martineau to Haydon, who felt that the Government ought to patronize the arts as a matter of course, and that it was beneath the dignity of a great poet to show humble gratitude to the Court for an award which chiefly honoured the giver. With the spitefulness of a hurt illusion, he recorded in his journal all the stories that went round about Wordsworth borrowing Samuel Rogers' court suit and having to be shoved and hauled into the breeches, of his falling on both knees at the Levée when the Queen passed by and being unable to stand up again without help, and commented "Fancy the High Priest of Mountain and of Flood on his knees in a Court, the quiz of Courtiers, in a dress that did not belong to him, with a sword that was not his own and a coat which he borrowed". He did not confine his feelings to his diary; he wrote to Talfourd and other friends about it too, with indiscreet vehemence.

He was not the only one. Browning, Elizabeth Barrett, Miss Mitford, Mrs Jameson, Miss Martineau, Talfourd, all exchanged anecdotes about the visit to the Levée and Samuel Rogers' breeches. Their comments sound malicious, even tittering; but it is not quite that, not just the envy of lesser writers against a greater one. When Elizabeth Barrett, who revered Wordsworth's poetry, wrote "I have heard such really desecrating things of him, of his selfishness, his love of money, his worldly *cunning* (rather than prudence)", she was expressing the feeling of a whole younger generation of poets. The legend of Wordsworth's apostasy has now been dispelled, but it did look like that to some of his contemporaries. His evolution

from his early liberal opinions, his conformism, his deliberate
Tory politics, his disapproval of Catholic Emancipation and the
Reform Bill and the Repeal of the Corn Laws, his defence of
capital punishment, were a real wound to his younger admirers, which desecrated what had been so sacred. To these
younger writers it seemed that it was Wordsworth who first
showed them that unquestionable genius can go with odious
opinions, that insight can exist without love. It was he who had
clouded their glad confident morning. Thirty years later
Browning, when he admitted that Wordsworth had been his
model for *The Lost Leader* (published in the winter before
Haydon's death), added that he still thought Wordsworth's
abandonment of liberalism, at such a moment in history, was
deplorable.

Elizabeth Barrett felt the same—she could have wept that
Wordsworth should write sonnets in favour of capital punishment, that "a hand which has traced *life*-warrants so long for the
literature of England should thus sign a misplaced *Benedicite*
over the hangman and his victim". It was not that Wordsworth
was a lesser man than they had believed; if he had been, it
would not have mattered so much. It was a real leader—whose
mild and magnificent eye they had lived in, whose great language they had learnt—who was lost to them for a handful
of silver. When they saw—or thought they saw—the justly
admired genius turn conformist, and vanish within the doors
of the Establishment, the young felt—and feel today, perhaps,
in parallel cases—the pain and fear worse than the scorn. They
kick their idol the more violently because, in spite of everything, it does not fall; it has a sheep's head, but still it is a
true and potent image of a god.

Mrs Jameson saw both Browning and Elizabeth Barrett on 1st July. During these days she was in lodgings in Mortimer Street with the niece whom she had adopted. Browning looked in on her in the course of a morning of calls—on Forster, on Mrs Procter and last at the office of the publisher Edward Moxon, where he managed, in a dexterous inquiry which did not reveal his special interest, to collect the information that Miss Barrett's poems were selling very well and would shortly be out of print. After which he went home and found that Carlyle had sent him a copy of the new edition of *Cromwell* with a friendly inscription on the first page; and better still, that there was a letter from Elizabeth Barrett showing that she was really thinking in practical, detailed terms about where they should go in Italy when they were married. Altogether it was a good day with him, and he was pleased with the world, and especially with Mrs Jameson. "I do extremely appreciate her, delight in her. . . . I never was just to her before, far from it".

Browning's confidence in Mrs Jameson had been increased by a recent conversation in which she had spoken to him with frank indignation about the irrational tyranny of Miss Barrett's father, who stubbornly refused his consent to her going to Italy for the winter for her health, though her doctors had said it was essential. Mrs Jameson had said to Browning about Miss Barrett "I feel unhappy when in her presence—impelled to do her some service, and impeded. *Can* nothing be done to rescue her from this? *Ought* it to continue?" Mrs Jameson did not know how near rescue was, nor that she was speaking to the future rescuer; she knew Browning only as a friend and visitor of Miss Barrett's. But Browning was grateful for her kind concern, and longed to tell her that a rescue was to be attempted, and soon; but he was withheld by the consideration that if Mrs Jameson knew beforehand of their plans, Miss Barrett's family would blame her afterwards for having kept the secret.

Having seen Browning on the Wednesday morning, Mrs Jameson took her niece at five o'clock that afternoon to call upon Miss Barrett, and here too she was much appreciated: "feeling and affectionate as ever . . . such kindness! The sense of it has sunk into my heart. You cannot praise her too much for *me*" Elizabeth Barrett told Browning. Mrs Jameson urged Miss Barrett to go to Italy for her health that winter. Miss Barrett could not confess how advanced her plans were for going to Italy, and with whom, but she admitted that there was a probability of her going.

"What are you counting on?" Mrs Jameson asked.

"Perhaps on my own courage".

"Oh, now I see clearly" exclaimed Mrs Jameson.

Miss Barrett smiled, and Mrs Jameson cordially offered help in any way that could be useful. She was off to France and Italy herself in the autumn. It was an affectionate but slightly tricky interview; and next day, Thursday 2nd, Miss Barrett was due to have another, with an older and dearer friend, Miss Mitford, but she confessed to Browning that she was not looking forward to it in the least. He had turned her heart into hard porphyry for everyone but himself. Once it had been the softest clay to every pressure of Miss Mitford's finger. They had known each other for ten years and had kept up a frequent fond animated correspondence, punctuated by Miss Mitford's visits to Wimpole Street. It was Miss Mitford who had given the spaniel Flush to Miss Barrett.

Mary Russell Mitford was now fifty-eight years old, and— free at last from the burden of her old vampire of a father— was living by herself in modest sufficiency in her beloved cottage at Three Mile Cross, near Reading. The days of her greatest fame as poet, playwright and essayist—the days of *Julian*, *Foscari*, *Rienzi*, those forgotten tragedies, and *Our Village*, that unforgotten series of country sketches—were now rather past, but she was still a respected literary figure, with a wide span of friends and acquaintances. They included Haydon, a close

friend; Wordsworth, Rogers, Landor, Talfourd—a most helpful ally and supporter in her early literary career—Forster,
Procter, Browning and Macready—who had succeeded in
quarrelling even with the good-natured Miss Mitford, and
subsequently described her as "false and base" in his diary.

Perhaps all Miss Mitford's books and literary contacts now
meant less to her than her garden, which was one of the
wonders of her neighbourhood, and at its very best in June
and early July, so that it must have been hard to leave it even
for a day to go up to London on the 2nd, now that the weather
was fine again, and there had been enough rain to revive all the
flowers except those that the earlier drought had withered
altogether. Miss Mitford was a great collector of newly im-
ported species of flowers, and had tall spires of vivid blue
delphinium, and dense tufts of orange erysimum, and azure
nemophilas, and white and lilac lupins, and fiery Oriental
poppies, and great clumps of glittering violet-blue Siberian
larkspur. But she also had the traditional English cottage
flowers in masses: monkshood, blue and white double Canter-
bury bells, sweet williams, steeples of hollyhock and white
foxglove rising against the horizon of low wooded hills and
cloudless sky, festoons of roses and honeysuckle hanging from
the pear trees and the dark brick walls of the cottage. Above
all she had geraniums—her speciality, her pride and joy; a
great pyramid of them, made up of dozens of different varieties,
was the central glory of her garden, under a special movable
canopy to protect them from the fierce sun. Flowers from the
Three Mile Cross garden were often taken or sent to Miss
Barrett in Wimpole Street, but on this Thursday it was a basket
of jam that Miss Mitford brought with her. She left Three
Mile Cross early enough to reach Wimpole Street by two
o'clock, and she was there till seven—she had a very great
deal to say to Miss Barrett about the terrible event of last week,
the suicide of their common friend.

Haydon and Miss Mitford first met in 1817, and they remained friends and correspondents ever after. "One of my
dearest friends" he called her in his diary, and she deserved it—
she was a faithful, sympathetic, if clear-sighted supporter and

encourager of him and his family. She liked and admired his wife—"How should you like to be 'Sir Benjamin'? *She* would become the 'Lady', would she not?" she wrote to Haydon when King George IV bought Haydon's picture *The Mock Election*. She was godmother to Haydon's eldest son, Frank. She warmly congratulated Haydon on every success, and heartily sympathized when he was imprisoned for debt. She praised him cordially to her friends—"He is quite one of the old heroes come to life again—one of Shakespeare's men—full of spirit and endurance and moral courage"; "he himself—oh! how you would like him!—is a creature of air and fire; the frankest truest man breathing; absolutely free from pretence or trickery". She thought his conversation dazzlingly brilliant in its boldness, vivacity, originality, keen observation of character. She had only two faults to find with him. One was his lack of taste, the want of moral elegance which coarsened his opinions. The other, surprisingly, was his appearance. She thought him a "fright", and was astonished that he could conceivably have used his own countenance, intellectual and spirited as it was, as a model for one of the versions of Christ's head which he made for his *Entry into Jerusalem*; it was "one of the very last human faces that anybody but the owner would think of copying for Jesus Christ".

Haydon's opinion of Miss Mitford's appearance was no more flattering than hers of his. He loved her goodness of heart, he enjoyed her wholesome judgment, her lack of affectation, her fine sympathy, but he considered her an ugly woman—intellectual-looking but ugly, with her big forehead and her little snub nose. It is not surprising that the only faint shadow that ever crossed their friendship was when he painted her portrait in 1825. She herself thought that his portrait, though unflattering, was not much unlike what she saw every day in the looking-glass, but her father refused to have it in the house and her friends could not bear it. They told her it made her look like a sixty-year-old kitchen maid, or like Falstaff disguised as an old woman. It remained on the hands of the painter, who always liked it, and sent it among the treasures which he entrusted to Miss Barrett for safe keeping just before his death;

even then, he said that he would only lend it to Miss Barrett, he could not bear to part with it permanently.

The news of Haydon's suicide appalled Miss Mitford. Her letters to her friends in the next few days are full of it, and describe herself as "shocked past expression", "completely upset by the terrible shock". She mourned over their thirty years of unbroken friendship, the many letters they had exchanged, his brilliancy, the unfulfilled promise of his early pictures, the sacrifice he had finally made to secure an income to the wife and children of whom he was so dotingly fond. One of the first letters she wrote was to Miss Barrett, who answered that she too had been quite overcome for several days by the news, and had imagined how much her friend must have suffered; "I knew that you would be shocked beyond all power of words". Both ladies perhaps felt a certain pride in how upset they had been. Miss Barrett told Miss Mitford about Haydon's deposit of his journals and portraits—including Miss Mitford's —with her, and went on to give the conclusions on the suicide which she had communicated to Browning.

"Never did I imagine that it" [the sending of the journals and pictures to her] "was other than one of the passing embarrassments so unhappily frequent with him. Once before he had asked me to give shelter to things belonging to him, which, when the storm had blown over, he had taken back again. I did not suppose that in this storm he was to sink—poor noble soul! And be sure that the pecuniary embarrassment was not what sank him. It was a wind still more east: it was the despair of the ambition by which he lived, and without which he could not live. In the self-assertion which he had struggled to hold up through life he went down into death. He could not bear the neglect, the disdain, the slur cast upon him by the age, and so he perished. The cartoon disappointment, the grotesque bitterness of the antagonism of Tom Thumb: these things were too much—the dwarf slew the giant. His love of reputation, you know, was a disease with him; and, for my part, I believe that he died of it. That is my belief".

It was not quite Miss Mitford's belief; she credited Haydon with a motive more deliberate and more unselfish, and she

hurried up to London to discuss it with her friend. She spoke of
the poem which their common friend Richard Hengist Horne
had written about Haydon's death, and which had appeared in
the *Daily News* on 29th June. Horne had taken up the line in
Wordsworth's sonnet to Haydon—

"Faith in the whispers of the lonely muse"

and had made of it a lamenting refrain to his elegy, every
stanza of which begins—

"Mourn, fatal Voice, whom ancients call'd the Muse!"

There are moving lines in the poem, giving some idea of why
Horne, now quite forgotten, was considered an outstanding
poet and dramatist in his day. It tells of the Muse's fiery
whispers which exalted the artist's heart with dreams of
power and beauty, led him through forests of ecstatic imagination, taught him to be strong, untiring—

"But teachest no man how to know himself,
His over-measure or his fallings short,
Nor how to know when he should step aside
Into the quiet shade, to wait his hour,
And foil the common dragon of the earth"

and therefore now the Muse must mourn the loss of a worthy
son whose eyes she had enraptured while his feet wandered
on to ruin and death, who "lost himself, remembering thee".
Horne's poem cannot match with Wordsworth's sonnet, but
they make together a frame for the opening and close of a
life astray.

Miss Barrett was much affected by Horne's poem on Haydon,
which she thought both just and touching. But the five-hour
talk with Miss Mitford that Thursday was not what it would
have been a year earlier—an absorbing exchange of thoughts
and feelings. Miss Barrett's attention wandered at times when
her friend was talking to her, and she forgot much of what she
herself had intended to say, and was exhausted by the end of
the interview. She felt guilty about it, and wrote an effusive
letter of thanks to Miss Mitford for coming, and giving her
"such a heap of golden hours", but it was not true, and her old

friend must have realized that some barrier had come down between them.

The barrier was Robert Browning, and Elizabeth Barrett's love for him. It was not merely the secret of the engagement, and the absorption of all Miss Barrett's thoughts by her love. Miss Mitford did not like or approve of Browning, and Miss Barrett knew it. Miss Mitford thought that Browning's poetry was obscure and overrated, and that he himself was an effeminate weakling, and the first opinion, at any rate, had been communicated to Miss Barrett, who had often defended his poetry in her letters to Miss Mitford. But recently they had kept off the subject. "All those hours you were not once mentioned" Miss Barrett told Browning, describing her five-hour session with Miss Mitford. "*I* had not courage—and she perhaps avoided an old subject of controversy. . . . It is singular that for this year past you are not mentioned between us. . . . No single person will be more utterly confounded than she, when she comes to be aware of what you are to me now. . . . She will be confounded and angry perhaps—it will be beyond her sympathies—or if they reach so far, the effort to make them do so will prove a more lively affection for me, than, with all my trust in her goodness, I dare count on. Yet very good and kind and tender, she was to me today. And very variously intelligent and agreeable. Do you know, I should say that her *natural* faculties were stronger than Mrs Jameson's—though the latter has a higher aspiration and, in some ways, a finer sensibility of intellect. You would certainly call her superior to her own books—certainly you would. She walks strongly on her own two feet in the world—but nobody shall see her (not even *you*) fly out of a window. Too closely she keeps to the ground, I always feel. Now Mrs Jameson can 'aspire' like Paracelsus; and believes enough in her own soul, to know a poet when she sees one".

Appreciation of Browning was the touchstone of all excellence for Miss Barrett now. Mrs Jameson passed that test, Miss Mitford did not, and the former was succeeding the latter as the really trusted friend.

Mrs Carlyle's friend Geraldine Jewsbury wrote at the end of June that Mrs Carlyle's last letter had made her really uneasy about the writer's health and spirits after her stay at Addiscombe with the Barings. "All those grand people may be very well—a great privilege to know, and all that—but just now you want to be out of the hearing of 'wits', and with somebody that loves you, and to whom you can speak".

Mrs Carlyle was ill and sleepless and miserable in that last week of June. She was ill with the heat, and from other causes. She had been fatigued and irritated by the houseful of lively idle guests at Lady Harriet Baring's, and when she got back to enjoy her own house and household duties at Chelsea, Carlyle began to talk of giving up the house and going to live in Scotland, taking away all her pleasure in the home on which she had spent so much effort. One pleasure she had in that miserable sultry week. "The most important thing that has *happened* to me since my return has been the gift of a splendid Indian scarf (from Lady Harriet) almost '*too* splendid for *anything*' " she wrote to her cousin on 26th June. "But I was greatly pleased with it because of its being the facsimile of one she got for herself. She rails at *sentiment* and never puts any into her *words*, but it peeps out often enough in her *actions*. She would not put an *affectionate* sentence in her letters for the world but she will put *violets*—leaves of the *flowers one likes*—sometimes sends me envelopes by post containing nothing else!! What a contrast I often think betwixt that woman and Geraldine! the opposite poles of woman-nature".

That was Mrs Carlyle's last letter about Lady Harriet Baring before, on 4th July, she had a violent quarrel with her husband, generally supposed to have been about Lady Harriet, and rushed off to Liverpool by herself to stay with friends. It is not the letter of a straightforwardly jealous woman. Her frame of mind was more complicated than that.

Lady Harriet Baring was one of those people whose power depends on some magic of personality which is felt by those who know them, but is incommunicable to anyone else. Her influence now seems inexplicable. She was rich and hospitable, but so were dozens of other Victorian hostesses. She was, we are told, extremely witty, but almost all the examples of her wit which have survived are cruel, and many are merely brutal, without finesse. A male guest of hers once boxed her ears in the presence of twenty people because of her intolerable rudeness. Everyone complained of her flaying tongue and her bossiness. She was not at all handsome; even Milnes, who was devoted to her, described her as "the best-looking ugly woman ever seen" and her portraits show a heavy-cheeked pudgy-nosed double-chinned woman with wavy—or more probably tong-waved—hair, and large heavy-lidded but penetrating eyes. Yet everybody was subjugated by her. "I like Lady H. Baring but I hate her" said Thackeray. Princess Lieven declared "qu'il vaudrait bien s'abonner pour entendre causer cette femme". Her houses were always full of guests, it was a great much-sought honour to be invited there.

Both the Carlyles succumbed. Lady Harriet captured Carlyle first, and he became a constant visitor and correspondent, a fascinated flattered stimulated admirer. Then she made a set at Mrs Carlyle, and cast a spell over her too. Mrs Carlyle's favourable reports after their first meetings were perhaps partly a conscious effort to seem unconcerned, impartial, not a victim of the jealousy everyone expected her to feel. But this attitude turned into real admiration—"A *grand* woman every inch of her—and *not* 'a coquette' the least in the world—if all the men go out of their sober senses beside her how can she help *that*?" Three months before the quarrel in July, Mrs Carlyle wrote of Lady Harriet—"for my part I *love* her now as much as I *admired* her in the beginning. She is the only woman of *genius* I have found among all our pretenders to it—I only wish I had got to know her twenty years ago when I was better capable of enjoying the advantages of such an acquaintance".

Yet Mrs Carlyle did undoubtedly require of her husband that he should break off his acquaintance with Lady Harriet. She did not believe him capable of a guilty passion for Lady Harriet, or of that kind of passion at all. What was wrong was something of which the Lady Harriet story was only a symptom, and not the worst, though it was the one which finally provoked the drawing of the surgical knife to cut away their marriage. The knife had been waved before—in 1844 when Mrs Carlyle had angry moods of threatening to leave her husband for good and all, in 1845 when she wrote to him "Husbands are so obtuse! They do not '*understand*' one's movements of impatience— want always to be 'treated with the respect due to genius', exact common sense of their poor wives rather than 'the finer sensibilities of the heart', and so the marriage state 'by working late and early, has come to what ye see'—if not precisely to 'immortal smash' as yet, at least to within a hair's breadth of it!" She was half joking, the use of their private catchwords and quotations proves that—it was always half a joke, but the undercurrent is there that made her entertain her friends with little stories at Carlyle's expense, expose his inconsistencies, make him look slightly ridiculous, chip into his long mono- logues with ironical comments. She was jealous of Carlyle, certainly, but not only with Lady Harriet. She was proud of him and of his achievements; but she was an intensely clever woman who had no real outlet for her cleverness, and that was intolerable. "I can't bear to be thought of only as Carlyle's wife" she told Espinasse. A month before the quarrel, she called on the Macready family, and made them laugh till they cried with her stories about Carlyle and his horse. Mrs Macready talked about her own depression of spirits, and was astonished when Mrs Carlyle admitted to having black moments too— she had supposed Mrs Carlyle was never sad. Mrs Carlyle made no reply but congratulated herself on having played her part so well, and said to her cousin, describing the incident, "I wish I could find some hard work I *could* do—and saw any sense in doing. If I do not soon it will be the worse for me".

Her fierce mental energy rusted in her unused, and the corrosion spread through her personality. The most revealing words, perhaps, that she ever wrote about herself were in a letter to Gavan Duffy: "I have sometimes thought that in a civil war I should possibly find my 'mission'—*moi*! But in these merely talking times, a poor woman knows not how to turn herself; especially if, like myself, she 'have a devil' always calling to her, 'March! march!' and bursting into infernal laughter when requested to be so good as to specify whither". She could have been another Florence Nightingale—she had as good a brain, nearly as much practical organizing ability, and health no worse. It was bad enough, though, and especially at this time of her life, when she sometimes thought she was going mad, was perpetually having headaches and vomiting and passing sleepless nights, and always took far too many medicines—tartar emetic, castor oil, mercury, and at this time a good deal of morphia too. No doubt the morphia contributed to her neurotic frame of mind. Life had not kept its promises to her, it was empty and meaningless, a futile restless flurry of noise and hard uncaring faces, and a black nothing at the end of it.

We do not know what she and Carlyle said to each other before she left for Liverpool on 4th July, except that as she left she did promise to let him know of her safe arrival. Their usual economical method of doing this was to post a newspaper— cheaper than a letter—and she duly did this on Sunday 5th, feeling too exhausted to write a letter. For some reason the newspaper did not arrive in Cheyne Row on the Monday morning, and Carlyle wrote her an anxious note. "My Dear, I hope it is only displeasure or embarrassed estrangement from me, and not any accident or illness of your own, that robs me of a Note this morning. . . . This is not good; but perhaps an unfriendly or miserable Letter would have been worse: so I will be patient as I can. Certainly we never before parted in such a manner! And all for, literally—Nothing! Composure, and reflexion, at a distance from all causes of irritation and freaks of diseased fancy, will show us both more clearly what the God's Truth of the matter *is*: may God give us strength to follow piously and with all loyal fidelity what that is!" He had been sadder than for ten years past, and ill too, and had worked away miserably enough, and had not been near the Barings since she left, whatever she might have been imagining; she must believe that she was and always would be, his dearest.

Mrs Carlyle had recovered enough on Monday to write him a calm sad faintly apologetic letter. "I shall do quite well here for a while, as I have the amplest tolerance granted me to be as ugly and stupid and disagreeable as ever I please,—the only satisfaction in life which I aspire to for the moment. For *you*, you must feel as if a millstone had been taken off your breast". She ended "Ever affectionately yours".

Carlyle got this letter and the newspaper after he had written his letter on the Monday, and on Tuesday he fired off a thankful letter of relief and affection. "So kind and good a little message! It has lifted a mountain from my poor inner-man. O if you could see *there*, the real fact of the thing, verily it would all be *well*. . . . And so, let us not say a word more of it", but he added many more words of gratitude and endearment, a brief mention that he had been at the Barings' on Monday night but hadn't enjoyed it, and ended "Adieu dear Jenny mine!"

Mrs Carlyle replied on Friday 10th, acknowledging his two letters, blaming the post for the delay in the arrival of the newspaper which had caused him so much anxiety, reporting on her health and her appetite and the weather, making a few faintly ironic remarks about arrangements for Carlyle's horse, and ending "I feel myself a dreadful bore—though Betsy's patience is enormous. Ever affectionately yours". There was not a syllable in reply to the assurances and endearments in Carlyle's letter.

About this time she also wrote to her friend Mrs Russell to say that the great heat of London had made her ill, "and as my husband would not make up his mind yet where to go or when, I made up my own mind one fine morning, and started off hither". She also wrote a letter to Giuseppe Mazzini, the exiled Italian patriot who was her friend and confidant; it was a short sad letter telling him that her life was empty, that she yearned after a happiness that she knew to be unattainable, to have no real existence. She got a very bracing reply from Mazzini telling her to do her duty and not dream about happiness, to trust in God and fill her so-called empty life with love and good deeds. He appealed to a sanction in which Mrs Carlyle did not believe; he called her grievances ghosts and phantoms; his letter cannot have helped her much.

Carlyle was not happy either. He could not really understand what had gone wrong between him and his wife, what it was that she wanted and was not getting. Of course she was not happy—no one was happy, there was no such thing as happiness for mortal men. Her violent bitter protests were irrational, the effects of "diseased fancy". His friendship with Lady Harriet was both innocuous and unimportant, but enjoyable, and he would like to keep it if he could, but would give it up if he must.

In any case it was not worth—nothing was worth—the violence of his wife's parting with him. Life was at best a miserable business, but to be endured with fortitude, in theory (and with querulous gloom in Carlyle's practice), not with outbursts of unavailing protest. Alone in London, he worked at home in the sticky heat, went out riding in a thunderstorm, arranged for publication of one of his books in America, walked out to the Barings' at Addiscombe and came back by river steamer in baking sunshine. Writing to a friend on Saturday of that week, seven days after Mrs Carlyle had gone off, he explained that the summer heat had driven her out of London in search of rest and fresh air, and added "I, too, am tattered and fretted into great sorrow of heart".

But if he could not understand his wife's trouble, he could feel for it. "His was the soft heart and hers the hard one" said Geraldine Jewsbury when both the Carlyles were dead. He made an effort to console his wife's inexplicable misery. He bought a card-case to send to her as a birthday present, and sent it off with a letter wishing her many happy returns "or if 'happy returns' are not in our vocabulary then 'wise returns', wise and true and brave, which after all are the only 'happiness', as I conjecture, that we have any right to look for in this segment of Eternity that we are traversing together, thou and I. God bless thee, Darling; and know thou always, in spite of the chimeras and delusions, that thou art dearer to me than any earthly creature. That *is* a fact, if it can be of any use to thy poor soul to know. And so accept my little gift, and kiss it as I have done; and say, in the name of Heaven it shall yet all be well; and my poor Husband *is* the man I have always known him from of old, is and always will be!"

However they had parted, Mrs Carlyle expected to hear from him on her birthday, and on 14th July she walked to the post office to collect the expected letter—but there was no letter for her. She walked home again in a tumult of wretchedness, and shut herself up in her room to imagine that Carlyle had finally lost patience and resolved to write to her no more, that he was enjoying himself at the Barings' and had forgotten her existence, that he was too ill to write. This last idea tortured her so much that she longed to rush to the station and take the train back to London. For two hours she tormented herself with these thoughts, and then she heard a voice crying "Mrs Carlyle! Mrs Carlyle! Are you there? Here is a letter for you".

The expected letter, and Carlyle's present with it, had come after all. She was so shattered by what she had gone through that she could scarcely write, but she had to thank him at once. "Yes, I have kissed the dear little card-case; and now I will lie down awhile, and try to get some sleep. At least, to quiet myself, I will try to believe—oh, why cannot I believe it, once for all—that, with all my faults and follies, I *am* 'dearer to you than any earthly creature'".

Nothing was really solved or settled. A day later she was writing miserably about her weariness and longing for death, a month later he was bitterly reproaching her for unfounded jealousy; but for an hour or two her life at any rate had not been empty.

The thirteenth clause of Haydon's will read "I leave Manuscripts and my memoirs in the possession of Miss Barrett, 50
Wimpole St., in a Chest which I wish Longman to be consulted
about. My Memoirs are to 1820, my journals will supply the
rest. The style, the individuality of Richardson, which I wish
not curtailed by an Editor. Correspondence and Journals for
the rest".

This clause, at first inattentively read by Haydon's executors,
caused a great deal of unnecessary anxiety. On Sunday 5th
July, another day of oppressive heat in the morning and a great
storm of thunder and rain in the afternoon, Miss Barrett's
cousin John Kenyon called on her with a message from Haydon's
executors that Haydon had bequeathed his manuscripts to her,
with a request that she would edit them and arrange with
Longmans for their publication.

Elizabeth Barrett was touched that Haydon should have
confided such a trust to her, but she was much embarrassed and
upset by it. She already knew enough about Haydon's autobiography to be certain that its editing would be a very responsible and difficult piece of work. Three and a half years
earlier, when she and Haydon were at the peak of their correspondence, he had sent her his autobiography to read. She read
it with great interest, and told him that it was delightful and
most moving, and that if he would cut out some of the "unmeasured words" it certainly ought to be published. She told
Miss Mitford at the same time, as a great secret, that she had
been allowed to see the autobiography and that it was "full of
blood and pulses—and of the detail of life—and of the *life-
agony* of genius". She hoped Haydon would also show her his
journals—the autobiography only covered his life up to 1820.
But he decided that he could not show her the actual diaries.

But a few months later he consulted her about the publication of his autobiography, and she gave him some business-like advice about which publishers to apply to, and the financial terms he should ask for, if he decided to publish immediately. She added a warning—"One previous consideration is that you could scarcely name the names of living persons and discuss their merits quite as frankly and freely now, as if the publication were to take place hereafter. If you publish now, you must soften a little—and I would moreover, if I were you, abbreviate and subdue certain parts of your MS . . . particularly the opening of it where you speak boldly and openly of your own genius. I like the consciousness of genius, and I do not object to truth under any aspect. But you must be aware that the world and the great mass of readers are irritated by assertion into denial; and are apt to call all such gloryings, if not mistaken vanity, mis-spoken bad taste. I would therefore, if I were you, *spare the provocative*. Now remember—this is not to advise insincerity, but simply one shade more of reserve".

Haydon replied that she wanted him to be hypocritical and feign humility. She wrote again, denying this, and repeating that she was simply advocating reserve, but that he might be right in his own case; certainly she believed that men with great powers always knew that they possessed them, "the lion knows always that he can roar". She was anxious that his autobiography should be a success when it was published, and she admired its style which "if not always correct and classical, is always characteristic and vivacious".

Three months after this, he sent her for the first time all his papers and journals for safe keeping, when he expected an execution for debt in his house after the failure of his cartoons in the House of Lords competition. There is no evidence that Miss Barrett read any of the journals while they were in her safe-keeping, and Haydon took them back a few weeks later.

So when Kenyon told her on this Sunday that the journals had been bequeathed to her to edit, her reaction to the bequest was based on the autobiography which she had read three years earlier. But her memory of that was alarming enough, as she wrote to Browning that night. "It was—with much that was individual and interesting,—as unfit as possible for the general reader—fervid and coarse at once, with personal references blood-dyed at every page". In any case she herself, as she told Browning, Miss Mitford and her brother George in letters describing Kenyon's announcement, was quite unqualified to edit the journals of a painter, whose famous friends and contemporaries were all older than her and personally unknown to her. She had seen hardly any of his pictures, and was very ignorant about art in general. She felt convinced that in mentioning her in his will, Haydon had only meant to indicate that his journals were actually in her possession, not that she was to edit them. If Haydon really had clearly said that he wanted her as editor, she ought not to shrink from the work, however unpleasant it would be, she told Browning. But she could not believe that he had. Serjeant Talfourd, who was actually one of Haydon's executors, would surely be the obvious person to do the job. In any case, her cousin Kenyon was going to try to see the will and discover exactly what it had said. So far, he had only had a message from Talfourd about it, through Forster. It was Forster who called on Kenyon to tell him about the bequest, and ask him to communicate the news to his cousin Miss Barrett.

It would have been John Forster. As the epitaph on his tomb in Kensal Green put it, he was

> "Noted in private life
> For the robustness of his character
> And the warmth of his affections
> For his ceaseless industry in literature and business
> And the lavish services in the midst of his crowded life
> He rendered to friends;
> For his keen appreciation of every species of excellence,
> And the generosity of his judgments
> On books and men"

If in the London of the 1840's there was a negotiation to be carried on about getting something published, Forster would be certain to have a hand in it. Busy as he was with his own work —in this summer he was editor of the *Daily News* which Dickens had founded in the spring, as well as literary editor and dramatic critic of the *Examiner*—he was also constantly involved in managing other people's affairs. He advised his friends about titles for their books, he corrected their proofs, he negotiated with their publishers, he supervised their contracts. "The beadle of the universe", Leigh Hunt's son called him— he organized everything and everybody. He sat on committees, he got up subscriptions, he launched appeals; in this month of July he was closely concerned in getting a pension awarded to Leigh Hunt. He acted as a theatrical agent for his literary friends, and had been instrumental in getting Macready to put on plays by both Talfourd and Browning. Browning owed a great deal to Forster's reviews of his poems, which had been admiring from the first, and had done much to raise his reputation. Forster had negotiated the publication of *Sordello*, had suggested that Browning should write a play about Strafford, had defended *Paracelsus* when all the other critics were attacking it, and had just, in April of this year, done a very friendly review of Browning's latest *Bells and Pomegranates*. Browning gave Forster the MS of *Paracelsus* with the inscription—"To John Forster Esq (my early understander), with true thanks for his generous and public Confession of Faith in me". Miss Barrett had reason to be grateful to Forster too; he gave a handsome review to her 1844 Poems. "He is the ablest of English critics, and for his kindness to my little volumes I am grateful" she wrote to Haydon. Haydon himself had cause to be grateful to Forster, who wrote a good review of his first series of lectures when they were published, and a kind notice of his last ill-fated exhibition at the Egyptian Hall. Even his powerful advocacy could not rescue Haydon, but it had launched other men of real but unrecognized merit—not only Browning but Tennyson, Thackeray, Dickens and Bulwer all owed much to his promotion of their work.

Forster, whenever one hears of him, seems always to have been a figure of such portentous influence that it is difficult to realize that in this summer of 1846 he was only thirty-four— two months younger than Dickens, one month older than Browning. He was a big broad-shouldered man with heavy strongly-marked features—a long upper lip, an aggressive lower lip and prominent chin, sharp eyes under jutting eye-brows. He had a loud domineering voice, began half his sentences with "Great God!", and had a burly laugh which made everyone else laugh too. Superimposed on this bluff natural manner was a painstaking imitation of Macready's voice and stage mannerisms; he would stride into a room where someone was waiting for him (he always kept everyone waiting, his overfull life made him perpetually late), apologizing in tragic tones for the delay and pressing his hand to his heart to show how overcome with shame he felt. It was particularly exasperating for Macready to be admonished and contradicted by Forster in a travesty of his own intonation and manner. Even total strangers were astonished at the dramatic violence of Forster's way of speaking. One friend of the Carlyles, on his way by bus to dine with them in Chelsea, noticed an important-looking man who got onto the bus shortly after he did and, because the bus went rather slowly, addressed the conductor "with singular vehemence . . . again and again, in rebuke of his dilatoriness and general depravity". This important-looking passenger got off the bus at the same stop as the Carlyles' friend, walked down the same lane, and turned up on the Carlyles' doorstep. It was Forster.

The hasty exaggeration of his temper was partly due to ill-health. Tall and strong as he looked—and he was endlessly energetic and a fearless rock climber too—he was not a healthy man; he suffered all his life from asthma and rheumatism.

It might have been supposed that such an expert negotiator and adviser was a model of tact and conciliation. But Forster was perpetually offending people and having rows with them. His loud overbearing manner, his frankness, his brusque dogmatic opinions, his hasty temper, his determination to have a finger in every pie, to run everything his own way, caused perpetual rows. Even Dickens once ordered him out of the house; even Browning once nearly threw a decanter at him at dinner. He quarrelled with Thackeray, he quarrelled with Tom Taylor (future editor of Haydon's journals), he quarrelled with Harrison Ainsworth, he was mainly responsible for embroiling Bulwer and Tennyson in their attack and counter-attack in *The*

New Timon and in *Punch.* As for Macready, with whom it was only too easy to quarrel, Forster had a violent disagreement with him this very summer, and was vilified in Macready's diary for rudeness, slights, questionable behaviour, and disagreeable manners.

But they were reconciled. Everyone always was reconciled to Forster. He annoyed them, but they trusted and relied on him. His judgment was so sound, and then he had such a way of getting you to do what he thought best, whether you meant to or not. Carlyle spoke with some contempt of Forster's lack of original or serious thought, but warmly praised his sincerity and friendliness, and made him his literary executor; had Forster survived Carlyle, it would have been Forster, not Froude, that wrote Carlyle's life. Mrs Carlyle made fun of Forster's "Brummigen enthusiasm", his deafening exclamations of "Great God!", but she was fond of him, and grateful for the good review he gave to Carlyle's *Cromwell*. She went to see him when he was ill, and actually danced with him at a party at the Macreadys', and went to see him and Dickens do their famous amateur theatricals, and smiled at Forster's "loftiest flights of *Macreadyism*".

Forster in 1846 was already formidable, but he was still good fun, too—not yet the pompous disapproving figure that a disillusioned Dickens was to portray as Podsnap in *Our Mutual Friend*. In this summer of 1846 Dickens was still consulting and informing Forster about every chapter that he wrote. A week before Kenyon called on Miss Barrett with Forster's message about Haydon's journals, Dickens wrote to Forster from Lausanne that on 27th June he

BEGAN DOMBEY!

as he informed Forster in capital letters in a separate line to do justice to the occasion. Forster was given the fullest preview of how the plot of *Dombey and Son* was to evolve, and what Dickens meant its underlying themes to be; and had his own say, too, on how the story turned out, for originally the hero Walter Gay was to have gone to the bad, but Forster protested and Walter was remodelled, and eventually married to the heroine. Forster's protest was made when Dickens had sent him the first four chapters of the book. When Dickens was writing the fifth chapter, on the day after he got Forster's letter commenting on the plan of the book, was it perhaps an indistinct feeling that Forster was really too managing, too much "the Beadle of the Universe", that made him, in this very fifth chapter, describe Mr Dombey as "the beadle of private life; the beadle of our business and our bosoms"?

This was the man whom Haydon's executor asked to advise Miss Barrett what to do about Haydon's papers. It was a delicate situation, since Miss Barrett was an invalid who received nobody but her cousin Kenyon (neither Forster nor Talfourd knew about Browning's visits to her). But she must be persuaded to give Haydon's papers up into safer hands; if in her innocence and ignorance of the world she were to hand them over to a publisher as they stood, there might be horrid revelations which would embroil half the literary and artistic world of London.

On the morning of Monday 6th July Browning wrote a rather
melancholy letter to Elizabeth Barrett. One reason for his
gloom was that there had been an abrupt change in the weather;
yesterday it had been oppressively hot, today it was windy and
cold, and he was afraid the sudden change would be bad for
Miss Barrett. But the worst cause for depression was that he
had not been able to see her on Saturday, which should have
been their day, and was not to see her on this Monday, which
he had hoped for when Saturday proved impossible; and now,
though Wednesday was promised, even that was not quite
sure. The thought that he might have to spend another whole
year in only seeing Elizabeth Barrett so rarely and under such
uncertain conditions was intolerable to him.

The last few days had certainly been tantalizing. On Thursday,
there had seemed a chance that they might meet twice in two
days; Miss Barrett was due to call on Mrs Jameson, and
Browning was invited at the same time, so they looked like
having that meeting as well as their regular one in Wimpole
Street on Saturday. But the threatened arrival of an aunt and
cousin of the Barretts to stay in Wimpole Street, and then
Miss Barrett's feeling rather unwell, made it impossible for
her to get to Mrs Jameson's, either on Friday or Saturday.
Browning waited for her there in vain on Saturday, and
daringly wrote a letter to her from there, under Mrs Jameson's
very nose; but when he heard afterwards that if she had come,
she might have fainted, he admitted that it was just as well she
hadn't come, since if she had fainted when he was there, he
would have found it impossible to keep the secret of his feelings
for her. But it was hard that he could not see her at home on
Saturday afternoon either; she had to put him off, as her
father would be at home then, which might produce complica-

tions, and the relations might arrive at any time during the afternoon, and expect to see her at once, and if they didn't, there would be "questions and answers à faire frémir". She and Browning were in a very dangerous situation, more and more dangerous as the time for their secret marriage and departure drew nearer, and they could not run any risks.

As it turned out, Mr Barrett went out early that afternoon after all, so that particular complication would not have arisen, but there were still the imminent relations; so Elizabeth Barrett spent Saturday afternoon disconsolately reclining in her chair with her feet on a stool, looking at the empty chair beside her which Browning ought to have been sitting in, and thinking about him, and that it had been a whole week since she had seen him, and even their Monday meeting was not safe. And on Sunday she was obliged to tell him that her aunt would want to spend Monday afternoon with her, and so Browning's visit would have to be put off till Wednesday.

That Sunday afternoon, her aunt exhausted her with floods of talk on family news. The hours of conversation with someone who did not know of Browning's existence made Miss Barrett feel that she was losing her identity as Browning's beloved, and was slipping back into her past self as the permanent invalid, the pale pitied niece who was the only side of her known to her aunt. There was however a moment of excited embarrassment during the interview. The aunt, Miss Clarke, looked at the vase of almost dead blue flowers that Browning had brought a week before, and said "I suppose Miss Mitford brought you those flowers?"

"No, she did not" Elizabeth Barrett answered in a non-committal voice.

"Oh no, not Miss Mitford's flowers" put in Arabel Barrett in a meaning voice, and her sister had hastily to change the subject.

She ended her Sunday letter to Browning "Dearest, do not leave off loving me. Do not forget me by Wednesday. Shall it be Wednesday? or must it be Thursday?" No wonder he was teased, tantalized, low-spirited when he replied on Monday morning.

He was also alarmed and annoyed at the news about the bequest of Haydon's journals to Miss Barrett. Browning thought that Haydon's passion for vindicating himself in writing had been the real cause of his troubles, and the idea of resurrecting all those vindications seemed to him insane, and of giving Elizabeth Barrett the responsibility of editing them was more insane still. He suspected that Haydon had chosen Miss Barrett as editor precisely because her innocence and isolation would make her unaware of how dangerous it was to print such journals. He had a recent proof of Haydon's unreliability—he had slandered Maclise without a shadow of justification—and how many more people would he have maligned in these journals? If they could be edited by an impartial discreet man who knew all the artists concerned, something might be made of them; but, even apart from the imposition on Miss Barrett, he hated the whole idea of "these posthumous revelations,— these passions of the now passionless, errors of the at length better instructed! . . . He is so far above it all now". Browning hated the idea of Miss Barrett being involved in these sordid revelations, and he loathed it all the more because he himself could do so little to extricate her. Although he knew Forster and Talfourd, he could not intervene with them without showing that he had a special interest in Miss Barrett's affairs. He was due to dine with Talfourd next day, and would have liked to give him a message from Miss Barrett, but he would have to leave it to Kenyon to handle.

In his angry tenderness for Miss Barrett's reputation and peace of mind, Browning imputed to Haydon a mean motive in choosing her as editor, a plot to take advantage of her ignorance of the world in order to get published what a more worldly-wise editor would suppress. But there is no evidence that Haydon wanted Miss Barrett to edit his journals; in fact, after what she had written to him in 1843 about discretion and reserve, he was very unlikely to have entrusted her with the task. He did not want an editor at all; he meant his journals to be sent to Longmans, who had already published his lectures, for publication in their entirety—"the style, the individuality of Richardson, which I wish not curtailed by an Editor" he had distinctly written in his will. He aimed at the style of Richardson, whom he had once described as "the Raphael of domestic life"; he intended the breathless vivacity of a Pamela, the persecuted nobility of a Clarissa, the inviolable superiority of a Grandison, to be united in his life-justification.

He had always, from the first, intended his journals for publication. As far back as 1812 he was writing "Whoever you are that read this, when I am dead . . .", and when he wrote up his early journals into an autobiography, he inserted specific addresses to readers. "I write this Life for the student. I wish to show him how to bear affliction and disappointment by exhibiting the fatal consequences in myself who did not bear them"; "my view is to give my readers a notion of my character, temperament, virtues, vices and infirmities". If his style was modelled on Richardson, his autobiography was intended to emulate Vasari's *Lives of the Painters*, with all their lively anecdotes and adventures—the frank immediacy which had kept them popular through centuries, while the biographies of English painters, with their stuffy decorum, never even went into a second edition.

Haydon, like many of his contemporaries, had ambivalent views about the publication of letters and memoirs. His theory was that all letters should be destroyed, but he was very far indeed from practising this; he stuck quantities of the letters he received into his journal—fortunately, or some of Keats' finest letters would have been lost.

It was a much-discussed topic in the 1840's. Some writers, like Tennyson, so detested the "publicities and gabblements of the nineteenth century" and felt so strongly about the use that might be made of any papers that they left behind them, that they specifically forbade publication of any rough notes or drafts. Tennyson had a horror of biographical revelations; even Milnes' affectionate and admiring *Life, Letters and Literary Remains of John Keats* was probably the source of Tennyson's bitter protest, in his poem *To* ——, *After Reading a Life and Letters*, against orgies over the tombs of the newly dead, violation of privacy; against the carrion vultures who wait greedily to tear a dead man's heart in pieces before the crowd.

Tennyson's resentment was against those who published private papers. Dickens looked at it from the other end; he despised men who kept private diaries which they really intended for publication, those who "jot down in diaries the events of every day, and keep a regular debtor and creditor account with heaven, which shall always show a floating balance in their own favour". Dickens was so disgusted with Haydon's diaries, when they came to be published, that he took Haydon as a model for one part of the character of Harold Skimpole, in *Bleak House*, who is last heard of as having "left a diary behind, with letters and other materials towards his Life; which was published, and which showed him to have been the victim of a combination on the part of mankind against an amiable child".

Peel felt as Tennyson and Dickens did about the publication of intimate papers. Some of the first days of his new leisure at Drayton after his fall from power were spent in going through his correspondence and setting apart the letters he had had from Queen Victoria and Prince Albert, to "ensure their exemption from the fate to which in these days all letters seem to be destined", the fate of being published.

Harriet Martineau even demanded that all her friends should destroy her letters, for fear of the use that might be made of them. When Mrs Jameson heard of this, she protested most strongly, on the point of principle. "You wish that I should burn or surrender your letters? The request seems to me so extraordinary, so inconsistent with the brave, honest, clear spirit I have always admired and respected in you, that I paused and waited till I should have your reasons at length". She added that Miss Martineau's attitude was "a deadly blow to mutual confidence. . . . Shall we openly allow that we are afraid to speak or write what we think and feel, lest our words be repeated and published to our own or others' wrong?" She admitted that accidents had happened, through indiscretion, treachery or carelessness, but that should only make one more discriminating in one's friendships. "I think it the most detestable treachery to keep or show some kinds of letters; I think it the extreme of weakness and cowardice to destroy

others of a different character and if, in the discrimination, I am
to have no right of judgment whatever, then I am not fit to be
trusted with anything, nor fit to be yours or any lady's friend''.
She added that she had kept some of Miss Martineau's letters
because they did her honour and contained valuable truths, and
might be a source of strength and comfort to others; and she
asked Miss Martineau to authorize her still to keep these
letters.

It is ironical that while Mrs Jameson herself destroyed
many of her private letters and papers because she disliked the
idea of her private life being paraded before the world, her
niece was induced to go against her aunt's known wishes, and
to publish a life of her, chiefly because of animadversions on her
which appeared in Harriet Martineau's autobiography when
that was posthumously published.

Samuel Rogers agreed with Mrs Jameson that letters ought
to be preserved and published, though his reasons for thinking
so were not the same as hers. Soon after Sydney Smith died,
Rogers was staying with Mrs Grote at Burnham, and Fanny
Kemble, who was also staying there, reports a conversation
between Rogers and Mrs Grote as to whether Sydney Smith's
letters, with all their witty remarks at the expense of his friends
and acquantainces, should be published. Mrs Grote, who herself
had many of Sydney Smith's letters, declared it would be impossible to publish what he had said about people still alive.
Rogers, on the other hand, thoroughly enjoyed the idea of the
mischief the letters would make, and urged her to give the
complete uncut text of the letters to the press.

"Oh but now" said Mrs Grote "here, for instance, Mr Rogers,
such a letter as this about ——; do see how he cuts up the
poor fellow. It really never would do to publish it".

Rogers took the letter and read it with a grin of devilish
delight, and said "Publish it! publish it! Put an R, dash, or an
R and four stars for the name. He'll never know it, though
everybody else will!"

Meanwhile Mrs Grote held out silently to Fanny Kemble,
who was sitting beside her on a low stool, another letter of
Sydney Smith's, which began with a ludicrous description of

Rogers' cadaverous appearance. Fanny Kemble glanced from
the letter to the ugly old man, grinning over Sydney Smith's
letter about the unfortunate R——, and burst out laughing.

Miss Barrett also agreed with Mrs Jameson that fine letters
should be preserved, and was equally indignant when she heard
of Miss Martineau's demand for the return of her letters. She
had a robust attitude to the squeamishness of her age about
personal details. "The shrieks on all sides because Mr such a
person tells the astonished public that Mrs such a person has
a nose, could scarcely be louder if he had attacked her character
in a public court. And as to the printing of letters, I never will
believe (for all Miss Martineau may re-iterate) that a man or
woman either, let them live ever so in perpetual presence of the
grand possibilities of Posterity, would write restrained sentences to their very intimate friend; under the idea that after
they are dead their letters will be printed by their executors".
Did Miss Mitford, to whom she was writing this, ever feel
restrained by such a thought, asked Miss Barrett, although she
must know that everybody kept her delightful letters? If everybody acted on Miss Martineau's principle, what treasures
would have been lost—the letters of Madame de Sévigné, of
Madame du Deffand, of Cowper. What did it matter, when one
was dead, what people thought of one? "As if, when we have
seen God, we shall care for man seeing *us*!" Miss Martineau,
with her clear logical mind, ought to have been able to see such
a truth as that.

So when Browning suggested, in the letter she got that
Monday afternoon, that Haydon's letters should be suppressed
because he knew better now, she maintained her opinion even
against him. She agreed that the journals were, as Browning
had called them, a "dispiriting bequest" to her, that she was
not a fit person to edit them, and that they could not possibly
go straight to a publisher's hands as they were. But Haydon
had had in him the stuff of greatness, and what he had left
behind deserved to be treated with respect. "True, he is above
it all—true, he has done with the old Haydon" but "this record
is not for the angels, but for *us*, who are a little lower at highest.
Three volumes perhaps may be taken from the twenty-six full

of character and interest, and not without melancholy teaching. Only some competent and sturdy hand should manage the selection; as surely as mine is unfit for it. But where to seek *discretion? delicacy?*" She would be glad if he would talk to Talfourd about it on her behalf; her cousin Kenyon was going to talk to Forster.

Browning acquiesced in her general principle. He was not, he said, against confessions and autobiographies in general— not even against the publication of some part of Haydon's journals, but with the petty complaints, the defensiveness, the fretful gestures cut out. And in this Elizabeth Barrett entirely concurred. When she remembered what Haydon had said in his autobiography about Shelley and Leigh Hunt, and the letters from Keats to Haydon about Hunt which she had seen, she agreed that it would be dreadful to publish such passages as those, for Leigh Hunt himself to read. Then, too, there were the imputations on Caroline Norton—it would be monstrous if they were published. Good, careful, discreet editing was entirely necessary.

Her letter, which began with these calm sensible observations, ended with anything but calm. She had not seen Browning for more than a week, and she could think of nothing but his coming—"let it be wise or unwise, I *must and will see you tomorrow* —I cannot do otherwise. It is just as if Flush had been shut up in a box for so many days. My spirits flag. . . . So come dearest, dearest".

We cannot tell what she would have thought about the publication of such an intimate letter as this one of hers. But we know what Browning thought. At the very end of his life, when he had destroyed all the other letters in his possession, he showed his son the letters he and Elizabeth Barrett had exchanged, lying in the inlaid box where he had always kept them, arranged and numbered in their consecutive order; and he said "There they are, do with them as you please when I am dead and gone".

The bequest of Haydon's journals, and the further details
about his death which Kenyon had related, depressed Miss
Barrett so much that on Tuesday 7th July she had to write to
her blind friend Boyd to say that she could not yet fix a date for
the second visit which she had promised to pay him. She had
managed one visit, in the previous week. She had gone up to
his dark little room and found him sitting in his chair with his
head bent down, chin against chest. She had kissed his forehead, and he had talked querulously to her about Ossian, and
forced her to drink Cyprus wine which she did not want. It
had been a sad occasion and her gratitude for his past kindnesses
could not make such visits any less painful.

This same morning of Tuesday 7th brought her a letter from
Forster, sent through Kenyon, advising her to write direct to
Talfourd about Haydon's journals. She much disliked the idea
of the letter to Talfourd, and wrote a hasty note to Browning
asking for his advice; she knew he was to dine with Talfourd
that evening. "*You* would manage it for me—but to mix *you*
up in it, will make a danger of a worse evil" she wrote.

Talfourd's house was a particularly dangerous place for
Browning's and Elizabeth Barrett's secret, because Talfourd
knew Miss Barrett's barrister brother George—Browning had
met him there several times; and George Barrett was the most
responsible of the Barrett brothers, and the one most in his
father's confidence, as far as any of Mr Barrett's children were
in his confidence, which was not at all far. Any sign shown by
Browning at Talfourd's of an undue concern for Miss Barrett's
affairs would be likely to come to Mr Barrett's ears, and he
might then cut her off entirely from any contact with Browning,
by letter or interview. Miss Barrett's reluctance to write to
Talfourd about Haydon's papers was chiefly because she did

not want to draw any attention on herself from that quarter at this juncture in her affairs; the fact that Talfourd was Haydon's executor made Haydon's bequest doubly embarrassing.

Thomas Noon Talfourd was not in himself an ill-disposed or even a very formidable figure, though Elizabeth Barrett, influenced by Miss Mitford, felt some distrust of him. He was the most obliging and urbane of men; upright, generous, equable, fluently chatty. By profession he was a barrister; he had been Member of Parliament for Reading; he was soon to be a Judge. But his real devotion was to literature rather than law, as a critic on the *New Monthly Magazine*, as the biographer of Charles Lamb, and as a dramatist. His plays *Ion* and *The Athenian Captive* had been staged by Macready and had brought him a high reputation. He was a friend of Browning, Miss Mitford, the Carlyles, Wordsworth, Forster, Macready and Dickens (who dedicated *The Pickwick Papers* to him). He was a considerate, philanthropic man whose last words (he actually died in Court, while charging a jury at the Stafford Assizes—the first Judge ever to die on the Bench) were an expression of regret for the want of sympathy which produced class hatred and consequently crime. Opposite his house in Russell Square, an old woman used to sit by a lamp-post selling fruit; Talfourd used to send out plates of food to her from his dinner-table, and one day, finding her sitting there in the rain, he bought her an umbrella. His kindness extended to animals; he used to dine with a cat sitting on his knee. Vanity over his literary achievements, a little jealousy over the literary successes of others, and a little insincerity due to the desire to please, seem to have been the only faults of this exemplary man. Elizabeth Barrett's comment on his play *Ion* might have been made on Talfourd himself—"beautiful rather morally than intellectually". Nothing that he wrote is read today; there was no enduring diamond in his mind and work. When he first made a speech in the House of Commons, Peel took out his pencil to make notes, and listened attentively for a few minutes, after which he put his pencil back in his pocket; he could tell that Talfourd had not the stuff in him to make a dangerous political opponent.

Talfourd has, however, two claims on us now. He was one of the very first to recognize and proclaim Wordsworth's genius, in defence of which he published *An Attempt to Estimate the Poetical Talent of the Present Age* in 1815, when he was only twenty and was supporting himself by journalism while he was reading for the Bar. His other claim, which deserves the gratitude of every English writer today, is that he did much to get the Law of Copyright amended in favour of authors. One of his most famous cases was his defence of the publisher Edward Moxon in a prosecution for blasphemous libel when he published *Queen Mab* in the first complete edition of Shelley's works. Talfourd's plea that offending passages must be considered in their context, and according to whether they contribute to the total effect of a real work of literature, anticipated the arguments put forward in the *Lady Chatterley's Lover* case.

Miss Mitford was deeply indebted to Talfourd for his help in getting her books published and her plays put on, and for many years she was a devoted admirer of his sincerity and integrity and the dazzling fluency of his conversation. "Listening to Mr Talfourd is like looking at the sun; it makes one's mind ache with excessive brilliancy. . . . To say that he harangues is nothing. All his talk is one harangue. It is impossible to slide in a word", "his eloquence is wonderful, so full, so genuine, so fresh". He introduced her to his literary friends, he read over her MSS, she stayed with him and his wife in Russell Square. Their friendship was cooled by his colossal conceit after the success of his play *Ion*, and there were now serious misunderstandings between them, though they still corresponded.

Talfourd even brought off the very uncommon feat of remaining on more or less good terms with Macready, and this although Macready had played the principal rôle in two of his plays; Macready practically always quarrelled with the dramatists in whose plays he appeared. Talfourd did not escape being occasionally described as envious, imbecile, treacherous and extremely disagreeable in Macready's diary, but this is comparatively mild, and they continued to meet frequently, and Macready once even made an unparalleled admission—that he had misjudged Talfourd. He thought very highly of *Ion*, though not of *The Athenian Captive*, in which his own rôle was less congenial; and on the whole he recognized Talfourd's amiability and good qualities.

Talfourd showed at his best in his relationship to Haydon. Miss Mitford introduced the two men, and for twenty years they had kept in touch. Talfourd contributed to a subscription to get Haydon out of the King's Bench Prison, and lent him money at intervals. Haydon always thought him eloquent, kind, good-hearted and full of fun—"the noblest Creature I ever knew, taking him in every way, Father, Husband, Brother, Son, Friend or enemy". In his will he named "my dear friend Serjeant Talfourd" as the first of his executors.

Haydon's executorship was a heavy and embarrassing load, but Talfourd undertook it with his usual good nature, organized the subscription for Mrs Haydon, and began the disentanglement of Haydon's debts and bequests. Haydon's will, being unwitnessed, was invalid. He had no assets, owed thousands of pounds, and all his pictures and papers were liable to be seized on behalf of his creditors. Talfourd had heard from Miss Mitford, who had sent him a copy of Miss Barrett's letter to her about the bequest of the Haydon papers, and he was much concerned lest Miss Barrett should get involved in a dispute with Haydon's creditors over the possession of the journals, if, without taking sound advice first, she simply carried out Haydon's wish that the journals should be sent to a publisher.

This was the situation when Browning arrived in Russell Square to dine with the Talfourds on this Tuesday evening. Three days earlier his host had had a new honour conferred on him: he had been sworn in as Queen's Serjeant by the Lord Chancellor, Lord Lyndhurst. Talfourd was considered by his friends to look more like a poet than a lawyer. He was thin and delicate-looking, with dark rather prominent eyes, a long Roman nose, a full lower lip and a dimpled chin. His voice was usually low and soft, but could take on a loud resonant ring when his feelings were stirred.

The conversation at dinner that night, when the ladies had withdrawn and the men were left to their wine, took a turn which provoked emphatic declarations from the host. Among the guests, as well as Browning, Edwin Landseer, and the mathematician Charles Babbage, was John Forster. Forster asked Talfourd how the subscription for Haydon's family was going. This led to a reference to the bequest of Haydon's papers to Miss Barrett, and Talfourd read out the letter about it which he had had from Miss Mitford, in which she quoted Elizabeth Barrett's lament over Haydon's death and commented "So speaks our great poetess".

"I suppose" added Talfourd dryly "that when Miss Barrett writes about Miss Mitford, she concludes 'And so speaks our great dramatist' ". Miss Mitford's letter, and her quotations from what Elizabeth Barrett had said about Haydon in the first horror of his death, were indiscreet and sounded foolish enough when they were read out to this company of men at the dinner table, and a good deal of ridicule of the two women writers followed. One of the men said that Miss Barrett was plainly a *very* particular friend of Haydon's; another said that her house appeared to be a refuge for his goods against his creditors. Talfourd confirmed this. "Haydon, it seems, was in the habit of using Miss Barrett's house to deposit his pictures and papers. She could never have known the nature of the transaction nor the very serious consequences it involved".

Talfourd probably meant chiefly to condemn Haydon's action in placing Miss Barrett in such a predicament, but Browning thought the phrase about "using Miss Barrett's house" had such an offensive implication, particularly after the previous insinuation that she and Haydon had been "very particular friends", that he could contain his anger no longer.

"Miss Barrett never saw Haydon" he broke in. "I suppose she could not bring herself to refuse admittance to what he chose to send to her house. Probably he selected her for the Editorship precisely on account of her isolation from the world".

Browning stopped here, and gave no explanation of how he came to know that Haydon and Miss Barrett had never met; but his outburst seems to have checked the conversation. Forster left soon afterwards, and when the men went upstairs

179

to the drawing-room, Browning cornered Talfourd and said that he knew Miss Barrett by correspondence, that she had told him a few of the circumstances of her contacts with Haydon, and that she had at once thought of Talfourd himself as the best person to ask for advice about the journals. Talfourd's reply was that Haydon's will, and consequently the bequest of his papers to Miss Barrett, was an absurdity. The papers were the undoubted property of the creditors, and if Miss Barrett made any attempt to publish them, or even let it be known that they were in her possession, she would subject herself to a legal prosecution. Talfourd agreed with Browning that Haydon had left them to Miss Barrett because he hoped that she would publish them in full with all their offensive passages. Haydon had first asked Talfourd himself to undertake the care of them, but Talfourd had refused. Eventually, if Haydon's creditors permitted, some part of the journals might be published, with advantage to Mrs Haydon, but she was not in immediate want of money as the subscription had provided for that.

"The course I would recommend Miss Barrett to adopt" concluded Talfourd "is to let the deposit—if she has such a deposit, which I do not *know*" (and here he paused, but Browning was restrained enough to say nothing) "lie untouched—not giving them up to anybody, any creditor, to Mrs Haydon's prejudice". He concluded by saying that if Miss Barrett would put him in possession of the facts "I can arrange everything with her brother, when I meet him on circuit—I know him—he is a very promising youth". This hint of what was the proper channel made it slightly more difficult for Browning to tell Talfourd he would transmit a message to Miss Barrett; but at seven o'clock next morning he wrote an account of the evening to her, advising her to write immediately to Talfourd, explaining the facts about her possession of the journals and asking for Talfourd's advice. If she preferred to write through her brother, he should be reminded that Talfourd did not know that Browning and Miss Barrett were personally acquainted, only that they corresponded with each other. How intricate, how dangerous it all was, and it was all Haydon's fault for having involved Miss Barrett in his miserable affairs; Browning added an angry description of what Talfourd had told him about Haydon's debts and his wild "Last Thoughts" about Wellington and Napoleon—"all this wretched stuff, in a room theatrically arranged,—here his pictures, there—God forgive us all, fools or wise by comparison!"

Browning's embarrassment in deciding how much he could say without revealing how close he and Elizabeth Barrett were, was a repetition on an enlarged scale of an incident at another dinner of Talfourd's, a few months earlier. At that dinner party Browning, Haydon, Maclise and Miss Barrett's brother George were present. After dinner Browning and George Barrett happened to look together at a big green morocco-bound book lying on a table in the drawing-room. It was majestically labelled *Volume II*, and they found that it consisted of congratulatory letters written to Talfourd about his play *Ion*—private letters, but they had been bound and indexed and laid out on the drawing-room table for the edification of visitors. Browning and George Barrett, astonished at such a notion, took up the book between them to examine it, and turning to the index, found there "Miss Barrett" and a little further on, "Browning". George Barrett read both the poets' letters with much amusement, and teased his sister about it afterwards. But Browning could not read Elizabeth Barrett's faint small handwriting at the distance at which George Barrett was holding the book, and did not dare to peer too closely for fear of revealing too much interest. He found his own resurrected letter embarrassingly enthusiastic when he read it, he felt the whole business was distasteful, and that close juxtaposition of BA- and BR- in the index gave him a feeling of danger, of privacy doubly invaded, so that he sheered nervously away. But next day the letters flew to and fro between him and Elizabeth Barrett, working in unwearying detail over the little incident and how it might arouse George Barrett's suspicions.

Browning's fairly frequent meetings with Miss Barrett's brothers and sisters at parties were interesting but uneasy experiences for him. There was the pleasure of talking them over with Elizabeth Barrett afterwards, of seeing her in another relationship, the conventional setting of his black pearl. But there was always danger of betraying how much he knew, how often he came to Wimpole Street, of dropping some resounding brick.

Now on this Tuesday evening Browning was back in Talfourd's drawing-room, with the same green-bound *Volume II* lying on the table, but in a situation far more dangerous for suspicion and betrayal of his secret engagement to Elizabeth Barrett. Moreover he had not seen her for eight long days. But when he got home after his dinner with the Talfourds, he found a letter from her saying he must come at three o'clock next day. She could not go any longer without seeing him. It might be dangerous, in a house more than ever full of watchful eyes, but he must come.

Browning saw Elizabeth Barrett on the afternoon of Wednesday 8th July, and told her more about the dinner at Talfourd's than his early morning letter had had time for, and abused Haydon very heartily to her, and told her that the way in which her name had been bandied about at the dinner party of the previous night had made him long more than ever for their marriage, so that he should have the right to speak out and protect her.

She defended Haydon, and she gave Browning Haydon's last letters to take away and read. He put them in his pocket and forgot them till after he had gone away, out of the house and along the street, because he was still thinking of her. When he remembered them, he stopped under a gateway to look through them. As he read them, his heart was pricked at what he had said against Haydon. He saw now that there was something admirable in Haydon's sense of vocation, and that when he was at his best—as he was in writing to Miss Barrett—he was good and even great. Browning still thought him a weak man, destroyed by griefs that were not really overwhelming or intolerable compared with what others had borne. His suicide must have been a sudden impulse—he could not have intended it when he wrote these letters.

Browning's recantation was a joy to Miss Barrett. She had felt sure that he would be touched by the letters, that he was too generous and pitiful to do injustice to Haydon, weak as he was. She agreed that "his conscience was not a sufficient witness— nor was God. He must also have the Royal Academy and the appreciators of Tom Thumb". But then she wrote her final word on Haydon, perhaps the most understanding of all the obituaries, published or private, that were dedicated to Haydon. "That he had in him the elements of greatness—that he looked

to noble aims in art and life, however distractedly—that his
thoughts and feelings were not those of a common man—it is
true, it is undeniable. . . . Poor Haydon! Think what an agony
life was to him, so constituted!—his own genius a clinging
curse! the fire and the clay in him seething and quenching one
another!—the man seeing maniacally in all men the assassins
of his fame! and, with the whole world against him, struggling
for the thing that was his life, through night and day, in
thoughts and in dreams—struggling, stifling, breaking the
hearts of the creatures dearest to him, in the conflict for which
there was no victory, though he could not choose but fight it.
Tell me if Laocoon's anguish was not as an infant's sleep, compared to this? . . . As to grief as grief—of course he had no
killing grief. But he *suffered*".

In some ways it was a pity that Elizabeth Barrett did not
undertake the editing of Haydon's journals. She understood a
good deal of how his mind worked. The comparison with
Laocoon is in Haydon's own vein of hero-personification. But
her personal preoccupations at this time, and her ignorance of
art and artists, made it impossible, and on this Wednesday
evening, after Browning left her, she wrote to Talfourd and
told him that she had the journals but could not accept responsibility for them, and asked for his advice and directions,
as Haydon's executor. After this, she and Browning put the
thought of Haydon behind them, and gave their minds and
hearts to their own increasingly critical situation.

The trunks full of the journals went back from Wimpole
Street to Mrs Haydon in Burwood Place. The Haydon family
decided that they would like Miss Mitford to edit the journals,
but she declined. To the Haydons she gave the excuse that she
was "not sufficiently conversant with the artist world", but she
told her friends that she knew the journals must contain much
that would hurt the feelings of Haydon's friends and acquaintances, and much about himself that no real friend of his would
wish to see published. Like all Haydon's friends, she was anxious
as to what letters and sayings of her own would be quoted in
Haydon's journals when they came to be published. Miss
Barrett had the same worry, and took pains to get back her

letters to Haydon; when they were returned, she kept them all her life and they were sold with all the rest of the Brownings' papers at the Sotheby sale in 1913. Miss Mitford was reassured about her letters to Haydon by Tom Taylor, who was finally chosen to edit the journals, and who wrote to Miss Mitford that he had read her letters to Haydon in the course of his editing, that they did her nothing but credit, but that he was not proposing to make use of them in his selection from Haydon's papers.

The versatile Tom Taylor, dramatist, editor and lecturer on English Literature, was responsible for the edition of Haydon's Autobiography and Journals which was the main source of information about Haydon for over a century. As a selector and arranger, he did well; his preliminary comments on Haydon are fair but not sympathetic. He found Haydon's claims to heroism and martyrdom unconvincing, and thought the book valuable chiefly as "a curious piece of psychological revelation, and a not uninteresting, though mournful, picture of artist life".

It had a stronger interest than that for Haydon's former friends. Milnes thought the book "as pathetic and strange as Rousseau's". Miss Mitford called it the book of the year, and its author a man whom it was impossible not to like. Mrs Browning wrote from Rome that she could hardly shake off the pain of the book, it was written in heart's blood.

When Tom Taylor had done his work, the journals went back to the Haydon family. Mrs Haydon died the year after they were published. She left the journals to her son Frank, who kept them in two metal chests and brooded over them, occasionally adding bitter footnotes to his father's flights of rhetoric. He allowed his brother Frederic access to them to make extracts for *Benjamin Robert Haydon: Correspondence and Table Talk* which he published in 1876. Frank Haydon killed himself in 1887, and his daughter, who inherited the journals, guarded them from all researchers till they were bought and taken to America after her death in 1935, and finally published in full by Professor Willard Pope in 1960 and 1963, in five huge volumes quite as long as the Richardson sagas which Haydon hoped to emulate. "The style, the individuality of Richardson, which I wish not curtailed by an Editor"—that one clause of Haydon's invalid will has been carried out at last.

The subsequent history of the pictures which Haydon left with Miss Barrett just before his death is curious and confused. The portrait of Miss Mitford was in Frederic Haydon's possession for many years, by his own account, but Miss Mitford's biographer Miss Vera Watson says that it remained in Mr Barrett's possession for some years after his daughter married and went to Italy, and there is some evidence that in the 1850's it was in the possession of Francis Bennoch, a friend and creditor of Haydon's, and was used by John Lucas as the basis for his picture of Miss Mitford which is now in the National Portrait Gallery and which, though dated 1852, shows Miss Mitford as a youngish woman, as she was when Haydon did his portrait of her in 1825. Haydon's portrait of her is now in the Reading Art Gallery. Haydon himself always liked this portrait as much as Miss Mitford and her friends disliked this "cookmaid" version of her, with its round jolly cheeks and snub nose and frilly cap.

Haydon's portrait of Wordsworth on Helvellyn, which he also sent to Miss Barrett just before his death, was afterwards sent to Kendal by his executors, as it was thought more likely to sell in the Wordsworth country. It was finally bought by Cornelius Nicholson, who then sent it to Rydal Mount for Wordsworth's daughter Dora Quillinan to see. She was dying, then, and it was shown to her as she lay in bed. "It is perfection" she said. Now it hangs in the National Portrait Gallery, and is the best known of all Haydon's pictures.

Haydon would have been outraged by the idea that the best known of his pictures should be a portrait. He hated painting portraits; if he had a day of it ahead of him, he woke with a sour taste in his mouth, whereas if he had a historical painting to work on, he tingled with excitement at the thought of getting down to it. The thought of the "meagre wrinkled accidents of booby faces" which he would have to reproduce in portraits made him feel sick. "What work! Miserable, namby stuff!— small—spiritless" he wrote angrily in his diary after a day spent in completing a portrait of Mrs Talfourd. Great historical events and the heroes that caused them should be portrayed in an ideal style, not with individual realism; he was entirely opposed to the "warts and all" theory. He would have found the principle behind the National Portrait Gallery—with the foundation of which, ten years after his death, his pupil Eastlake and Thomas Carlyle were so much concerned—a rather vexatious one. It was right that the State should patronize art and honour its great men; Palmerston's dictum, when proposing to the House of Commons the founding of the National Portrait Gallery, that "there cannot, I feel convinced, be a greater incentive to mental exertion, to noble actions, to good conduct on the part of the living, than for them to see before them the features of those who have done things which are worthy of our admiration", would have been entirely sympathetic to Haydon. But to his thinking, the mighty dead should be shown in the act of doing the things worthy of our admiration, not in the mere accident, the unheroic irregularity, of their natural appearance. It would not be in the National Portrait Gallery that he would have chosen to have his work best known to posterity; it would be bitter indeed for him to know that anyone in London can see his portraits of Wordsworth and Leigh Hunt, but his grandest work, *The Raising of Lazarus*, is inaccessibly stacked away on a roller in the cellars of the Tate Gallery.

As Haydon's journals and pictures were dispersed from Wimpole Street, the men and women whose lives were interwoven with the last days of his life scattered from the stuffiness of a London July to seek fresh air and quiet nights, green countrysides and snowy mountains, in the North or across the Channel.

Carlyle prepared to join his wife at Liverpool, on his way to Scotland. He left London after a dismal struggle with his packing—he had run out of tobacco, a waistcoat lacked a button, he had to find an address that his wife wanted him to bring, he had to write letters altering his plans and arranging about his horse, he had to fit in far too many interviews and callers before he left London, he had somehow to convey to Lady Harriet Baring that Mrs Carlyle was determined to break off their relationship, and yet not quite to break it off himself, either. He was full of chagrin and depression, and of anxiety about the black confusions of his wife's mind. Consequently when he arrived at the seaside house, quiet and airy among its lawns and woods, where Mrs Carlyle was staying, he neither found nor brought peace. He was miserable, and Mrs Carlyle—headachy and short of sleep—was sharp and touchy, especially when he revealed that he was going to meet the Barings during his time in Scotland. Lugubriously he went on to stay with his mother in Scotsbrig, where he could not sleep; when he did meet the Barings at Moffat, it rained all the time and everything went badly; his wife's letters went astray and he thought she was deliberately keeping silent to punish him for the meeting with the Barings. Their marriage was on the verge of shipwreck, even in his eyes.

But Mrs Carlyle was recovering. She had gone on from Liverpool to stay with Geraldine Jewsbury at Manchester, and had

there been so tactfully handled, so fully occupied, that she began
to feel better in health and calmer in spirits. The shipwreck,
after all, was averted. Like a good many other middle-aged
couples, they had reached a crisis in their marriage, of a kind
which seems at the time the final wave which must sink the
ship, but which is seen afterwards to be one wave of many,
driving the ship onto a different course, leaking and listing
perhaps but still afloat, and gradually righting itself.

When both the Carlyles were dead, and Froude had published Carlyle's self-accusing account of the difficult side of
their marriage, the friends who had known them well at that
time spoke out about it. Browning, who always revered Carlyle,
defended him against the charge of unkindness to his wife.
Mrs Carlyle, he said, was a hard unlovable woman; if there
were any domestic quarrels, she was the more to blame of the
two. Milnes wrote to his daughter—"You ask me about Mrs
Carlyle. The book makes the case worse than it was. She was
really very fond of Lady Ashburton" [as Lady Harriet Baring
became] "and certainly not jealous in the vulgar sense of the
word". The final verdict is perhaps Tennyson's—"Mr and
Mrs Carlyle on the whole enjoyed life together, else they
would not have chaffed one another so heartily".

The Carlyles' recent guest, Gräfin Hahn-Hahn, also went north
in July. We hear of her in York, very well satisfied with her
stay in London, with the welcome she had received, and with
England altogether; she found the healthy strong-willed indivi-
dualism of the English as reviving to her as a chalybeate spring,
she told a German friend. But the great beautiful empty
cathedrals of the North confirmed the leanings towards the
Roman Catholic Church which she was already beginning to
feel. She was shocked by the riches of the ecclesiastical digni-
taries, and compared them with the Catholic priest who has
"no beautiful wife to be adorned with diamonds". Her acquaintances in the North of England were clearly the Arch-
deacon Grantleys of the day, rather than the perpetual curates;
Mrs Josiah Crawley of Hogglestock had not much chance of
being hung with diamonds, nor had Charlotte Yonge's Mrs

Edward Underwood of Bexley. As Amely Bölte wrote waspishly about Gräfin Hahn-Hahn, "in such a short visit one sees only the outside of things . . . one ought not to want to write about a country till one has seen a little deeper". But Gräfin Hahn-Hahn was quite satisfied that she understood the English, and she liked them very well on the whole—and they liked her. Monckton Milnes' summing up of her visit was "The only lion in the way of literature has been Gräfin Hahn-Hahn, a plain woman with one eye, but so intelligent and light in hand that she won favour in all eyes, although encumbered with a Reisegefährte whose name she did not bear, and who was thus difficult to place in an intelligible position in England".

Milnes himself, who normally went abroad or to his family home in Yorkshire in the summer, could not make any plans this July because his mother was at Brighton, seriously ill, and because of the political situation; the Liberals, whom he had joined when Peel fell, were now in power. Peel, at last at leisure down in Staffordshire, felt no envy for his successors. "I find the day too short for my present occupations, which consist chiefly in lounging in my library, directing improvements, riding with the boys and my daughter, and pitying Lord John and his colleagues" he wrote from Drayton late that summer, and in August he told Prince Albert how much he was enjoying the contrast between his present repose and his past official life. The Queen and Prince Albert, too, were enjoying their summer holidays; they had had to go up to London in early July to take leave of the outgoing Government and install the new one, but now they were thankfully back in the Isle of Wight, walking, driving, sitting out in the beautiful island weather.

One of their less loyal subjects, Macready, was also island-bound for as much of a holiday as he ever had. After a breakfast with Samuel Rogers, a tremendous orgy of feeling over George Sand's *Consuelo*, and a visit to Kensal Green Cemetery to the tomb of his little daughter Joan who had died six years earlier, he left London for the Channel Islands. He performed in both Jersey and Guernsey, appearing in Bulwer's play *Richelieu*, now eight years old, which had caused such trouble when it was first produced, and when Forster gave dire offence to Bulwer by falling asleep when Macready read it aloud after dinner. Mrs Macready did not accompany her husband to the Channel Islands; three weeks later another daughter was born to them, and was christened Cecilia Benvenuta.

Some were going further afield for their holidays that summer, or would like to have gone. The Wordsworths hoped to go to the Pyrenees, but they were detained in Westmorland by the approaching death of Wordsworth's nephew John, and the convalescence—or what seemed the convalescence—of their daughter Dora, back at last from Spain and Portugal. Wordsworth felt he needed a change from home, but everything around him was soothing and beautiful, and also, though he could still walk all day in the hills, he could not bear the motion of a carriage, rheumatic as he was. He was seventy-six, and had less than four years to live.

"I understand you are going on a summer excursion with Alfred Tennyson" he wrote to his publisher Moxon. "I hope all will go well with you and that you may enjoy yourselves". Tennyson, after many hesitations, left London with Moxon on 2nd August and went by Ostend, Bruges and Liège to Cologne, where they took a boat up the Rhine, and went on by train and diligence to Switzerland. They rode and climbed in the mountains round Lucerne, and then took a circuit through the Bernese Alps to Chamonix and on to Geneva. Tennyson was edgy and bored by chattering travellers at first, it was hot and he could not sleep; there were fleas, the beer was bad, and the hotels were noisy. He and Moxon were untidy and travel-stained by the time they took a steamer from Geneva to Lausanne to see Dickens, who hardly recognized them as they came up his drive one wet evening late in August, as he was walking in the loggia after dinner, thinking about *Dombey and Son*. When he saw who it was, he gave them a hospitable welcome; they had dined on the steamer, but he gave them Liebfraumilch and crisp unsweetened biscuits and a great many cigars. Moxon was wearing a deplorable straw hat, and talked in bursts with "you know" at the end of every sentence, and

altogether seemed to Dickens—who was still piqued that
Tennyson had refused to come abroad with him and his family—
"an odd companion for a man of genius". The man of genius
himself was at ease and well pleased with the evening, but
refused to go into raptures over the Mer de Glace, as Dickens
expected. His talk about it, Dickens told Forster, was much
like that of the man who had seen Niagara and said it was
nothing but water. Moxon later told Kenyon, who told Miss
Barrett, that Tennyson had been disappointed with the mountains, and Tennyson said as much himself to Fitzgerald of the
great mountains. He was very short-sighted; he saw huge
bright distant objects, stars and mountain peaks, as haloed
pencilled outlines. And he and Moxon were unlucky in their
weather; dawns were dim, sunsets feeble, low-lying clouds
often hid the lakes. But sometimes the great red rock ledges,
the plunging outline of the crags, seemed to Tennyson utterly
satisfying, and all through his journey he was observing and
remembering the effects of flowing water and shifting cloud
which always meant most to him in a landscape—the shimmer
on the moonlit Rhine at Cologne, the green river roaring against
the piers of a bridge, dark lake waters marbled with cloud
reflections, mists smoking up from the mountain slopes and
shutting out and then revealing the valleys below. The silver
horns and icy ravines of the mountains, the woods and villages
far down in the valleys, brought out a pattern of feeling which
was latent in his imagination, and while he was at Lauterbrunnen
and Grindelwald, he wrote *Come down, O Maid, from yonder
mountain height*.

The Talfourds also visited Dickens at Lausanne. They left
London in August, and had a wet and miserable crossing from
Brighton to Dieppe, went partly by diligence and partly by
train to Rouen, Paris and Chalons, then by river steamer down
the Rhône to Lyons and to Avignon. Talfourd wrote it all up
afterwards in his *Vacation Rambles*, noticing all the interesting
monuments, making all the right quotations, working in all the
historical references, and bringing in humorously resigned
anecdotes about the discomforts of a diligence or an inn, at
calculated intervals to vary the tone. The Talfourds stayed

with the Dickens family "and I think they were very happy" wrote Dickens to Forster. "He was in his best aspect; the manner so well known to us, not the less lovable for being laughable; and if you could have seen him going round and round the coach that brought them, as a preliminary to paying the *voiturier* to whom he couldn't speak, in a currency he didn't understand, you never would have forgotten it". They set off again after two days, and Dickens—just recovered from a spell of giddiness and headache and bloodshot eyes—plunged back again into *The Battle of Life* and *Dombey and Son*.

Mrs Jameson left London in early September with her niece on a trip that was to take them to France and Italy. She went first to Paris and was there on Monday 21st September when a surprising message from Browning was given to her at her hotel in the Rue de la Ville-l'Evêque. She had seen Elizabeth Barrett several times before she left London, and had urged her to go to Italy for her health's sake, and offered to accompany her. Miss Barrett's evasive and embarrassed refusal had shown Mrs Jameson that her friend had some secret plan of her own for getting away from Wimpole Street; Mrs Jameson had even mentioned an elopement, but she meant it as a joke.

Browning and Elizabeth Barrett had discussed again and again whether to tell Mrs Jameson their secret, whether even to ask her to accompany them to Italy. But the fear of involving her in blame from the Barrett family always held them back. Their danger was growing; increasingly observant eyes were all round them. They were almost sure that Kenyon knew their secret; Boyd had had to be told; an old family friend, Miss Trepsack, had guessed; Arabel Barrett, who knew the secret, kept making "I could an if I would" remarks about it in front of others not supposed to know; Elizabeth Barrett's eldest brothers, Charles John and George, were full of conjectures. Worst of all, Mr Barrett was beginning to be suspicious and resentful of Browning's frequent visits. All through August the dangerous game went on; and then on 9th September Elizabeth Barrett heard that her whole family were to be carried off to the country. Three days later, she went out with her maid to

St Marylebone Church and was married to Browning. A week
after that, she left Wimpole Street for ever, and went away
with Browning.

They were in Paris thirty-six hours later, and Browning sent
for Mrs Jameson and told her he was married, and to whom.
She found Mrs Browning tired and ill after the journey from
London, but after a week's rest they all went on together to
Orleans, where Mrs Browning found savage letters from her
father and her brother George about her marriage. Then they
all travelled by boat down the Rhône to Avignon as the
Talfourds had done a month earlier, past castle-crowned vine-
terraced hills veiled in downpours of rain, and so to Marseilles,
to Genoa and to Pisa.

When Mrs Jameson heard of the marriage, she told the
Brownings that they were "wise people, wild poets or not".
But she wrote to Lady Byron that she did not feel sure the
marriage would end well, because she had no faith in the
poetic temperament as a means of permanent happiness. Mrs
Browning thought differently; she told her sister that it was
good for a woman to be loved by a man of imagination, because
he saw her in the lustre that his own ever-changing inspiration
shed on her.

All the friends whose opinion they most valued—Miss
Mitford, Kenyon, Milnes, Procter—wrote kind letters of con-
gratulation to the Brownings on their marriage. They heard
that it had been discussed at a dinner at the Carlyles', and that
Carlyle had declared he had more hopes of Browning than of
any other writer in England; but for almost a year there was
no letter from him. At last he sent a letter which gave the
Brownings more gratification than any other they had received.
He told them that not for years had any marriage among his
circle given him such pleasure as the Brownings' marriage had,
and went on—"Certainly if there ever was a union indicated
by the finger of Heaven itself, and sanctioned and prescribed
by the Eternal Laws under which poor transitory sons of Adam
live, it seemed to me, from all I could hear and know of it,
to be this! . . . Perpetually serene weather is not to be looked
for by anybody; least of all by the like of you two—in whom

precisely because more is given, more also in the same proportion is required: but unless I altogether mistake, there is a life-partnership which, in all kinds of weather, has in it a capacity of being blessed".

Haydon was buried in Paddington New Churchyard, and they put on his tombstone

> SACRED TO THE MEMORY
>
> OF
>
> BENJAMIN ROBERT HAYDON
>
> BORN JANUARY 25TH 1786
>
> DIED JUNE 22ND 1846
>
> HE DEVOTED FORTY TWO YEARS
>
> TO THE IMPROVEMENT OF THE TASTE
>
> OF THE ENGLISH PEOPLE
>
> IN HIGH ART
>
> AND DIED BROKEN HEARTED
>
> FROM PECUNIARY DISTRESS

The epitaph ended, not with a quotation from the Bible, but with the line from *King Lear* which was the last words he wrote in his diary before he killed himself.

Haydon had written an epitaph for himself twenty years earlier; it was longer and much more explicit, more a manifesto than an epitaph, calling on the Government to give due dignity to historical painting and describing himself as a victim to his own enthusiasm, since he had been destroyed for telling truth to power. After the date of his death in this epitaph was to come the statement that he died "believing in Christ as the Mediator and Advocate of Mankind". In the will which he made twenty years later, in the last hours of his life, he declared that he believed in the efficacy of the Atonement, hoped for forgiveness, and had no fear of appearing before the "Awful Consciousness of the invisible God".

Some of those who have written about Haydon have questioned whether he ever had any real religious experience. He

196

professed in his diary to be a deeply religious man. God was his refuge and his consoler, in whose justice and compassion he trusted in the worst moments of trouble. He told Wordsworth that Christianity was so closely interwoven with his whole nature that he knew it was the revealed Will of God as distinctly as if he had heard God's own voice telling him so. "It is in my heart, my brain, my blood". To Keats he wrote "*Trust in God* with all your might", and when Shelley, Hazlitt and Leigh Hunt tried to argue with him in favour of atheism, he refused even to discuss it. All his diary from beginning to end is full of prayers. "Prayer is available and can alter the apparent destiny of man" he wrote, and so he prayed for health and good eyesight, he prayed that he might be able to paint good pictures, he prayed for patrons who would buy them, he thanked God if a creditor had been staved off or a piece of drapery had worked out well in a picture or he had had a good idea for a background. Such petitions are not in favour today even with those who believe in the efficacy of prayer. We do not pray that we may catch a train, or be able to pay our income tax, or even, perhaps, that we may be able to write a good book. We think that such prayers diminish God into a mumbo-jumbo—or is it in fact that we feel them to be beneath *our* dignity? Haydon had no such patronizing consideration for the status of the Almighty. He was always ready to fling himself down on his knees and plead or be grateful for immediate material things to the God of whose close presence he was conscious all his life. God was there, at his elbow almost, listening, understanding, encouraging, singling him out. "Seeing Him that nobody else sees is the thing for me" he wrote, referring once again to a text that was specially favourite with him, and which he quoted again and again, the text from the *Epistle to the Hebrews* about Moses who "endured, as seeing Him who is invisible".

It is hard to say whether Haydon actually had true mystical experiences. He thought that he was vouchsafed visions and voices. The voices were audible startlingly distinct whispers bidding him—"On, on!"; "Go on!"; "Get up!"; urging him not to despond, not to give up, to do his duty, to trust in God; they even gave him such explicit instructions as to put his last sovereign in the collection plate at church. When Wordsworth wrote his sonnet to Haydon telling him to have faith in the whispers of the lonely Muse, he penetrated into the secret of Haydon's soul.

Sometimes Haydon would see instead of hear the words of encouragement, in the form of glittering fiery letters against a background of darkness, spelling out "Trust in God!", "Go on!" As a young man he had some visionary experiences— when he stood in Westminster Abbey and seemed to hear, beneath the roaring of the organ, the spirit of God breathing behind the altar; when Death appeared to him in the night in floating undulations of harmony, beams of sunny light and blasts of power; when he spent a day in the fields at Richmond and suddenly saw the flowery grass and hedges alive with millions of winged genii, shouting and adoring in a shifting haze of golden cloud. All his visions were lit by fire; often it seemed to him that a great fiery Eye was watching him. Sometimes it was the all-seeing eye of God, fixed, scintillating, glaring like a heated furnace at his youthful lust. Sometimes it was the Devil's eye that started out at him through the wall of a room, or rose up fiery and cruel in the darkness of his midnight bedroom, or looked out, tremendous, globular and black, from the face of a ruined man. Sometimes he would feel that the Devil was crushing his heart in "black, bony, clammy, clenching fingers". When he left his home in Plymouth, he passed the first night of his new life "in burning dreams of future glory, but at the end I saw a demon with his malicious and fiery smile, that seemed to warn and welcome me. He looked as if in the midst of a sun that, while it shone on my path, increased the brilliant darkness of his own figure".

Haydon lived, as his son Frederic said, in "an atmosphere of extraordinary interferences and miraculous inspirations, intimations and presentiments". A nineteenth-century Samuel, he lay in bed and heard a voice denouncing the iniquities of the house of Eli, in the shape of the Royal Academy. The words that were whispered in his ear always produced in him an access of strength, energy and courage. The question that has to be asked is, were the voices entirely ventriloquial, or did he perhaps hear a real Voice but one that was saying something different from what he thought he heard?

Most commentators have thought that he deceived himself entirely, that his God was nothing more than a gambler's mascot or lucky charm, that his prayers were begging letters despatched to the Almighty. The most charitable verdict is that of Mr Edmund Blunden: "Nor let us accept the complaint that his vehement religion, and habit of prayer, was only rhetoric, or Haydono-morphism". Did the God in whom he said he trusted, the people for whom he said he had sacrificed himself, did anyone at all, have any real existence for him outside himself?

"On 1st October 1806, setting my palette and taking brush in hand, I knelt down and prayed God to bless my career, to grant me energy to create a new era in art, and to rouse the people and patrons to a just estimate of the moral value of historical painting". When a man sees himself as divinely inspired to save a nation, is he able to see the salvation of the nation as a good in itself, separable from his mission to bring it about? Could Haydon ever have said with sincerity "So long as it is done, it doesn't matter who does it"?

Such questions would have been completely meaningless to Haydon himself. He knew with absolute conviction that Providence worked in History through the heroic actions of divinely-called great men. History itself was a series of historical paintings of great events, and to suggest that so long as a good is achieved, it does not matter who achieves it, would make no more sense than to suggest that the whole composition of his picture of *The Assassination of Dentatus* could just as well be centred on the distant trumpeter as on the lunging hero in the foreground and the boulder poised above his head. In the mind of Providence, the great historical moment had a composition like a picture. Haydon would have seen nothing ludicrous in the idea of a thirtieth-century painter choosing as the subject of a picture *Haydon Creating a New Era in Art*. Men could fail to seize their great moment when it came, as Haydon blamed Napoleon for doing, but then the whole composition fell to pieces, there was no question of its re-forming like a kaleidoscope. The nation to be saved, the man chosen to save it, the God who chose the man, were linked together. Perhaps the nation, and even the God, had no separate reality for the man outside their relationship to him, but they were not merely his tools, his stepping-stones. If they had no existence without him, he had no value in his own eyes except as he was called by and for them.

The heroes of History filed through Haydon's imagination, smiling and shaking their heads at him in "awful encouragement"—Alexander and Napoleon, Columbus and Cortez, Aristides and the Black Prince, Eucles, Dentatus and Curtius, whom Haydon painted leaping into the gulf, with his own face as the model of the calm resolute face between the helmet-flaps. He felt that he too was "Rome's greatest treasure", a brave citizen who had flung himself into a gulf for his country's good, and over whom the earth would close.

"He had much talent, of which he was very conscious" wrote Procter after Haydon's death; "violent passions; proud irrepressible hopes; delusions, if you will, on this head in an unreasonable degree. The very extent and character of these carried him beyond the limit of common sufferers. It is not enough to argue that a man's own ambition has no solid foundation in other minds. There it was, in the mind on which it was destined to operate".

One extended attempt has been made, in a brilliant novel, to penetrate the mind that was operated on by these delusions and suffered from them. The character of Casimir Lypiatt in Aldous Huxley's *Antic Hay* is based on Haydon, whose personality always fascinated Huxley. Casimir Lypiatt thought of himself as a Great Man. He felt the exultant consciousness of power growing in himself as he dreamed about a forthcoming exhibition of his paintings, which turned out to be a dismal failure. At the end of the book he is shown as preparing to shoot himself, and admitting in his farewell letter that he had misjudged his own powers, and deserved to be laughed at, though what seemed ludicrous to the onlookers was still agony to him.

Haydon sometimes doubted his own powers, but I do not think it ever crossed his mind that anyone could laugh at him.

Since he died, laughter—condescending, nervous, mocking, puzzled—has been his portion. Three weeks after his death, on Monday 13th July 1846, Browning had a dream that he was in a gallery of Haydon's pictures, one of which was a portrait of his wife. In the dream, Browning was convinced that Haydon was alive and well, and working somewhere near at hand. Browning's mother, who slept next door, heard him crying out in his sleep "Bravo! Bravo!" over and over again, with bursts of laughter.

APPENDIX

Note A. Chapter I, pages 18–19. *Two Supper Parties at Lord Jeffrey's House in March* 1846

The first party, on 3rd *March* 1846. Mentioned by Haydon under this date in his Diary (edited Professor Willard Pope, Vol. V pp. 522–3). Frederic Haydon, in *B. R. Haydon, Correspondence and Table Talk*, Vol. I pp. 463–4, gives his father's description of this party under the heading "Extracts from Letters to His Wife. Edinburgh, 13th March 1846", but it is clear from the coincidence of events described (dinner with Walter Scott's publisher Cadell, reference to the painter Watson Gordon, Haydon's sitting next to a beauty at Jeffrey's party) that the day in question is the same as the one entered under 3rd March by Haydon in his diary, and that Frederic Haydon (who was a very slapdash editor) has run together several letters from his father to his mother under the date of the latest. By a further piece of careless editing he has given the date "Wednesday 3rd March 1843" to a letter from Jeffrey to Haydon (*Correspondence and Table Talk*, Vol. I pp. 461–2) which must actually belong to March 1846, as (i) Haydon was not in Edinburgh in March 1843, but the letter ends "Let us see you again some evening before you go" (ii) it refers to the engraving of Haydon's portrait of Wordsworth, which was not engraved till 1846 (iii) it refers to "the fair creature you sat by", an obvious reference to the beauty whom Haydon sat next to at Jeffrey's party on 3rd March 1846. Jeffrey adds that she was "Mrs Forrest, the wife of the moustached American who was at the other table". The American actor Edwin Forrest, who had noticeable blue-black whiskers, was in Edinburgh at the beginning of March 1846, when he made himself conspicuous by hissing Macready's performance of Hamlet.

Appendix

The second party. Haydon gives the date of this as 11th March (*Diary*, Vol. V p. 525). Miss Rigby gives it as 9th March (*Letters and Journals of Lady Eastlake*, Vol. I p. 179). It was probably 10th March, as that was a Tuesday; Jeffrey's soirées were always on Tuesdays and Fridays. Macready makes no mention in his diary of having attended a supper party of Jeffrey's and has no entry at all for 10th March. He records in his diary that he played Hamlet on the 2nd, 9th and 16th March, Lear on the 4th, Richelieu on the 5th, Othello on the 6th, Macbeth on the 13th.

Note B. Chapter VIII, pages 79–81. Accounts of Haydon's Last Hours

My description of Haydon's last hours has been extracted from:

The *Morning Chronicle* Wednesday 24th June 1846

Life of B. R. Haydon, Historical Painter, from his Autobiography and Journals edited Tom Taylor

B. R. Haydon: Correspondence and Table Talk edited F. W. Haydon

The Life and Death of B. R. Haydon by Eric George

The accounts do not entirely coincide, especially as to whether the visit to the gun-maker or the conversation about the letter to the Duke of Sutherland came first, or as to the actual details of the suicide. In general I have followed the *Morning Chronicle* account which was the earliest full account to be published, before the inquest, and has details obviously supplied by someone closely connected with the Haydon family, perhaps Coulton.

Note C. Chapter XI, pages 104–105. Leigh Hunt on Haydon's Death

Leigh Hunt's letter about Haydon's death is dated "11th and 12th August 1846" in Thornton Hunt's 1862 edition of his father's letters (Vol. II pp. 84–89) but this must be a mistake. Leigh Hunt could hardly have seen an announcement of Haydon's death in a newspaper appearing six weeks after the event, and if he had, it could not have been news to him, as he had seen Forster since Haydon's death (*Letters*, Vol. II pp 80–81) and it is inconceivable that Forster—whose paper the *Daily News* had been reporting and commenting on Haydon's death, the inquest and the subscription for his widow, all through the weeks after 22nd June, and who had been involved in negotiations over the dead man's papers—would not have discussed the tragedy with Haydon's old friend Leigh Hunt at their next meeting after the event. Hunt's letter, which has been dated "11th and 12th August", is nearly all about his claim to a pension and reads as if it followed closely on the letter dated 15th June on the same subject (*Letters*, Vol. 11 pp. 79–80). The later letter refers to a forthcoming visit by Forster to Wimbledon, probably the one which took place at the end of June (*Letters*, Vol. II pp. 80–1), and it should probably be dated about 26th June, which would be a reasonable date for Leigh Hunt to have seen an announcement of Haydon's death.

Note D. Chapter XXII, page 186. Haydon's Portraits of Words-
    worth

It has been suggested by Professor Shackford in her edition of Elizabeth Barrett's letters to Haydon, and by Professor Pope in Note 2 on page 552, Vol. V of his edition of Haydon's diary, that the Wordsworth portrait which Haydon left with Miss Barrett just before his death cannot have been the *Wordsworth on Helvellyn* which is now in the National Portrait Gallery because Haydon said in his Will, written four days later, that the picture was in the possession of the engraver Lupton. But the actual sentence in the Will reads—"Lupton has a Portrait of Wordsworth, my property, engraved. He is to be paid 80 gns". I take this to mean that Lupton had the block of the Wordsworth engraving; the block was Haydon's property but had not been paid for. There is no implication that the portrait from which the block had been made was still in Lupton's possession. The engraving had already been fairly widely circulated; the Wordsworth family had seen a version of it (*Letters*, edited de Selincourt, Vol. III p. 1276, letter of 24th January 1846), so had Lord Jeffrey (see Note A above), so had Miss Rigby (*Letters and Journals of Lady Eastlake*, Vol. I p. 179). Miss Barrett had the *Wordsworth on Helvellyn* portrait in her possession twice, once in 1842 and once in June 1846; she was also lent Haydon's other, seated, *Wordsworth on Helvellyn*, in April 1843 (Elizabeth Barrett, *Letters to Haydon*, letter of April 1843). This picture was subsequently in the possession of Francis Bennoch and is now in Dove Cottage (*Portraits of Wordsworth* by Frances Blanshard).

Note E. Chapter XXIII, pages 191–192. Tennyson's Visit to Dickens at Lausanne

I have assumed that the "A." and "N." of Dickens' letter of 24th August 1846 to Forster (*Letters*, edited Dexter, Vol. I p. 781) are Alfred Tennyson and Edward Moxon. Dickens describes two travellers who arrived for an evening at his house at Lausanne on 23rd August, having come from Geneva by steamer. This fits with the dates and route of Tennyson's and Moxon's journey. Tennyson recorded in his letter of 12th November 1846 to Fitzgerald (*Alfred Lord Tennyson, a Memoir* by his Son) that he and Moxon had visited Dickens during their Swiss tour, and had been given Liebfraumilch to drink. Dickens says that he gave "some fine Rhine wine" to "A.", and also "cigars innumerable", which would fit Tennyson, an inveterate smoker. "A." and "N.", Dickens complained, were unimpressed by the Mer de Glace; Tennyson is known to have been disappointed by the Swiss mountains (letter of 12th November 1846 to Fitzgerald. Elizabeth Barrett, letter of 3rd September 1846 to Robert Browning). "A." and "N." had missed much fine mountain scenery because of low cloud, reported Dickens; so had Tennyson and Moxon, as the former told Fitzgerald. Dickens found "N." vulgar; on a previous occasion he had complained of Moxon's "coarse and vulgar babbling" (letter of 22nd May 1840 to Talfourd. *Letters*, Vol. I p. 258).

LIST OF SOURCES

Note: biographies are listed under their subject, not under their author; thus—
>
> HAYDON, B. R.
>> George, Eric. *The Life and Death of B. R. Haydon*
>
> but with a cross-reference to the author of the biography; thus—
>
> George, Eric. See under HAYDON.

Acland, Alice. See under NORTON, Caroline.

ALLINGHAM, William. *A Diary*. Macmillan. 1907.

Armour, R. W. See under PROCTER, B. W.

Balston, T. See under MARTIN, John.

BARRETT, Elizabeth. *Letters*, edited F. G. Kenyon. 2 vols. Smith Elder. 1897.

> *Letters to B. R. Haydon*, edited M. H. Shackford. O.U.P. 1939.

> *Elizabeth Barrett to Miss Mitford*, edited Betty Miller. John Murray. 1954.

> *Letters to her Sister, 1846–1859*, edited Leonard Huxley. John Murray. 1929.

> *Elizabeth Barrett to Mr Boyd*, edited. B. P. McCarthy. John Murray. 1955.

> Taplin, G. B. *The Life of E. B. Browning*. John Murray. 1957.

Batho, Edith. See under WORDSWORTH, William.

BEWICK, William. *Life and Letters*, edited T. Landseer. 2 vols. Hurst & Blackett. 1871.

Blanshard, Frances. See under WORDSWORTH, William.

BLESSINGTON, Lady. Sadler, Michael. *Blessington d'Orsay*. Constable. 1933.

List of Sources

Blunden, Edmund. See under HAYDON, B. R. and HUNT, Leigh.

Blunt, Reginald. See under CARLYLE, Thomas.

BOASE, T. S. R. *English Art 1800–1870*. Clarendon Press. 1959.

Brain, J. A. See under TALFOURD, T. N.

BROOKFIELD, C. H. E. and F. M. *Mrs Brookfield and Her Circle*. 2 vols. Pitman. 1905.

BROWNING, Robert and BARRETT, Elizabeth. *Letters*. 2 vols. Harpers. 1899.

    Letters of the Brownings to George Barrett, edited Paul Landis. University of Illinois Press. 1958.

BROWNING, Robert. *Life and Letters*, edited Mrs Sutherland Orr, revised F. G. Kenyon. Smith Elder. 1908.

    Letters, edited T. L. Hood. John Murray. 1933.

    Ritchie, Lady. *Tennyson, Ruskin and Browning*. Macmillan. 1896.

    Miller, Betty. *Robert Browning, a Portrait*. John Murray. 1952.

    De Vane, W. C. *A Browning Handbook*. Appleton-Century-Crofts, New York. 1955.

Buckley, J. H. See under TENNYSON, Alfred.

Burdett, Osbert. See under CARLYLE, Thomas.

Butt, John. See under DICKENS, Charles.

BYRON, Lady. Moore, Doris Langley. *The Late Lord Byron*. John Murray. 1961.

CARLYLE, Thomas. *Past and Present*. Dent. 1912.

    Reminiscences. Longmans. 1887.

    New Letters of T. Carlyle, edited Alexander Carlyle. 2 vols. John Lane. 1904.

    Letters to Varnhagen von Ense, 1837–1857, edited Richard Preuss. Longmans. 1892.

    Letters to His Wife, edited Trudy Bliss. Gollancz. 1953.

J. A. Froude. *Thomas Carlyle: A History of his Life in London, 1834–1881*. 2 vols. Longmans Green. 1884.

Duffy, Charles Gavan. *Conversations with Carlyle*. Sampson Low, Marston. 1892.

Wylie, W. H. *Thomas Carlyle: the Man and His Books*. Fisher Unwin. 1909.

Burdett, Osbert. *The Two Carlyles*. Faber 1930.

Symons, Julian. *Thomas Carlyle: the Life and Ideas of a Prophet*. Gollancz. 1952.

Blunt, Reginald. *The Carlyles' Chelsea Home*. G. Bell. 1895.

Carlyle's House. Illustrated Catalogue and Descriptive Notes. Country Life, for the National Trust. 1954.

CARLYLE, Jane Welsh. *Letters and Memorials of Jane Welsh Carlyle*, edited J. A. Froude. 3 vols. Longmans Green, 1883.

New Letters and Memorials of Jane Welsh Carlyle edited Alexander Carlyle. 2 vols. John Lane the Bodley Head. 1903.

Letters to her Family, 1839–1863, edited Leonard Huxley. John Murray. 1924.

A New Selection of her Letters, edited Trudy Bliss. Gollancz. 1949.

Hanson, Laurence & Elisabeth. *Necessary Evil: the Life of Jane Welsh Carlyle*. Constable. 1952.

Scudder, Townsend. *Jane Welsh Carlyle*. Macmillan 1939.

Cecil, Lord David. See under NORTON, Caroline.

Claydon, P. W. See under ROGERS, Samuel.

Cockburn, Lord. See under JEFFREY, Lord.

Cornwall, Barry. See under PROCTER, B. W.

CREWE, Annabel. *Unpublished Diary*. Houghton Papers, Trinity College, Cambridge.

DICKENS, Charles. *Letters*, edited Walter Dexter. 3 vols. Nonesuch Press. 1938.

Letters to Angela Burdett-Coutts, edited Edgar Johnson. Cape. 1953.

———————————

Forster, John. *Life of Charles Dickens*. 2 vols. Dent. 1927.

Pope-Hennessy, Una. *Charles Dickens, 1812–1870*. Chatto & Windus. 1945.

Pearson, Hesketh. *Dickens, His Character, Comedy and Career*. Methuen. 1949.

Butt, John and Tillotson, Kathleen. *Dickens at Work*. Methuen. 1957.

Tillotson, Kathleen. *Novels of the Eighteen-Forties*. Clarendon Press. 1954.

Duffy, Charles Gavan. See under CARLYLE, Thomas.

EASTLAKE, Lady (Miss Rigby). *Journals and Correspondence*, edited C. E. Smith. 2 vols. John Murray. 1895.

Elwin, Malcolm. See under FORSTER, John and HAYDON, B. R.

ESPINASSE, F. *Literary Recollections and Sketches*. Hodder & Stoughton. 1893.

Finberg, A. J. See under TURNER, J. M. W.

FORSTER, John. Elwin, Malcolm. *Victorian Wall-Flowers*. Cape. 1937.

Renton, Richard. *John Forster and His Friendships*. Chapman & Hall. 1912.

FRITH, W. P. *My Autobiography and Reminiscences*. 3 vols. Bentley. 1887.

Froude, J. A. See under CARLYLE, Thomas and Jane Welsh.

George, Eric. See under HAYDON, B. R.

Gittings, Robert. See under KEATS, John.

GREVILLE, Charles. *Memoirs (Second Part, 1837–1852)*. Longmans Green. 1885.

Guedalla, Philip. See under WELLINGTON, First Duke of.

HAHN-HAHN, Gräfin Ida. *The Countess Faustina, A Novel*. Translated from the German by A.E.I. 2 vols. John Ollivier. 1845.

From Babylon to Jerusalem. Translated by Elizabeth Atcherley. T. C. Newby. 1851.

Letters of a German Countess. 3 vols. London. 1845.

Jacoby, A. *Ida Gräfin Hahn-Hahn*. Mainz. 1894.

Schmid-Jurgens, Dr Erna. *Ida Gräfin Hahn-
Hahn*. Germanisches Studien. Berlin. 1933.

HALL, S. C. *Book of Memories of Great Men and Women of the
Age*. Virtue & Co. 1871.

Retrospect of a Long Life. 2 vols. Bentley. 1883.

Hanson, Laurence and Elisabeth. See under CARLYLE, Jane
Welsh.

HAYDON, Benjamin Robert. *The Diary of B. R. Haydon
1808–1846*, edited W. B. Pope. 5 vols. Harvard
University Press. 1960 and 1963.

Lectures on Painting and Design. 2 vols. Longman,
Brown, Green. 1844 and 1846.

*Life of B. R. Haydon, Historical Painter, from His
Autobiography and Journals*, edited Tom Taylor.
3 vols. Longman, Brown, Green. 1853.

Autobiography and Memoirs, introduction Edmund
Blunden. O.U.P. 1927.

Autobiography and Journals, introduction Malcolm
Elwin. Macdonald. 1950.

Autobiography and Memoirs, introduction Aldous
Huxley. Peter Davies. 1926.

Autobiography and Memoirs, introduction A. P. D.
Penrose. Bell. 1927.

Correspondence and Table Talk, with a Memoir by
his son F. W. Haydon. 2 vols. Chatto & Windus.
1876.

George, Eric. *The Life and Death of B. R. Haydon
1786–1846*. O.U.P. 1948.

Paston, G. *B. R. Haydon and His Friends*. James
Nisbet. 1905.

Olney, C. *B. R. Haydon, Historical Painter*.
University of Georgia Press. 1952.

List of Sources

Huxley, Aldous. *Antic Hay*. Chatto & Windus. 1923.

The Tillotson Banquet (*Collected Short Stories*) Chatto & Windus. 1957.

HORNE, R. H. *A New Spirit of the Age*. O.U.P. 1907.

Howe, Susanna. See under JEWSBURY, Geraldine.

HUNT, W. Holman. *Pre-Raphaelitism and the Pre-Raphaelite Brotherhood*. Macmillan. 1905.

HUNT, Leigh. *Correspondence*, edited by his Eldest Son. 2 vols. Smith Elder. 1862.

Blunden, Edmund. *Leigh Hunt, a Biography*. Cobden-Sanderson. 1930.

Huxley, Aldous. See under HAYDON, B. R.

Jacoby, A. See under HAHN-HAHN, Ida.

JAMESON, Anna. *Companion to the Most Celebrated Private Galleries of Art in London*. Saunders & Ottley. 1844.

Memoirs and Essays Illustrative of Art Literature and Social Morals. Bentley. 1846.

Anna Jameson, Letters and Friendships, 1812–1860, edited Mrs Stuart Erskine. Fisher Unwin. 1915.

Letters to Ottilie von Goethe, edited G. H. Needler. O.U.P. 1939.

Macpherson, G. B. *Memoirs of the Life of Anna Jameson*. Longmans Green. 1878.

JEFFREY, Lord. Cockburn, Lord. *Life of Lord Jeffrey*. A. & C. Black. 1852.

JERDAN, William. *Autobiography*. 4 vols. Hall, Virtue. 1852.

JEWSBURY, Geraldine. *Selection from the Letters of Geraldine Jewsbury to Jane Welsh Carlyle*, edited Mrs Alexander Ireland. Longmans Green. 1892.

Howe, Susanna. *Geraldine Jewsbury*. Allen & Unwin. 1935.

KEATS, John. *The Letters of John Keats*, edited M. Buxton
Forman. O.U.P. 1947.

Rollins, H. E. *The Keats Circle: Letters and Papers
1816–1878*. Harvard University Press. 1949.

Gittings, Robert. *John Keats: the Living Year*.
Heinemann. 1954.

Ward, Aileen. *John Keats: the Making of a Poet*.
Secker & Warburg. 1963.

KEMBLE, Frances Anne. *Records of Later Life*. 3 vols.
Bentley. 1882.

LANDSEER, Edwin. Stephens. F. G. *Memoirs of Sir Edwin
Landseer*. London. 1874.

LESLIE, C. R. *Autobiographical Recollections*, edited Tom
Taylor. 2 vols. London. 1860.

MACKAY, Charles. *Through the Long Day*. 2 vols. W. H.
Allen. 1887.

MACLISE, Daniel. O'Driscoll, W. J. *Memoir of Daniel
Maclise*. Longmans Green. 1871.

Macpherson, G. B. See under JAMESON, Anna.

MACREADY, William. *Diaries*, edited William Toynbee.
Chapman & Hall. 1912.

Reminiscences, edited Frederick Pollock. 2 vols.
Macmillan. 1875.

Trewin, J. C. *Mr Macready*. Harrap. 1955.

MARTIN, John. Balston, Thomas. *John Martin, his Life and
Works*. Duckworth. 1947.

MASSON, David. *Memories of London in the Forties*. Blackwood. 1908.

MAZZINI, Giuseppe. *Letters*. Translated by A. de R. Jervine.
Dent. 1930.

Miller, Betty. See under BROWNING, Robert.

MILNES, Richard Monckton. *Commonplace Book for 1846*. Unpublished. Houghton Papers, Trinity College,
Cambridge.

Die Briefe Richard Monckton Milnes an Varnhagen

von Ense, 1844–1854, edited Dr Walther Fischer. Heidelberg. 1922.

Life and Letters of John Keats. Dent. 1927.

Monographs, Personal and Social. London. 1873.

Reid, T. W. *Life, Letters and Friendships of R. Monckton Milnes, 1st Lord Houghton*. 2 vols. Cassell. 1890.

Pope-Hennessy, James. *Monckton Milnes: the Years of Promise, 1809–1851*. Constable. 1949.

MITFORD, Mary Russell. *Recollections of a Literary Life*. 3 vols. London. 1852.

Life of M. R. Mitford in a Selection from Her Letters to Her Friends, edited A. G. L'Estrange. 3 vols. Bentley. 1870.

Letters of M. R. Mitford, 2nd Series, edited Henry Chorley. 2 vols. Bentley. 1872.

Friendships of M. R. Mitford, edited A. G. L'Estrange. Hurst & Blackett. 1882.

Watson, Vera. *Mary Russell Mitford*. Evans. Undated.

NATIONAL PORTRAIT GALLERY CATALOGUE. Foreword.

NORTON, Caroline. Acland, Alice. *Caroline Norton*. Constable. 1948.

Cecil, David. *Lord M*. Constable. 1954.

O'Driscoll, W. J. See under MACLISE, Daniel.

Olney, C. See under HAYDON, B. R.

Paston, G. See under HAYDON, B. R.

Pearson, Hesketh. See under DICKENS, Charles.

PEEL, Robert. *Memoirs*, edited Stanhope & Cardwell. 2 vols. John Murray. 1856–7.

Sir Robert Peel from his Private Papers, edited C. S. Parker. 3 vols. John Murray. 1899.

Ramsay, A. A. W., *Sir Robert Peel*. Constable. 1928.

Pitt, Valerie. See under TENNYSON, Alfred.

Pope-Hennessy, James. See under MILNES, R. M.

Pope-Hennessy, Una. See under DICKENS, Charles.

POST OFFICE MAP OF LONDON. 1846.

PROCTER, B. W. *An Autobiographical Fragment and Bio-graphical Notes*, edited Coventry Patmore. Bell. 1877.

Armour, R. W. `Barry Cornwall: a Biography of B. W. Procter*. Meador Publishing Co. Boston. 1935.

Ramsay, A. A. W. See under PEEL, Robert.

Rannie, D. W. See under WORDSWORTH, William.

REDDING, Cyrus. *Fifty Years' Recollections*. 3 vols. London. 1858.

Past *Celebrities Whom I Have Known*. London. 1866.

REDGRAVE, Richard and Samuel. *A Century of Painters*. Phaidon Press. 1947.

Reid, T. W. See under MILNES, R. M.

Renton, Richard. See under FORSTER, John.

Ritchie, Lady. See under BROWNING, Robert.

Roberts, R. E. See under ROGERS, Samuel.

Robinson, H. Crabb. See under WORDSWORTH, William.

ROGERS, Samuel. *Recollections*, edited William Sharpe. London. 1859.

Recollections of the Table Talk of Samuel Rogers, edited Alexander Dyce. Appleton. 1856.

Clayden, P. W. *Rogers and His Contemporaries*. 2 vols. Smith Elder. 1899.

Roberts, R. E. *Samuel Rogers and his Circle*. Methuen. 1910.

Rollins, H. E. See under KEATS, John.

RUSKIN, John. *Works*, edited E. T. Cook & A. Wedderburn. George Allen. 1903–12.

Sadler, Michael. See under BLESSINGTON, Lady.

Schmid-Jurgens. See under HAHN-HAHN, Ida.

SCOTT, William Bell. *Autobiographical Notes of the Life of W. B. Scott*. 2 vols. Osgood, McIlvaine. 1892.

List of Sources

Scudder, Townsend. See under CARLYLE, Jane Welsh.

Stephens, F. G. See under LANDSEER, Edwin.

Symons, Julian. See under CARLYLE, Thomas.

TALFOURD, Thomas Noon. *Supplement to Vacation Rambles*. Moxon. 1854.

  Miscellanies (*Modern British Essayists*, vol. vii). Carey & Hunt, Philadelphia. 1848.

  Brain, J. A. *A Lecture Entitled An Evening with Thomas Noon Talfourd*. Reading Observer. 1889.

  A Member of the Oxford Circuit. *A Memoir of Mr Justice Talfourd*. Butterworths. 1854.

Taplin, G. B. See under BARRETT, Elizabeth.

Tennyson, Charles. See under TENNYSON, Alfred.

Tennyson, Hallam. See under TENNYSON, Alfred.

TENNYSON, Alfred. *Alfred Lord Tennyson, a Memoir* by his Son. 12 vols. Macmillan. 1898.

  Tennyson, Charles. *Alfred Tennyson*. Macmillan. 1950.

  Buckley, J. H. *Tennyson: the Growth of a Poet*. O.U.P. 1960.

  Pitt, Valerie. *Tennyson Laureate*. Barrie & Rockcliff. 1962.

Tillotson, Kathleen. See under DICKENS, Charles.

Trewin, J. C. See under MACREADY, William.

TURNER, J. M. W. Finberg, A. J. *The Life of J. M. W. Turner*. O.U.P. 1961.

De Vane, W. C. See under BROWNING, Robert.

VICTORIA, Queen. *Letters*, edited A. C. Benson and Lord Esher. 3 vols. John Murray. 1908.

VIZETELLY, Henry. *Glances Back Through Seventy Years*. 2 vols. Kegan Paul. 1893.

Watson, Vera. See under MITFORD, M. R.

Wellesley, Muriel. See under WELLINGTON, First Duke of.

WELLINGTON, First Duke of. *Letters to Miss J. 1834–1851*, edited C. T. Herrick. Fisher Unwin. 1890.

Guedalla, Philip. *The Duke*. Hodder & Stoughton. 1931.

Wellesley, Muriel. *Wellington in Civil Life*. Constable. 1939.

Gibbs-Smith, C. H. and Percival, H. V. T. *A Guide to the Wellington Museum, Apsley House*. H.M.S.O. 1959.

WHITLEY, William. *Art in England 1821–1837*. C.U.P. 1930.

WORDSWORTH, William. *Letters of William and Dorothy Wordsworth: the Later Years*, edited E. de Selincourt. Clarendon Press. 1939.

Batho, Edith. *The Later Wordsworth*. C.U.P. 1933.

Blanshard, Frances. *Portraits of Wordsworth*. Allen & Unwin. 1959.

Rannie, D. W. *Wordsworth and His Circle*, Methuen. 1907.

Robinson, H. Crabb. *Diary Reminiscences and Correspondence*, edited T. Sadler. 3 vols. London. 1869.

On Books and their Writers, edited E. J. Morley. 3 vols. Dent. 1938.

Correspondence with the Wordsworth Circle, 1808–1866. Clarendon Press. 1927.

Wylie, W. H. See under CARLYLE, Thomas.

WYNN, Charlotte Williams. *Memorials*, edited Harriot Lindesay. Longmans Green. 1878.

YOUNG, G. M. and Others. *Early Victorian England*. O.U.P. 1934.

NEWSPAPERS

Daily News 18th–27th, 29th June, 1st July 1846.

Morning Chronicle 24th, 25th June 1846.

Standard 18th–26th June 1846.

Times 18th–26th June, 1st, 4th July 1846.

List of Sources

JOURNALS

Art Union Monthly Journal July, August, December 1846,
March 1847.

Athenaeum 18th July 1846.

Examiner 27th June 1846.

Illustrated London News 20th June 1846.

Punch June 1846.

INDEX

Addison, Joseph, 75
Adelaide, Queen, 130
Aeschylus, 23
Ainsworth, Harrison, 164
Albert, Prince, 20, 44–5, 78, 132, 171, 190
Alexander the Great, 23, 91, 200
Alvanley, Lord, 72
Anglesey, First Marquess of, 43, 44
Apsley House, 44–5
Arbuthnot, Mrs, 45
Ariosto, *Orlando Furioso*, 119
Aristides, 200
Arnim, Bettina von, 34, 126
Ashburton, Lady (see Baring, Lady Harriet)
Athenaeum, The, 52, 143

Babbage, Charles, 179
Bailey, Benjamin, 117
Baring, Lady Harriet, 27, 28, 32, 36, 40, 121, 122–3, 153–5, 156, 157, 158, 159, 188, 189
Barnum, Phineas Taylor, 21
Barrett, Alfred, 102
Barrett, Arabel, 22, 60, 62, 168, 193
Barrett, Charles John, 193
Barrett, Edward, 103, 146, 167, 168, 175, 186, 193, 194
Barrett, Elizabeth, 15, 17, 22–4, 25–6, 30, 31, 34, 39, 43, 46, 47, 48, 51, 52, 54, 55, 60, 62, 63, 64, 65, 66–7, 71–2, 77, 82, 83, 85, 87–8, 91, 92, 99, 101, 102–3, 114, 115, 126, 134–6, 143, 144, 145, 146–7, 148, 149, 150–2, 160–2, 163, 165, 166, 167–9, 172–3, 175–6, 178, 179–82, 183–5, 186, 192, 193–5, 205, 206
    Poems, 1844, 30, 66, 146, 163
Barrett, George, 64, 162, 175, 180, 181, 193, 194
Barrett, Henrietta, 22
Barrett, Henry, 103
Barry, James, 43
Beaufort, Seventh Duke of, 42, 43, 112
Beaumont, Sir George, 140, 141
Beerbohm, Max, 11
Bennoch, Francis, 186, 206
Bentinck, Lord George, 40–1, 56, 57, 78, 106, 131
Bewick, William, 79, 114
Blackwood, Mrs, 96

Blessington, Lady, 97, 138
Blunden, Edmund, 199
Bölte, Amely, 32, 35, 124, 125, 126, 190
Bonaparte, Joseph, 45
Bonaparte, Napoleon (see Napoleon)
Bonington, Richard, 74
Booth, Junius Brutus, 118
Boyd, Hugh Stuart, 62–3, 66, 75, 135, 175, 193
Brantling, Fanny, 118
Bright, John, 40
Brontë, Anne, 11, 12. *Agnes Grey*, 11, 86
Brontë, Charlotte, 11, 12. *The Professor*, 11
Brontë, Emily, 11, 12. *Wuthering Heights*, 11
Brougham, Lord, 42, 43, 112
Browning, Robert, 25–8, 30–1, 34, 36–7, 39, 46, 47, 48, 51–5, 62, 63–6, 71, 72, 77, 82, 83, 87, 88, 99–100, 101, 102, 114, 121, 124, 125, 126, 127, 134–6, 144, 145, 146–7, 148, 152, 161, 162, 163, 164, 166, 167–9, 173, 174, 175, 176, 178, 179–82, 183–4, 189, 193–5, 201, 206
    Bells and Pomegranates, 26, 30, 65, 66, 163
    Bishop Orders His Tomb, The, 65
    Blot in the 'Scutcheon, A, 52
    Colombe's Birthday, 55
    Home Thoughts from Abroad, 65
    How They Brought the Good News, 65
    Lost Leader, The, 65, 145
    Luria, 66
    Paracelsus, 152, 163
    Pied Piper, The, 65
    Pippa Passes, 11, 26
    Sordello, 26, 65, 163
    Soul's Tragedy, A, 66
    Strafford, 163
Bryant, Dr, 94, 108
Bulwer, Edward Lytton, 36, 63, 144, 163, 164, 190, 191
    New Timon, The, 63, 165
    Richelieu, 190, 204
Burke, Edmund, 88
Burwood Place (Haydon's house in), 15, 61, 76, 94, 95, 102, 103, 104, 108, 184

Index

Byron, George Gordon, Lord, 17, 44, 55, 68, 73, 85, 88, 138
Byron, Lady, 23, 85, 86, 88–9, 194
Bystram, Oberst Baron A. von, 35–6, 74, 75, 121, 125

Cadell, Robert, 203
Caligula, 88
Canning, George, 41, 56, 57
Carlyle, Jane Welsh, 25–31, 32, 33–4, 38, 39, 47, 51, 53, 61, 62, 63, 64, 65, 72, 83, 121–5, 129, 153–9, 165, 176, 188–9, 194
Carlyle, Thomas, 25–31, 32, 37–8, 39–40, 42, 46, 51, 53, 61, 62, 63, 64, 65, 66, 73, 78, 82–3, 87, 119, 121, 122, 124, 125–9, 143, 144, 146, 153–9, 164, 165, 176, 187, 188–9, 194–5
    Cromwell, 30, 42, 78, 122, 146, 165
    French Revolution, The, 27, 126, 128
    Past and Present, 119, 127, 128–9
Cartoon Competition for the House of Lords frescoes, 17, 19, 20, 74, 134, 150, 161
Castelcicola, Prince, 45
Castlereagh, Viscount, 69, 79, 114, 115
Cato, 69
Chantrey, Francis, 74
Chaucer, Geoffrey, 23
Cheyne Row (the Carlyles' house in), 26, 28, 37, 38, 61, 122, 123–4, 153, 156, 164
Chorley, Henry, 52
Clarke, Arabella Graham, 168
Cobden, Richard, 39, 40, 131, 133
Cockburn, Vice Admiral Sir George, 79, 94, 130
Columbus, Christopher, 127, 128, 200
Comic Almanack, The, 138
Corn Laws, Repeal of, 39, 40–2, 44, 57, 131–4, 145
Cornwall, Barry (see Procter, B. W.)
Cortez, Hernando, 200
Coulton, D. T., 76, 80, 94, 103, 204
Cowper, William, 173
Craigenputtock (the Carlyles' house at), 27, 124
Crewe, Annabel, 36, 49
Croly, Rev George, 138
Cruikshank, George, 29, 138
Curtius, Mettius, 23, 200
Cushman, Charlotte, 124

Daily News, The, 48, 52, 57, 108, 112, 134, 151, 162, 205
Darling, Dr George, 94
Darwin, Erasmus Alvey, 38
Deffand, Madame du, 173
Dentatus, 199, 200
Dickens, Charles, 22, 28, 29, 48, 52, 53,

60, 61, 63, 64, 66, 71, 85, 105–6, 130, 139, 162, 163, 164, 165–6, 171, 176, 191–3, 206
    Battle of Life, The, 193
    Bleak House, 61, 105, 171
    Dombey and Son, 71, 165–6, 191, 193
    Martin Chuzzlewit, 85
    Nicholas Nickleby, 53
    Our Mutual Friend, 165
    Pickwick Papers, 176
Dino, Duchesse de, 89
Disraeli, Benjamin, 36, 39, 40–1, 42, 56, 57, 78, 106
Drayton (Peel's house in Staffordshire), 41, 74, 89, 136, 171, 190
Duffy, Gavan, 143, 156
Dumas, Alexandre, Monte Cristo, 47
Dürer, Albrecht, 124

Eastlake, Charles, 19, 116, 130, 187
Eastlake, Lady (see Rigby, Elizabeth)
Eastlake, William, 116
Edward the Black Prince, 200
Eglinton Tournament, The, 96
Egyptian Hall, The, 21, 58, 106, 111, 112, 163
Elgin Marbles, 16, 18, 88, 116
Eliot, George (see Evans, Mary Ann)
Emerson, Ralph Waldo, 125
Espinasse, F., 155
Eucles, 200
Evans, Commissioner Joshua, 43, 68
Evans, Mary Ann, 11, 12
Examiner, The, 105, 137, 138, 163

Fitzgerald, Edward, 192, 206
Flush (Elizabeth Barrett's spaniel), 31, 46, 47, 67, 71, 72, 147, 174
Forrest, Edwin, 18, 19, 203
Forrest, Mrs, 18, 203
Forster, John, 28, 29, 52, 53, 54, 60, 61, 64, 66, 105, 138, 139, 146, 148, 162–6, 169, 174, 175, 176, 179, 190, 192, 193, 204–5, 206
Fouquet, Jean, 88
Fox, Charles James, 88
Frederick, Empress, 29
Frith, W. P., 104
Froude, James Anthony, 165, 189
Fuseli, Henry, 18

Garrick, David, 119
Gaskell, Mrs, 12
George III, King, 118
George IV, King, 149
Gielgud, John, 54
Giorgione, Giorgio, 88
Glynne family, 29
Goethe, Johann Wolfgang von, 137
Goethe, Ottilie von, 33, 34, 83, 86
Gordon, Watson, 203

Index

Gray, Thomas, 88
Greville, Charles, 56, 133
Grey, Earl, 44
Grote, Mrs, 77, 172
Gurwood, Colonel John, 70, 115

Hackett, Mary, 94, 110
Hahn-Hahn, Gräfin Ida von, 32–6, 38,
    39–40, 51, 54, 55, 74–5, 77, 87, 121,
    122, 123, 124, 125, 126, 127, 189–90
    Countess Faustina, The, 33–4, 35,
        46, 51, 77, 121
    From Babylon to Jerusalem, 39
Hall, Samuel Carter, 73, 85, 91, 106
Hallam, Arthur, 63
Hallam, Henry, 63
Hamilton, W. R., 138
Havilland, Mrs, 70, 89
Haydon, Alfred, 96
Haydon, Benjamin Robert, 15–24, 25,
    31, 42–4, 46, 50–1, 56, 58–60, 61,
    63, 66, 67, 68–71, 72, 74, 75–6,
    78–81, 88–92, 93–100, 102–7, 108–
    113, 114–20, 126, 127, 128, 129,
    130, 134–5, 137–44, 145, 147, 148–
    151, 160–1, 162, 163, 164, 165, 166,
    169–70, 171, 173, 174, 175, 176,
    178–81, 183–7, 188, 196–201, 203,
    204, 205, 206
    Autobiography, 117, 160–2, 170,
        185
    Journals, 15, 80, 92, 102, 106,
        111–13, 115, 119, 142, 150,
        160–2, 165, 169–70, 173–4, 175,
        178–81, 184–6
    Lectures on Painting and Design,
        24, 137–8, 163, 169
    Pictures:
    Alexander Taming Bucephalus, 23
    Alfred and the First British Jury,
        24, 58, 59, 80, 108
    Assassination of Dentatus, 199
    Banishment of Aristides, 20, 113,
        138
    Byron Musing at Harrow, 43, 68
    Christ's Entry into Jerusalem, 16,
        141–2, 149
    Curse on Adam and Eve, The, 17, 22
    Curtius Leaping into the Gulf, 23,
        200
    Edward the Black Prince Entering
        London with John of France, 17
    George IV and Wellington Visiting
        Waterloo, 43
    Judgement of Solomon, The, 16, 23,
        112
    Mary Russell Mitford, 15, 23, 24,
        186
    Meeting of the Anti-Slavery Con-
        vention, 89
    Mock Election, The, 149

    Napoleon Musing at St Helena, 21,
        89–90, 91, 92
    Nero at the Burning of Rome, 20,
        106
    Raising of Lazarus, The, 16, 79,
        187
    Reform Banquet, The, 138
    Study from Memory of an Expres-
        sion in Insanity, 115–16, 119
    Study for Wordsworth in Jerusalem,
        142
    Uriel Revealing Himself to Satan,
        17, 18
    Wellington Musing on the Field of
        Waterloo, 15, 43, 44, 142
    Wordsworth on Helvellyn, 15, 18,
        22, 142–3, 186, 203, 205–6
    Wordsworth on Helvellyn (full-
        length), 143, 205–6
Haydon, Frank, 68, 70–1, 94, 100,
    103, 110, 111, 112, 130, 149, 185
Haydon, Frederic, 18, 90, 94, 100, 112,
    115, 116, 119, 130, 142, 185, 186,
    198, 203
Haydon, Georgiana, 96
Haydon, Harry, 90, 97
Haydon, Mary (wife of B. R. Haydon),
    15, 19, 20, 23, 71, 76, 78, 80, 93, 94,
    95–100, 104, 106, 109, 110, 111, 112,
    114, 130, 139, 140, 149, 150, 178,
    180, 184, 185, 201, 203
Haydon, Mary (daughter of B. R.
    Haydon), 15, 93–4, 108–10, 112, 139
Hazlitt, William, 17, 95, 137, 197
Herald, The, 21
Herrick, Robert, Gather ye rosebuds, 136
Hobhouse, John Cam, 138
Holbein, Hans, 88
Hope, H. T., 43
Horne, Richard Hengist, 30, 64, 151
    New Spirit of the Age, A, 30, 64
Hunt, Holman, 107
Hunt, John, 79
Hunt, Leigh, 16, 61, 68, 104–5, 117,
    137, 163, 174, 187, 197, 204–5
Hunt Marianne, 68, 124
Hunt, Thornton, 163, 204
Huxley, Aldous, 200
Hyman, Rev Orlando, 94, 110–3, 139,
    140

Illustrated London News, The, 49
Irish Coercion Bill, 41, 57, 131–2

Jameson, Anna, 25, 32, 33, 34, 36, 52,
    54, 55, 62, 74, 75, 82–9, 124, 144,
    146–7, 152, 167, 171–2, 173, 193,
    194
    Companion to the Most Celebrated
        Private Galleries of Art in Lon-
        don, 82, 86, 87–8

Index

Jameson—*continued*
    Diary of an Ennuyée, 83
    Memoirs and Essays Illustrative of Art, Literature and Social Morals, 85–6
Jameson, Robert, 83–5
Jeffrey, Lord, 18, 19, 203, 204, 205
Jerdan, William, 138
Jewsbury, Geraldine, 27, 47–8, 121, 122, 153, 158, 188
Johnson, Samuel, 88
Jonson, Ben, 64

Kean, Edmund, 119
Keats, John, 16, 23, 43, 68–9, 115, 116–18, 142, 170, 174, 197
    Great Spirits now on earth are sojourning, 16, 116
    Haydon! forgive me that I cannot speak, 16, 116
    I stood tip-toe upon a little hill, 23
    My spirit is too weak—mortality, 116
    Ode to a Nightingale, 68
    On Sitting Down to Read King Lear Again, 118
Kemble, Fanny, 73, 172–3
Kemble, John Philip, 119
Kenyon, John, 52, 60, 66, 140, 160, 161, 162, 165, 166, 169, 174, 175, 192, 193, 194
Kirkup, Seymour, 117
Knowles, Sheridan, 63

Lamb, Charles, 118, 142, 176
Lance, George, 130
Landor, Walter Savage, 66, 148
Landseer, Charles, 130
Landseer, Edwin, 22, 52, 130, 179
Landseer, Thomas, 130
Lawrence, D. H. *Lady Chatterley's Lover*, 177
Lieven, Princess, 154
Literary Gazette, The, 138
Lockhart, J. G., 17
Londonderry, Marchioness of, 46
Longman, Brown, Green and Longmans, 160, 169
Lucas, John, 186
Lupton, T. G., 205
Lyndhurst, Lord, 178

Macaulay, Thomas Babington, 87
Maclise, Daniel, 52, 104, 169, 181
Macready, William, 18, 22, 29, 39, 50, 52–4, 56–7, 60, 61, 64, 104, 119, 133, 134, 137, 148, 163, 164, 165, 176, 177–8, 190, 191, 203, 204
Macready, Mrs, 155, 191
Mantegna, Andrea, 74, 88
Martin, John, 29, 60, 75, 76, 95

Martin, Leopold, 75–6, 95
Martin, Richard, 95
Martineau, Harriet, 144, 171–2, 173
Masson, David, 127
Mazzini, Giuseppe, 28, 39, 157–8
Medici, Lorenzo di, 87
Melbourne, Lord, 98, 99
Michelangelo, 87, 88, 113
Milnes, Richard Monckton, 29, 32, 34, 35, 36–8, 40, 41, 49, 52, 62, 63, 64, 74, 75, 77, 87, 117–18, 143, 144, 154, 170, 185, 189, 190, 194
    Life, Letters and Literary Remains of John Keats, 117–18, 170
Milnes, Robert, 41
Milton, John, 88, 96
Mitford, Mary Russell, 22, 23, 48, 53–54, 91, 95, 96, 104, 114, 139, 143, 144, 147–52, 160, 162, 168, 173, 176, 177, 178, 179, 184, 185, 186, 194
    Foscari, 147
    Julian, 147
    Our Village, 147
    Rienzi, 147
Mitford, Dr, 23, 147, 149
Morgan, Lady, 36
Morning Chronicle, The, 112, 126, 204
Morning Post, The, 112
Morpeth, Lord, 138
Moxon, Edward, 64, 66, 117, 139, 146, 177, 191–2, 206

Napoleon I, Emperor, 17, 24, 43, 44, 45, 69, 74, 81, 89–92, 105, 120, 181, 199, 200
Necker, Jacques, 42
Nero, 88, 106
New Cross (Browning's house at), 26, 46, 48, 51, 52, 62, 66, 71, 135
New Monthly Magazine, The, 176
Newton, William, 15
Nicholson, Cornelius, 186
Nightingale, Florence, 156
Norton, Caroline, 17, 36, 75, 96–100, 174
Norton, George, 98, 99

d'Orsay, Count Alfred, 45, 65, 113, 138–9
Ossian, 62, 175

Palmerston, Lord, 36, 187
Patmore, Coventry, 64
Peel, Sir Robert, 20, 24, 37, 40–3, 44, 56–7, 63, 70, 74, 78, 79, 89, 94, 103, 104, 106, 107, 111, 112, 113, 130–134, 136, 139, 171, 176, 190
Peel, Lady, 78, 131, 136
Pitt, William, 73
Plato, 23
Pope, Alexander, 63, 74, 87

Index

Pope, Willard, 185, 205
Poussin, Nicholas, 74
Procter, Bryan Waller, 51, 52, 54, 55, 60, 75, 148, 194, 200. *Mirandola*, 54
Procter, Mrs, 29, 51, 52, 54, 55, 60, 146
Prout, Samuel, 19
Punch, 55–6, 165

Quillinan, Dora, 186, 191

Raphael, 88, 170
Rembrandt, 74, 87
Reni, Guido, 74, 87
Reynolds, J. H., 16
Reynolds, Joshua, 88
Richardson, Samuel, 160, 169, 170, 185
Richmond, George, 73
Rigby, Elizabeth, 19, 204, 205
Riviere, Isaac, 79, 204
Robinson, Henry Crabb, 49, 77
Rochfort, Frank, 58
Roebuck, J. A., 57
Rogers, Samuel, 22, 25, 62, 63, 64, 72–5, 82, 83, 87, 89, 92, 101, 144, 148, 172–3, 190
Romilly, Sir Samuel, 69, 114, 115
Roubiliac, Louis François, 74, 87
Rousseau, Jean Jacques, 185
Royal Academy, The, 16, 20, 22, 23, 95, 104, 105, 139, 183, 198
Royal Commission on the Fine Arts, 17
Rubens, Peter Paul, 74, 88
Ruskin, John, 12. *Modern Painters*, 11
Russell, Lord John, 41, 56, 190
Russell, Mrs, 157
Rydal Mount (Wordsworth's house at), 49, 186

St James's Place (Rogers' house in), 62, 72, 82, 87–8
Sand, George, 33, 121, 122, 125, 126, 190. *Consuelo*, 190
Scott, Walter, 18, 95, 203
Sévigné, Marquise de, 173
Seymour, Lady, 96
Shackford, M. H., 205
Shakespeare, William, 86, 118, 149
    Hamlet, 19, 203, 204
    King Lear, 29, 50, 80, 118–20, 196, 204
    Love's Labour's Lost, 117
    Macbeth, 204
    Othello, 204
Shelley, Percy Bysshe, 124, 174, 177, 197
Sheridan, Richard Brinsley, 73
Smith, Sydney, 72, 73, 172, 173
Standard, The, 112
Stanfield, Clarkson, 22, 52
Sterne, Laurence, 88, 133

Stratton (see Thumb, General Tom)
Sutherland, Second Duke of, 79, 89, 204

Talfourd, Thomas Noon, 22, 60, 61, 79, 94, 114, 138, 139, 140, 144, 148, 162, 163, 166, 169, 174, 175–82, 183, 192–3, 194, 206
    Athenian Captive, The, 176, 178
    Ion, 176, 177, 178, 181
    Vacation Rambles, 192
Talfourd, Mrs, 177, 186, 192, 194
Talleyrand, Charles Maurice de, 89
Tate, Nahum, 199
Taylor, Bayard, 22
Taylor, Tom, 164, 184
Tennyson, Alfred, 37, 63–5, 66, 73–4, 144, 163, 164, 170, 171, 189, 191–2, 206
    Come down, O Maid, from yonder mountain height, 192
    Locksley Hall, 65
    To ——, After Reading a Life and Letters, 170
    Two Voices, The, 65
Thackeray, William Makepeace, 12, 52, 53, 55, 61, 64, 154, 163, 164
    Vanity Fair, 11, 55
Three Mile Cross (Miss Mitford's house at), 48, 147, 148
Thumb, General Tom, 21, 24, 112, 134, 135, 138, 150, 183
Times, The, 21, 55, 56, 102, 103, 112, 137
Tintoretto, 74, 87
Titian, 88
Trelawney, Edward, 98, 99
Trepsack, Mary, 193
Trollope, Anthony, 189
Turner, J. M. W., 60, 62, 104

Varnhagen von Ense, C. A., 32, 33, 34, 35, 77, 125, 126
Vasari, Giorgio, 170
Velasquez, 74, 88
Verdi, Giuseppe, 45. *Aida*, 21
Vere, Aubrey de, 64
Veronese, 88
Victoria, Queen, 20, 21, 36, 61, 78, 119, 132, 144, 171, 190

Wakley, Thomas, 106–7, 108–13
Waterloo Banquet, 44–6
Watson, Vera, 186
Watteau, Antoine, 88
Wellington, First Duke of, 15, 21, 40, 43–6, 70, 81, 91, 103–4, 132, 133, 134, 181
Western, Elizabeth, 111
Wilberforce, Samuel, Bishop of Oxford, 132, 133
Wilkie, David, 18

Index

Williams-Wynn, Charlotte, 33
Wilson, Elizabeth, 31, 193
Wimpole Street (Elizabeth Barrett's
house in), 15, 22, 43, 60, 66–7, 71,
77, 147, 148, 160, 167, 182, 184,
188, 193, 194
Wordsworth, John, 191
Wordsworth, William, 16, 17, 18, 20,
22, 23, 41–2, 49, 63, 77, 90, 96, 108,
139–45, 148, 151, 176, 177, 186,

187, 191, 197, 198, 205–6
  *Haydon! let worthier judges praise
  the skill*, 90
  High is our calling, Friend, 140–1,
  151, 198
  *On a Portrait of the Duke of
  Wellington*, 142

Yonge, Charlotte, 189